Distribution of ESTATE ACCOUNTS Washington County Maryland 1778-1835

ORIGINALLY PUBLISHED BY TRACES IN FOUR VOLUMES

Compiled by
Dale Walton Morrow and
Deborah Jensen Morrow

HERITAGE BOOKS
2007

HERITAGE BOOKS
AN IMPRINT OF HERITAGE BOOKS, INC.

Books, CDs, and more—Worldwide

For our listing of thousands of titles see our website
at
www.HeritageBooks.com

Published 2007 by
HERITAGE BOOKS, INC.
Publishing Division
65 East Main Street
Westminster, Maryland 21157-5026

Copyright © 2001 Dale Walton Morrow
and Deborah Jensen Morrow

Other books by the authors:

Marriages of Washington County, Maryland: An Index, 1799-1860

Washington County, Maryland Cemetery Records: Volumes 1-7
Dale Walton Morrow

Wills of Berkeley County, West Virginia, 1744-1880

Wills of Jefferson County, West Virginia, 1801-1899

Wills of Washington County, [Maryland], 1776-1890

All rights reserved. No part of this book may be reproduced or transmitted in any form or by any means, electronic or mechanical, including photocopying, recording or by any information storage and retrieval system without written permission from the author, except for the inclusion of brief quotations in a review.

International Standard Book Number: 978-1-58549-211-4

DISTRIBUTION OF ESTATE ACCOUNTS
Washington County, Maryland

INTRODUCTION

The Distribution Books were used until 1835 to record the settlement of estates in Washington County, Maryland. This practice was abandoned either during or after 1835, and only the four volumes exist. All information recorded in the Distributions Book is contained in these printed volumes.

The volumes are Volume I, 1778-1805; Volume II, 1806-1816; Volume III, 1817-1827; and Volume IV, 1828-1835.

In the first two volumes, the monetary system, for the most part, was pounds, shillings, pence represented as follows: 16.19.5. The rate of exchange was 12 pence equal a shilling and 20 shillings equal a pound. The monetary system changed to dollars and cents sometime around the period 1810-1820. There is a span of years during this period that both monetary systems were used. All amounts of money reported in dollars and cents are accompanied by a dollar sign ($).

Explanation of the Entries

ALLEN, James,* Adm. Martha K., Elisha Easton** 10/12/15;*** widow****, Archibald, Martha Easton, Henry, James, Benjamin A.P.,*****, T57.12.9½******

*Name of decedant
** Administrator(s)
*** Date of the distribution; "n.d." indicates no date appeared. The dates range from 1778-1835. The date numbers for the years 1778-1799 are 78-99; for the years 1800-1835, they are 00-35.
**** Widow, received 1/3 of the total distribution unless otherwise stated. In most cases, the widow is not named.
***** The other heirs received an equal share of the remaining 2/3; or equal amounts of the total if there was no widow; or each named heir received an equal share if not otherwise stated. A given name appearing alone, such as Martha K., Archibald, Henry, James and Benjamin A.P. above, have the same surname (Allen) as the decedant. (See Special Heirs)
****** "T" indicates the total amount of the distribution
"?" - a question mark following a name or word indicates that the spelling is questionable.

Special Heirs
In some cases, the reader will see among the heirs an entry such as "the heirs of Elizabeth Smith, (John, Lawrence, Elizabeth Battaile, Sally)." In these cases, the surname of those in parenthesis is Smith, with the exception of Elizabeth who probably married a Battaile.

Pencil Notes
In several instances, the compiler found pencil notes in the margins of the distribution books, undoubtedly placed there by a previous researcher. I have included these notes where they appeared and have identified them as such. I cannot vouch for their authenticity.

DISTRIBUTION OF ESTATE ACCOUNTS
Washington County, Maryland 1778 - 1805

1. AKELBARGER, Michael. Adm. Catherine 7/30/85; widow, Rebecca, John, Jacob, Michael, David, Elizabeth, Catherine, Enoch. T56.11.1
2. ALBERT, Frederick. Adm. Elizabeth 8/9/85; widow, John, Elizabeth, Jacob. T25.3.10
3. ANCHONY, Davalt. Adm. Christian 4/9/82; 21 children. T584.9.2
4. ANDREWS, John. Adm. Peter Reed 5/8/84; Barbara, Christian. T10.10.10
5. ANKENEY, John. Adm. Magdalena 10/11/04; widow, Henry, Andrew, Elizabeth, Polly, John, Magdalena, Devalt, Christiana. T1175.15.2
6. AVEY, Barbara. Adm. Peter Newcomer 5/28/05; eldest son John Snevely; Eliza of John, Mary and Anna of John, Fironica Houser, Anna Houser, Rachel Houser of John Houser T90.2.8
7. BAKER, Andrew. Adm. Peter, Conrad n.d.; 7 children. T7.14.3½
8. BAKER, Margaret. Adm. William Jones 2/6/96; William, Jane, Thomas, Margaret Willburger, Elizabeth Tice, Catherine Flener, Susanna Fisher, Ann Fisher. T141.17.2
9. BARKMAN, Jacob. Adm. Frederick Barkman 6/16/98; Frederick, Henry, Catherine Wise, Elizabeth Rape. T15.17.9
10. BARR, Martin. Adm. Barbara, John 2/15/02; widow, Elizabeth Stone, John, Jacob, Andrew, David, Mary, Otilla Newcomer. T336.13.5 3/4
11. BARTON, Richard. Adm. Benjamin Johnson 1/20/98; widow, Ann Rutledge, Elener, Mary, Thomas. T136.18.7½
12. BAUGH, Elizabeth. Adm. John Spawn. 10/22/82; Catherine, Barbara, John, Henry, Susanna T14.2.6
13. BEELER, Abraham. Adm. Christian, Jacob Ringer 8/17/05; Jacob, Elizabeth, Sarah, Mary, Samuel, Susannah, David T184.3.7
14. BELL, Peter. Adm. Lodwick Young, Baltzer Gale 7/14/92; widow, Frederick, Elizabeth, Margaret, Peter, Daniel T255.18.11   A second distribution, n.d., names John Protzman T233.7.4
15. BENSON, Thomas. Adm. John Shower 10/16/81; Distributed 3/14/89 to Ann Abinett T45.10.9
16. BETTS, Frederick. Adm. Mary 2/12/91; widow, Frederick, Ann, Mary, William, Christian, John T90.16.5
17. BISHOP, Jacob. Adm. William, David Harry 4/?/98; William, Jacob, George, Catherine, Margaret, Susanna T883.7.5
18. BISSETT, Thomas. Adm. Susanna Murphy n.d.; Thomas, heirs of Samuel, Susanna Murphy, Elener Mullen, Mary Anderson's heirs T119.13.8
19. BLAIR, John. Adm. John Lear, John 3/14/04; widow, Elizabeth Brotherton, John, Andrew, Samuel, Sarah Jaffer T248.17.2
20. BOND, George. Adm. Edmund Rutter, John, Walter 2/11/83; George T902.14.11
21. BOND, Walter. Adm. Lucy 11/12/85; widow, George, Edward, Joseph, Ann T330.6.10
22. BOWER, Jacob. Adm. Magdalen, William Philbe 3/29/83; widow, Jacob, Barbara, Conrad, John, Catherine, Mary, George, Susanna; Susanna Aulebaugh paid 5/31/99 T156.14.14
23. BOWMAN, Simon. Adm. Thomas Shuman, Henry Arnold 11/2/02; widow, John, Jacob, Mary Arnold, Catherine T345.5.1
24. BOYER, Philip. Adm. Jacob, Jacob Snevely 1/15/03; John, Magdalena, Christian T610.2.5
25. BRENT, George. Adm. John Reed and wife 1/14/03; widow, Thomas, Elizabeth Grayham T808.3.11
26. BRETT, Henry Sr. Adm. Henry Jr. n.d.; widow, Henry, Frances, Margaret T295.9.0
27. BURKART, Christopher. Adm. Jonas Hogmire, John Nigh 3/8/00; George, Christopher, Mary Penn, Catherine Nigh, Margaret Snell, Elizabeth, Samuel, Daniel T200.16.3/4
28. BURKHART, John. Adm. Robert Davison and wife; 3/17/98; widow, Daniel T277.16.3
29. CARVER, Christopher. Adm. John Barr 3/22/00; widow, 19 heirs not named T272.17.6
30. CHENEY, Charles. Adm. Jeremiah 10/16/81; no names T92.3.6
31. CHARLTON, John. Adm. William Webb n.d.; Agreeable to will, no names T47.4.4
32. CHEYNEY, Ezekiel. Adm. Joseph, Ann 12/9/83; widow, 5 children not named T165.9.7
33. CLAPPER, Harman. Adm. John 11/17/92; widow, Catherine, John, Mary, Elizabeth T219.8.7

1

DISTRIBUTION OF ESTATE ACCOUNTS

34. CLARKE, Mathew. Adm. John Ingram 8/13/82; James, Sarah, Isabella, James White, 14 grandchildren not named T784.0.0
35. CLEMM, Adam. Adm. Christian Lantz Jr. 10/27/91; Barbara Baum, Elizabeth Keifer, Hester Bower, Farancia Lantz, Catherine T1174.13.1½
36. CLOPPER, John. Adm. Christian, Christian King n.d.; widow, Elizabeth's representative, only child T199.10.8½
37. COX, Ezekiel. Adm. Abraham 5/12/83; widow 1/3, no others named T85.14.10
38. CREEBAUM, Adam. Adm. Eve Mary 6/8/79; widow, Phillip, Barbara, Adam, Christian T15.10 3/4.0
39. CRESAP, Michael Capt. Adm. John, Jeremiah, Jacob and wife 10/12/90; widow, Mary, Elizabeth, Sarah T2214.16.4
40. DARR, John Adm. Phillip, Mathias Beckley 2/10/87; Philip, John, Jacob, Ann Mary Zimmerman, Elizabeth, Hester Sites T197.15.0
41. DAVIS, John Adm. Conrod Cossroth, Jacob Bower 5/31/03; Hanson, John, Catherine, David, Frederick Merchand, Henry son of Nicholas, Elizabeth Miller, Margaret Conrod, Jacob Conrod, John Conrod, Elizabeth Conrod, John Clopper, John Leight, Jacob Bower, Catherine Conrod, Andrew Grubb, Daniel Conrod, the poor of Mr. Rauhauser's congregation, the poor of Baltimore, the poor of Sharpsburg, Margaret Snyder T649.0.7¼
42. DAVIS, Joshua. Adm. Richard 12/10/78; Richard, Ruth, Joshua, Caley T83.18.6
43. DELL, John. Adm. Christian 8/8/95; widow, Catherine, John, Jacob, Polly, George T9.9.11
44. DICK, Peter. Adm. Jacob Houser, George Kiper 5/9/98; George Kritzinger, John, Elizabeth, Mary, Rebecca T415.12.11
45. DOIL, Henry. Adm. Mary n.d.; widow, Adam, Catherine and two children not named, George, Conrad, Henry, Mary T107.2.3
46. DOUGLAS, William. Adm. Samuel 6/19/90; Samuel, Robert, Joseph, William, Rachel, Mary T334.1.7
47. DOWLER, Edward. Adm. James Grimes 1/6/89; Thomas, Frances, Joseph, John, Robert, Richard, Jane, Sally (who is dead, balance to George) T29.8.10; 2/15/94; John Protzman, David Harry for the above distribution share
48. DOWNEY, Joseph. Adm. Benjamin Light and Catherine, his wife 10/16/02; 1/3 to Adm., Robert, Samuel T16.16.0
49. DOWNEY, Robert. Adm. William Baird, Susanna Baird 8/13/93; Balance due on final settlement T819.8.11 Maryland currency
50. DOWNEY, William. Adm. Jean, David Dumwodie 10/9/92; widow, Polly, Isabella, Elizabeth T399.5.8
51. DREELING, John. Adm. Christian Stover n.d.; heirs of Mary Lopah, sister of deceased living in Pennsylvania (name unknown) T45.11.10
52. DUSING, John. Adm. Philip 7/25/89; Paul, Elizabeth, Susanna, Mary T46.19.5
53. DUVALT, Jeremiah. Adm. Elener Moore 5/6/86; Ann Davis, Richard, Elioner T148.13.5
54. EAKLE, Harmon. Adm. Robert Smith 9/12/01; Philip, Harmon, Peter, John, Mary Grove T17.14.8¼
55. EASTER, Adam. Adm. Simon Bowman, Joseph Smith 4/22/83; Mattelena, Craile? Painter, Peter, Jacob T1316.2.4
56. EMRICH, Jonas. Adm. David Harry 8/14/05; John's heirs, Jacob, Magdalena, Elizabeth, Roxanna, Dorothy, Margaret T27.10.8 Register's fee 1/7th deducted from each child's part
57. FAGAN, John Adm. John, Barbara 5/25/78; widow, remainder divided among children, not named T813.14.8¼
58. FEIRY, John. Adm. John, Henry n.d.; widow, John, Henry, Jacob, Joseph, Catherine, Elizabeth Houk, Mary Ash T1097.12.2¼
59. FISHER, Jacob. Adm. John 4/9/91; widow, John, Molly Warble, Ann, Elizabeth, Mary, Jacob, Daniel T62.16.9

1778 - 1805

60. FLECK, William. Adm. Andrew, David Miller 6/20/01; Elizabeth Piper, Mary Bardona, Andrew, Gattraat Hetrick, Catherine Miller, Christina Salety T97.16.18 Pencil note: All lived Sharpsburg, MD Name changed to Flick; Eliz. Piper w/o Jacob; Marg. Bardona w/o Jacob Barton; Gattraat Hetrick w/o Varner; Cath. Miller w/o David; Salety changed to Solladay.
61. FOARD, Henry. Adm. Rachel 4/5/88; widow, James, Esther, Hugh, Robert, Hannah, John, Henry T118.19.6
62. FOGLER, Andrew. Adm. Ludwig Young, Hester Wimer 4/9/82; widow only T34.6.6
63. FOGLESONG, Christian. Adm. Barbara 3/24/92; widow, Eve Yanders, Frederick, Christian, Catherine, John, David T48.19.9
64. FOGLESONG, Frederick. Adm. Barbara, Christian 9/29/98; his mother, Eve Gentice, Christian, Catherine Arnold, John T44.11.8
65. FRENCH, John. Adm. William Albright, Barbara n.d. (but probably 89); widow, Peter, John, George, Catherine, John Smice (s/o John) T324.10.11
66. FRY, Christian. Adm. John Miller 6/18/91; Christian, Rebecca (these children lived with their grandfather since 1784) T334.3.10
67. FUGATE, Peter. Adm. William Webb 2/27/02; widow, John, James Knowles, William Ditto, heirs of Thomas Charlton (4 in number) T273.11.3
68. FUNK, Henry. Adm. Martin, Henry 2/15/02; widow; add advancement to Elizabeth Newcomer 119.10.0, and Martin 73.0.0, divide equally 53.15.8 3/4 to Martin, Henry, Elizabeth Newcomer, John, Susanna, Ann, Catherine T430.5.10
69. FUNK, Henry (of John) Adm. John Rohrer and wife 4/10/04; widow, John, Daniel, Mary, David T313.9.10
70. FUNK, Henry Sr. Adm. Henry, John 3/14/89; Henry Jr., Susanna Snevely w/o Andrew, David, Joseph, Esther Stotler w/o John, Catherine Winger w/o John, Jacob. Each 15.18.9½. John received 17.12.12½ T129.3.8
71. FUNK, Joseph. Adm. Susanna, David Stoner 2/15/02; widow, Margaret, Susanna, Elizabeth, David, Mary Ann, Sarah T868.19.7½
72. GABLE, Abraham. Adm. Isabella, John McGlocklan 10 or 11/?/85; agreeable to will T292.2.5: 8/8/89; Adm. John McGlaughlin, Ann, William, Abraham T686.14.1
73. GARDENOUR, Jacob. Adm. Jacob 11/7/95; Jacob, Mary McName, Catherine, John T391.15.4
74. GLOSSBRENNER, Gutlep. Adm. Gadfrey, Henry Strause n.d.; Christina Strause, Godfrey, Abraham, Susanna, Adam, Preston, Jacob, John T78.3.10 3/4: 9/6/05 T41.19.2 3/4
75. GOLDING, Palmer. Adm. Josiah Brown n.d. T279.14.1 Nothing else written
76. GRAY, Catherine. Adm. Abraham Roland 1/13/98; Peter, Abraham 4.9.4½ each; Barbara Roland, Catherine Colleflower, Elizabeth, Easter 11.18.6¼ each; Samuel 0.15.01; John, for a stone, 2.10.0; T59.17.14
77. GRAY, Joseph. Adm. Abraham. 4/4/95; his mother; Barbara Rowland, Catherine Colleflower, John, Samuel, Peggy, Abraham, Elizabeth, Easter T49.9.9
78. GUISER, Frederick. Adm. Martin Ridenour 8/12/90; Mathias, Catherine Koler, Christina Bear, Rozana Hoover, Elizabeth, Mary Hoover, Frederick T504.16.4
79. HAFLEY, Christian. Adm. Daniel Rouderock and wife. n.d.; widow T76.3.6
80. HAGERMAN, Christopher. Adm. John Kimmerly and wife 12/?/90; widow, John, Sarah, Christian T66.7.10
81. HAMMETT, Sarah. Adm. James 12/13/05; McKelbie, Sarah, Mary, Catherine, James, William. T290.1.4
82. HARRY, Martin. Adm. Iona, David 3/28/95; Iona, David, Charles, Martin, Jacob, John, Andrew T1380.6.7 Note: the widow had received her legacy for which the Executor has got an allowance in this account.
83. HARTLE, George. Adm. Frederick, Martin 2/1/80; widow, Martin, Frederick, Michael, Bostian, Eave, Peggy all listed as children T422.13.6½
84. HARWOOD, John. Adm. Josiah Riley 12/7/99; widow, 80.9.5; George 80.9.5, To the part agreeable to will; To Mary Atkinson 20.0.0 and Margaret Atkinson 60.9.5 T160.18.0

DISTRIBUTION OF ESTATE ACCOUNTS

85. HAUSER, Mary. Adm. Paul Varner n.d. (probably 12/?/04); Paul Varner, Henry Varner, Mary Capper, Sauer or Lauer (?), Elizabeth Jamison, Sarah Ridenour T87.7.8½
86. HAWLEYBOWER, Balsor. Adm. Abraham Troxell 8/12/83; the widow 19.8.9, each child 5.11.1 T58.6.3 Note: T58.6.3 minus 19.8.9 equals 38.17.8; 38.17.8 divided by 7 equals 5.11.1, suggests there were 7 children
87. HEAFER, Frederick. Adm. John 12/30/97; equal shares to widow, brothers and sisters here named: John, Jacob, Phetty, Peter, Howard, Rebecca, Elizabeth, Catherine, Susannah T84.16.8½
88. HEDDRICK, Warner. Adm. John Heddrick 11/12/05; widow, John, Jacob, George, Joseph, Peter Hann T399.17.5
89. HEFFLEY, Michael. Adm. Frederick Alter 8/14/05; widow, Samuel, Jacob, Elie T165.12.1
90. HEIM, Joseph. Adm. John Langley and wife 10/14/88; widow, Thomas T226.2.6
91. HELTZER, Mary. Adm. David 8/13/05; received of David, full and complete satisfaction of demands against estate; witnesses Peter Henraeth, Elizabeth (her mark) Forquer, Daniel, John; John Bowles, John Cushwa Jr., Thomas Belt, Register.
92. HOGG, Thomas. Adm. Christian Orendorff between 12/04 and 5/05; Christian, John, Aron T119.11.8
93. HOUSEHOLDER, George. Adm. Adam, Jacob 2/27/81; widow, remainder divided among 6 children T182.12.4
94. HOUSER, Jacob. Adm. George Keefer, Christian Bealer 8/17/05; widow, Caty Stassler, Mary Kister, to daughter ___? Bleacher's children (Magdalena, Barbara, John, Caty, Jacob, Mary) T484.8.11 Between 6/04 and 12/04, another dist. T336.5.0
95. HURST, Joseph. Adm. Robert Clark. 9/16/86; Joseph, Ann, Morgan, Ruth T921.19.11
96. HYNES, William. Adm. Hannah, Thomas Hines 2/12/82; Hannah Lynn, Mary Rose, Lettina Gillet, Sarah Yates, Suzannah Powell, Charity Fitzpatrick, Ann Cole T350.0.0
97. INDEY, John. Adm. Catherine 4/9/82; widow, 4 children T431.18.6
98. ITNIRE, John. Adm. Nicholas Hockey and Dorathy, his wife 11/14/91; widow, John, Henry, George T111.6.5 Note: George Shafer and Wendle Shaketer bond.
99. ITNIRE, John. Adm. Henry Schnebly 5/3/87; Elizabeth, Mary, Martin, Daniel, John, Catherine, Leonard T330.5.4
100. JOHNSON, Barnet. Adm. Peter, William, Joshua 2/11/94; Peter, William, Joshua, John, Joseph, Elizabeth, Nancy, Denton, Elinor, Mary T203.19.5
101. JONES, David. Adm. David, John 4/14/88; widow, David, Hannah, John, Peter, Mary T201.16.11
102. JONES, David (whose wife was executrix of Christian Core's estate). Adm. John, David 4/14/88; Christian Core, Rozanna Core, Elizabeth Core T198.10.2
103. KAGY, Michael. Adm. Jacob Snevely, Ludwick Reyday and wife 2/19/85; widow, 57.8.6; 4 children each 9.1.7½ T93.15.0 1/13/98; Barbara, Fransy, Michael T110.7.0
104. KARSON, Richard. Adm. Margaret, Samuel Gray 10/14/05; widow, Esther w/o Thomas Deakin, Richard T50.11.9 3/4
105. KEDERMAN, Michael. Adm. Simon Keseker 2/12/88; widow, 7 children T166.0.6
106. KEEBLER, Jacob. Adm. Jacob 10/16/81; widow, 2 children T51.0.0
107. KENISTRICK, John. Adm. Henry, Nicholas Shefler 10/1/85; Frederick 1.10.0; John, Henry, Catherine Titwiler, Margaret, Mary Easter each 82.1.10½ T411.19.4½
108. KERSHNER, George. Adm. Mary 9/3/05; widow, Benjamin, Mary T277.14.8
109. KEYLER, Frederick. Adm. John Sybert 10/22/82; widow, 6 children T48.12.6
110. KEYSERMAN, Michael. Adm. Simon Kesaker 8/9/83; widow, John Kedomon, George, Michael, Simon, Catherine, Elizabeth, Rebecca T86.8.6 (distribution voided)
111. KNOKEL, Frederick. Adm. Philip Shilling 6/6/95; Hannah Abbonet, Catey Shilling T50.17.10
112. KOALER, George. Adm. Ludwick Emerick 8/17/99; Catherine, George, Daniel, Mary, John, Elizabeth, widow 1/7 T230.1.10½

1778 - 1805

113. KOALER, John. Adm. Catherine Between 8/14 and 8/16/05; widow, Christian, John, George, Catherine, Esther, Jonathan T361.12.10
114. KOHLER, George. Adm. John Hoober, Andrew Stephens 11/11/92; Catherine Coleback, Elizabeth Stephens, George, Barbara Heafner, John T374.4.9
115. LAMBERT, Jacob. Adm. Henry Shaver and wife 10/11/06; widow ½, ½ to son when of age, to bear interest from time he is of age until he is paid T96.11.11
116. LAUDENBERGER, George. Adm. Charles Oldwine, Adam Ott, Peter Waltz 6/21/00; widow, Mary T55.17.6
117. LECKRON, Dorathy. Adm. Jacob 12/7/87; Jacob, Simon, Dorathy T209.6.0
118. LEIGHTER, Peter. Adm. Martin Greider, Eve 5/10/04; widow, Jacob, John, each 46.4.0½ T138.12.1½
119. LINCH, Andrew. Adm. Mary Craver, John Craver 10/29/81; widow, Elizabeth, Peter T19.2.0
120. LONG, Isaac. Adm. Christian Newcomer 8/18/87; Advancement to Isaac 32.5.8; widow, John, Isaac, Jacob, Mary, Elizabeth, Joseph, Emmanuel, Sarah T403.1.0
121. LORSHBAUGH (LOSHBAUGH), Harman. Adm. Devolt Eckelberger 6/29/05; widow, John, Mary, Catherine, Margaret, George, William T206.8.11 Note: a second entry gives the widow 68.16.3½. Both entries are crossed out in the book.
122. LUCKETT, Samuel. Adm. Thomas, Huzza 2/27/81; Executor paid estate 13.10.0
123. LYNN, John. Adm. Abigail 12/21/93; widow, Edmond, Elijah, Clark, Dianah Nance, Mary T218.2.7
124. McCLANNAHAN, Alexander. Adm. Jane, Alexander 5/23/78; Dist. agreeable to will T218.10.10
125. McCLANNAHAN, Alexander Jr. Adm. Jane 6/8/79; Dist. agreeable to will T221.4.3
126. McNAMEE, Hugh. Adm. Alice, Job 6/22/05; widow, Job, Thomas, Hannah, Mary Baker, Adam, George, Gettee, Moses, Alice T126.19.6
127. MAINS, Thomas, Adm. Joseph, Mary 6/11/82; Dist. agreeable to will, bond taken with two Securities T265.3.0
128. MAPHET, William. Adm.William Baird, Abraham Troxell 4/18/80; widow 1/3, Elizabeth, Margaret, unborn child (received equal share) T1023.0.8
129. MARTIN, Jacob. Adm. John, Jacob Rowland 10/24/89; widow 257.17.6¼; Henry, Jacob, Christian each 89.9.4; John, David each 64.9.4; Barbara Rodes, Mary Bear, Elizabeth each 39.9.4 T773.12.7
130. MAYER, Felix. Adm. George Shunk, John Bridenbaugh 2/3/98; whole balance to John Bridenbaugh T11.8.10½
131. MEEK, Thomas. Adm. Thomas, Ann 10/13/78; agreeable to will T1094.18.5
132. MILES, Shaderick. Adm. Robert Barnes and wife 4/10/90; widow, Samuel, Margaret, Mary, John, Morris, Catherine, Benjamin T146.3.11
133. MILLER, Adam. Adm. Mary 2/26/83; widow, Philip, Catherine Gontz, Sarah Gontz, Barnett Swop,Barbara T303.10.0
134. MILLER, Christian. Adm. David, Abraham 6/11/82; Abraham, Fronica, Henry, Samuel, Barbara, Ester, Mary, Christina T584.16.7
135. MILLER, John. Adm. Henry Shyrock 2/26/83; widow, Catherine T29.6.5
136. MILLER, John. Adm. Daniel, John Fisher 4/9/99; Daniel, Jacob Fisher, John, Susanna Wissinger, Mary Studanbaker, Elizabeth Cameron, Jacob, Abraham, Lodwick, David T2010.5.9
137. MONG, Devalt. Adm. Catherine, Peter 12/5/04; widow, Mary Harbaugh, Margaret Crist, Godfred, Peter, Elizabeth Harbaugh, Jacob, Devalt, Catherine T1007.19.0
138. MONG, G.N. Adm. Adam, John Seibert 10/26/92; Adam, Catherine Horn, Eve Hughit, Mary Hughit, Jacob, Margaret Seibert, Henry, John, George T190.17.6
139. MOUDY, Baltzer. Adm. George, Casper between 8/13 and 8/16/05; Amount of judgment vs. estate yet unpaid 34.6.4; George, Henry, Martin, John, Michael, Peter, Adam, Jacob, Casper, Abraham Ash T62.11.1 Note: Deduct 2/7 from each child's part for debt (0.27.0½) due Harmon Loshbaugh

DISTRIBUTION OF ESTATE ACCOUNTS

140. MOYER, Conrod. Adm. Jacob Schnebly 5/28/99; Christian, Barbara, Eve, Peggy, Betsey, Catherine T45.7.6
141. MOYER, Simon. Adm. John, Henry Funk 4/8/83; John 5 pounds of stouff is 8.6.8; 8 children 9.12.10½ each; namely John, Jacob, Christian, Ann, Mary, Barbara, Abraham, Henry T85.9.7
142. MYERS, Lud (probably Ludwig). Adm. Peter Dick, Frederick Fox 9/28/80; 50.0.0 to Pegie; widow 648.14.0; remainder 1297.8.1 to Pegie, Elizabeth, George T1996.2.1
143. MYERS, Michael. Adm. Adam 8/16/05; ½ to widow Catherine, Jacob, Adam, Frederick, Sarah Robinson, Magdalena Showman, Elizabeth Long, Barbara Middlekauff, heirs of Daniel Tinkle, each 5.16.7 T93.5.6
144. NAVE, Abraham. Adm. Jacob, Michael Capp 7/10/04; Jacob, Abraham, George, Leonard, Henry, Catherine Capp, Anne Maria Tuping, Magdalena Smith, Christina Graffin, Margaret Reese's (deceased) 4 children, Sophia Hogmire's (deceased) one child, T188.1.8; In a second distribution between 12/04 and 5/05 each received 76.19.3. The name Tuping spelled Tussing; the name Graffin spelled Griffin.
145. NEAD, Mathias. Adm. Daniel 3/19/91; widow, Daniel, Barbara Clinesmith, Jacob, Charlotte, Uliana English T492.19.8
146. ORNDORFF, Christian. Adm. Eliza 12/3/99; Margaret Hess, Elizabeth Stitta, Barbara Ragan, Catherine Rohrer, Rose Rohrer, Mary Hager T2496.0.3
147. OSTER, Philip. Adm. Joseph Toner (Tower?) between 12/04 and 5/05; 2/3 to Henry, 1/3 to Elizabeth Leighter T237.1.6
148. OSWALD, Philip. Adm. John, Benjamin 4/3/02; the widow's legacy 15.5.7½; John, Adam, Benjamin, Catherine, Eve, Elizabeth each 1.13.5½; Peter 51.13.5½ T76.19.10
149. OTT, Michael. Adm. Adam, John Miller 8/9/86; widow, Jacob, Michael T65.8.3
150. PEAL (PEEL), Nicholas. Adm. Christian Lantz, Henry Summers 8/4/92; widow 21.12.8; Frederick 15.10.1; Elizabeth Lamy, John, Catherine, Eve, George each 5.10.10½ T64.17.11
151. PECK, Jacob. Adm. Jacob 12/12/05; Jacob, Catherine Mankaman, Barbara Momeltorff, Casper, John T347.12.6
152. PERREN, Joseph. Adm. Rachel between 8/85 and 10/85; widow, Deborah, Catherine, Rachel, John, Eliner, Joseph T155.3.7
153. PERRY, Joseph. Adm. Richard Dowlar 6/9/95; widow, Martha McCoy 0.4.5 1/10; This distribution had two figures; the first figure was a legacy; the second figure appears to be what each received after a deduction of some kind. I have lettered the parts to keep them separated:
(a) Perry McCoy legacy 50 received 22.2.8; (b) Daniel McCoy, Jacob McCoy, John McCoy, William McCoy, Martha McCoy m. Fackler, Elinor McCoy m. E. Foard, Margaret McCoy m. Beard, legacy 10 received 4.8.6 4/10; (c) Allien Charlton legacy 400 received 177.1.3 2/10 and her 4 children each, legacy 10 is 40 received 10.14.1 4/10; (d) Elenor Perry legacy 400 received 177.1.3 2/10 and her 3 children each, legacy 10 is 30 received 13.5.7 3/10; (e) Richard Dowlar in right of his wife formerly I. Morehead legacy 200 received 88.10.8; (f) John, James, Ann, children of Ann Perry each, legacy 30 received 13.5.7 2/10; (g) John Perry legacy 100 received 44.5.4; (h) John Darling executors legacy 30 received 13.5.7 2/10; (i) Isabella Perry for Ann legacy 18 per annum, legacy 300 received 132.16.0; (j) Ann Perry ditto 166.13.4 is 73.15.6 6/10?;(k) 0.8.10 3/4 for legacy or 1817.3.4 is legacy 804.7.10 legatee's part (this statement complicates matters); (l) Samuel Jones signature at bottom of distribution
154. PETER, Michael. Adm. Jacob 9/10/91; widow, Jacob, Elizabeth, Abraham T1160.6.6
155. PETERBRENNER, Leonard. Adm. John 9/30/97; Balance due upon passing final account T167.9.10 specie, with interest from 7/1/97, interest paid Leonard Ball, security for the balance
156. PETTICOAT, Nathan. Adm. Hannah 6/5/90; widow, Nathan, William, Laken, Althea Davis, Rachel T230.10.0

1778 - 1805

157. PETTYCORT, Hannah. Adm. Dennis Davis 10/12/04; no distribution listed T188.19.0
158. POFFENBERGER, Valentine. Adm. Henry Yeakles 8/13/05; widow, Polly, Christiana, John, Elizabeth, Henry, Catherine T129.4.10
159. POWERS, Joshua. Adm. Benjamin 10/14/83; widow, to the children Benjamin, Hesley, James, George, Thomas, William, Elizabeth, Mary T86.13.0
160. PRATHER, Richard. Adm. Thomas, Samuel 2/8/94; widow 210.0.0; Elizabeth Pream legacy 31.2.6 and share 153.14.4 3/4; Rebecca legacy 46.7.6 and share 153.14.4 3/4; Thomas, James, Samuel, Henry each 153.14.4 3/4 T1259.16.4
161. PRATHER, Thomas. Adm. Jennett, Basil 10/22/87; widow 330.13.11; Basil, 1 Negro, legacy 90.0.0 and residuary legacy 182.5.4; Thomas, 1 Negro, legacy 25.0.0 and residuary legacy 182.5.4; Elizabeth 182.5.4 T992.9.11
162. PRATHER, Thomas. Adm. Rush, Samuel 12/10/05; widow, Jane, Lucy, Richard, Benjamin, Henry, Thomas, Samuel T89.11.2
163. PUTNAM, Andrew. Adm. Samuel Baker, Coonrod Snibely 3/1/79; agreeable to will T261.11.7
164. RAMER, John. Adm. Jacob Whiteman between 10/29/91 and 3/24/92; widow 25.6.3; John Frederick 27.6.3; John, Benjamin each 24.6.3 T95.5.0
165. RAYNER, John. Adm. Joseph Whiteman 9/30/86; widow 55.6.9; Frederick 18.3.0; John, Benjamin each 15.3.0 T103.15.9
166. REIGH, Mathias. Adm. Barbara 10/25/88; widow, Barbara T234.16.11
167. REYNOLDS, John. Adm. Joseph 6/11/82; 103.9.4 Specie, to give security bond taken 8/13/82
168. RICKENBAUGH, Martin. Adm. Jacob Feller 4/9/03; widow, Henry, Martin, Samuel, David, Daniel, Jacob T1188.13.6 Note: with interest from 11/29/02 until paid
169. RIDENOUR, Daniel. Adm. Philip Kershner 12/9/00; widow 5.6.10 3/4; Nicholas, Henry, Jacob, Mathias, David, Conrod, Valentine Ackenbarger, John's heirs each 0.13.4¼ T10.13.9
170. RIDENOUR, John. Adm. Martin Kershner 4/18/01; widow, 4 children T132.17.4
171. RIDENOUR, Martin. Adm. Martin Kershner 10/9/98; widow, Elizabeth, Magdalena Ault, Dorathy Koogle, Martin, Catherine, Benjamin, Susannah, Barbara T36.1.9
172. RIDENOUR, Matthias. Adm. Martin Kershner, Nicholas 2/14/95; Nicholas, Henry, Jacob, John, Mathias, Daniel, David, Eve Oster, Rosena Echelberger T531.12.8 3/4
173. RODERICK, Lodwick. Adm. Peter Miller. 10/27/98; widow 18.14.10; to each of ten children 32.15.6½ T346.10.6
174. ROME, Henry. Adm. Mary 5/17/99; ½ to widow 104.8.6; Susanna, Elizabeth, Jacob, Catherine, David each 41.15.4 3/4 T213.5.6
175. ROUGH, Henry. Adm. Peter Renold and Eve his wife 5/6/03; widow, John, Henry, Polly, Catherine, Ann T72.11.11
176. RUSSELL, John. Adm. Jacob 12/19/01; 1/3 to widow 206.14.0 3/4; add advancement 413.8.1½; Peter Barkman 70.8.10; Jacob 163.5.9; George 134.5.5; John Fluke 14.12.0; Henry 37.19.2; John 157.0.0; Henry Fluke 0.7.3; Balance to be divided into 9 equal parts for the above, plus Christian Middlecof and Peter Thomas T999.14.5
177. RUTTER, Edmund. Adm. Charles McKown 3/2/81; widow 1157.16.5; balance to heir Alexander 2315.12.10 T3473.9.3
178. SCHNEBLY, Leonard. Adm. Henry Feb. term 88; widow 19.5.7; Elizabeth Miller 33.4.2; Catherine, Susanna, Christina, Leonard each 75.5.6 T353.11.11½ Note: written in margin "lived near Hancock in 1756."
179. SCHNELL, Philip. Adm. Judith, Henry 6/14/91; widow 20.9.3; John 85.9.3; Henry, Phillip, Jacob each 70.9.3; Eliza, Sarah each 20.9.3 T358.4.11
180. SHAFER, Davolt. Adm. Lodwich Young, William Shanefelt 4/29/87; widow 287.5.10; D. 48.13.6; C. Winter 48.11.10½; M. Bumgarner 88.11.10½; A., G., P. Hassen, E. Row, A., S. Yost, B., M., each 48.11.10½ T861.18.6 Note: Initials only in the dist.

7

DISTRIBUTION OF ESTATE ACCOUNTS

181. SHAFER, John. Adm. Barbara 12/18/84; widow 65.12.7½; 101.15.1 divided between John, Henry, Catherine, Elizabeth, Mary, George, Leonard T196.17.11
182. SHANEFELT, Frederick. Adm. William 5/17/99; Frederick, Mary, Catherine, Margaret, Eve with interest from year 1785 till paid. T245.10.6
183. SHANEFERT, John. Adm. William 4/9/85; widow 228.9.0; Elizabeth 27.12.0; John 18.0.0; fees of commission 1.9.8; for Frederick, Mary, Catherine, Margaret, Eve, each 49.2.0½ T521.1.8
184. SHAVER, Peter. Adm. George, Philip Earhart 7/25/95; widow, Philip, George, Peggy T235.9.11
185. SHECTER, Andrew. Adm. Wendle 5/15/84; Wendle, Mary Dick, Doratha Eatenire, Henry T169.0.5
186. SHEES, Peter. Adm. Lodwich Young 4/10/90; Peter 15.3.5; widow 7.11.8½; to Switzer 7.11.8½; to Weaver, Elizabeth (Pence) each 7.11.8¼ T45.10.3
187. SHEETS, Frederick. Adm. Jacob Cale, Barbara Cale 8/10/84; widow, 3 children T105.3.10
188. SHOCKEY, Abraham. Adm. Henry Bougher and Elizabeth his wife 1/30/90; widow, Christian, Ann, Catherine T14.3.10
189. SHOTT, Philip. Adm. Margaret, Anthony Roof 2/15/79; nothing written T602.19.4
190. SHULTZ, George. Adm. Elizabeth 3/12/81; time prayed to pass a 2d account; 12/15/83; Adm. Martin Harry, Elizabeth Harry; widow 112.10.1; Mary 68.15.0¼; 3 daughters each 18.15.01¼; 2 sons each 75.0.0 T387.10.4; 12/15/84; widow 102.0.3; Mary 75.10.1; 2 sons each 51.10.1½; to other 3 girls each 25.10.1½ T356.0.11
191. SHYROCK, Leonard. Adm. John, Michael Fockler 10/29/91; 1/3 to widow, Henry, John, Catherine, Mary, Michael, Elizabeth, Susanna T105.6.7; 5/26/98 T142.11.1
192. SIMMONS, Jacob. Adm. Lodwick Davis and wife 10/6/98; widow, Sarah T170.4.6
193. SIMMONS, Jonathan. Adm. Joseph 11/30/05; Joseph, Thomas Wheeler T25.18.10
194. SMISER, Mathias. Adm. Ann 10/15/81 (see number 197)
195. SMITH, Jacob. Adm. Jacob Konsler 3/24/04; widow 13.6.2; Christian, Andrew, John, David, Betsey Kensler, Polly, Mary each 1.18.0¼ T26.12.4
196. SMITH, John. Adm. George 10/12/79; nothing written T479.14.1
197. SMYSER, Matthias. Adm. Frederick Fible, Ann Fible 8/13/82; widow, 7 children T209.7.0
198. SNAVELY, Conrad. Adm. Adam between 12/04 and 5/05; Catherine Showman, Susannah Seibert, Elizabeth Echart each 250.0.0; John, Henry each 300.0.0; Elizabeth Snyder 200.0.0 for total 1550.0.0; Residue 1010.11.11; Casper, Henry, John, Catherine Showman, Adam, Jacob, Susannah Seibert, Elizabeth Echart each 133.16.6 T2620.11.11 Note: pencil note "settled near Keedysville 1760, Schnebly original name."
199. SNYDER, Abraham. Adm. George Shaver, John Cushwa 10/3/89; widow 87.12.10; Balance between heirs, brothers and sisters and Bequest Relatives 175.5.8 T202.18.6
200. SNYDER, Daniel. Adm. Casper 8/25/87; Daniel, Casper, Mary Jones, Catherine Miller T210.4.5
201. SNYDER, John. Adm. Adam between 3/24/92 and 7/14/92; Adam, Elizabeth Gillium, John, George, David T317.7.9
202. STEPHEN, Leonard. Adm. Andrew, George Winters 2/15/79; widow 10.0.0; to daughter 19.7.4; to five children each 3.2.2; to oldest son 3.11.6 T19.7.4
203. STEFFEE, Andrew. Adm. Nicholas, George 11/14/01; widow, Andrew, Nicholas, George, Michael, Catherine Augustine, Peter, Elizabeth T762.9.2½
204. STOVER, Michael. Adm. Catherine between 9/01 and 11/01; widow, John, George, Jacob, Frederick, Margaret, Catherine T503.8.6 3/4
   8/13/04; Payments made to divisees of deceased Frederick 23.18.6; Jacob, John each 15.18.8; Catherine 18.13.9; George 37.4.11; Margaret 22.14.5 and 33.4.3 T141.14.6

1778 - 1805

205. STREIGHT, Leonard. Adm. Rev. George Young, Leonard 4/12/94; Christian, Laurence, M. Young deceased, Leonard, William, Sarah T198.9.10
206. STRUMBAUGH, Philip. Adm. Magdalena, Mathias Young 4/18/01; widow, George, Magdalena Young T350.11.7
207. STUCKEY, Simon. Adm. George Shaver and wife 3/19/96; widow legacy 70.0.0; Jacob 216.6.11; Susanna Benter 432.13.10; Samuel, Abraham, Rebecca Miller, Simon, Daniel, Eliza, Mary each 216.6.11 T2233.9.4
208. SUMMERS, John. Adm. John 6/2/04; 1/3 to mother of deceased 52.11.5¼; Mary, Peter, Elizabeth Petery, Jacob each 26.5.5 3/4 T157.14.4 3/4 Note: Pencil note in margin: "Elizabeth Petery w/o Ludwick, lived Boonsboro."
209. TETERICK, Peter. Adm. Peter 8/13/82; 11 children each 30.16.7½, namely Peter, Francis, Isaiah, John, Philip, Conrad, Catherine Shedler, Elizabeth Cave, Margaret Statsman, Barbara, Magdalen T340.0.0
210. THOMAS, Jeremiah. Adm. Mary 9/3/03; widow, Sarah Waller (Walter?), Ann Harper, William, Leonard Walters, Joseph, Polly Harper, Elizabeth Board, Jeremiah, John T49.18.4½; n.d.; 1/3 to widow, no indication as to disposition of other 2/3 T49.16.4½
211. THRALLS, Richard. Adm. Joseph 10/11/00; widow 107.6.10; John Olliver, Mary Olliver each 75.0.0; Casandra 0.5.0; Joseph, Richard, Sigmund, Joan, Jacob each 42.17.9 T472.0.7
212. THUSDY, Ann. Adm. William Heyser, Jacob Nicholls 11/3/81; Jacob 11.9.1; 3 remaining children each 39.4.6 T129.2.6
213. TRESLER, John. Adm. Barbara 11/17/98; ½ to widow 82.1.3½; Frederick,Jacob, George, Adam, Elizabeth Sunday, Mary, George Sr. each 11.14.5½ T164.2.7
214. TROUP, Adam. Adm. John Funk, Henry Funk 11/6/90; 0.16.8 widow's part personal estate; 476.4.6 widow's part real estate; David 135.0.0 legacy, 114.2.9¼ d.s.; Adam 100.0.0 legacy, 6.15.0 wearing apparal, 114.2.9¼ d.s.; Henry 100.0.0 legacy, 114.2.9¼ d.s.; Henry son of Jacob 30.0.0; Esther Musselman legacy 10.0.0; the poor 30.0.0; Catherine Shively 66.2.9¼ d.s.; Mary Brewors 114.2.9¼ d.s. T1402.10.1 Note: d.s. means distributive share
215. TROXELL, Abraham. Adm. David Troup, John Hager 1/15/91; widow 142.4.3; David, 2 shares 80.5.3; Catherine, Magdalena, Anna, Sarah, Susanna each 40.12.7 T426.12.11: 6/22/93; 1/3 to widow 170.9.11¼; David 97.8.6½; Catherine Swilar, Magdalena, Anna, Susanna, Salome each 48.14.3¼ T511.9.10
216. TROXELL, George. Adm. John Cellars, Jacob Rowe 6/18/85; widow 30.11.1; Peter, Abraham, Daniel, Catherine, Philip Olinger each 22.11.1 T216.5.2
217. TUG, Frederick. Adm. Jonas Hogmire, Peter Avey 6/17/99; widow 70.0.0; John 162.19.11; Jacob, David each 187.19.11; Catherine Woolf, Elizabeth Long, Susanna Martin, Sarah Haflebower, Mary each 137.19.11 T1298.18.5½
218. TUG, Jacob. 9/17/96; Names of heirs are same as Frederick Tug. Distribution voided.
219. TUTWILER, Henry. Adm. Jacob, Jacob Harry 9/27/94; to the children of the deceased's brothers and sisters, to... (nothing more recorded) T417.0.6
220. TWIGG, John. Adm. Rebecca 3/9/79; widow 30.16.10; children (not named) divided remainder T92.10.6
221. WAGONER, Philip. Adm. Regana 12/27/88; widow, 10 heirs T58.17.9
222. WALLS, Martin. Adm. Mary 4/11/80; ½ to widow 36.12.11; remainder to Catherine, Christina and Jacob, the children T109.8.9
223. WASHBAUGH, Dealmer. Adm. Samuel Bachtell, John Bowman 2/11/83; widow 100.0.0; Margarette Schnebly (Christian), Christina Rohrer (Jacob), Feronica Cochenour (Jacob), Elizabeth Shank (Christian), Mary Lowery (Michel), Susanna Rush (John), Catherine each 181.18.8; Ann 191.18.8 T1569.9.4 Note: Male names in parentheses are husbands

DISTRIBUTION OF ESTATE ACCOUNTS

224. WEIMER, Solime. Adm. Peter Kline, I. Schnebly 7/27/02; Catherine Delmar, legacy 35.0.0; Peter Kline legacy 30.0.0; Jacob Fisher of John 5.0.0; John Fisher 0.5.0; Eliza Fisher 4.0.0; to the poor 15.0.0; additional to each named above 13.2.3 T154.16.3
225. WELLS, Jeremiah. Adm. Rezin, Frederick Shaw 9/21/05; Rezin, Aaron, Elenor Shong, Kipey Brand, Rebecca Bayly, Mary Jones, Milly Jones T775.16.1 3/4
226. WELTY, Christian. Adm. John Wolganst, Christian Palmer 10/21/97; 1/3 to widow 221.5.2; Elizabeth Weaver, Ann Palmer, Barbara Teckerhoof, Magdalena Boster, Christly, Mary, Henry, Catha, John, Susanna, Joseph T663.15.0
227. WHETSTONE, Peter. Adm. Michael Ruff 10/12/79; agreeable to will T191.3.5
228. WHITMORE, Christian. Adm. Mary 2/13/82; widow, 5 children T209.3.8
229. WIANT, Joseph. Adm. Catherine 3/17/87; 1/8 to Elizabeth Forney and her six children, each 0.11.8; To Susa Brown and her five children (Peter, Susa, Jacob, John, Henry) each 0.10.0; Sary Angel and her four children (Margaret, Elizabeth, John, Susa) each 0.8.4; balance to the widow 20.9.1 T21.9.1
230. WILES, Frederick. Adm. Jacob 3/23/99; to the mother, John, Henry, Jacob, David, Elizabeth Hoover each 10.2.9 T60.16.6
231. WILES, William. Adm. Susanna, David 6/7/00; widow, John, Elizabeth Hoover, Henry, Jacob, David T248.7.1
232. WILLISON, Rebecca. Adm. Edward 6/23/79; agreeable to will T64.8.9
233. WILLSON, Walter. Adm. James Chapline, Walter 9/6/83; Balance due on passing final account... (Note: nothing else written)
234. WINTER, George. Adm. John, Martin Ridenour 5/12/04; Balance due estate 2980.12.2½; they have alledged to have distributed and paid to the widow and heirs, with 53.12.11 remaining...(space missing in original record) ...in their hands and also, the sum of 47.13.16½, the difference between money received for the rent and monies paid Fitzhugh, added equals 101.6.5½, to be distributed as 1/11 part to widow and 10 children or each 9.12.9½ T101.6.5½
2d distribution, n.d....all monies paid by a former distribution; money from land sold to Peter Crouse, 63.17.6; 1/11 to widow and 10 children, each 5.16.8¼ T63.17.6
235. WITMYER, George. Adm. Mary, Henry Funk 9/3/03; widow, Barbara Funk, Ann Myers, Mary Stover, Francy Grove, Metlena Fryor, Esther Horine, Elizabeth, Susanna Mason T77.2.8¼
236. WOOLF, John. Adm. Michael Lugh, Jacob Rohrer 12/22/92; Jonathan, Esther Seagrist, Jacob, Daniel, Joseph, Susanna, Hannah, John, Elizabeth Note: No distribution until land is charged
237. WOOLFORD, Adam. Adm. Henry 6/24/99; David, Elizabeth, Mathias, Catherine, Henry, Roseena, Susannah T188.11.1
238. WORLEY, John. Adm. Martin Harry Sr. 3/12/81; 72.9.8 in administrator's favor
239. YAKLY, Jacob. Adm. Barbara 10/21/86; widow, Tobias Ritter, Leonard Knave, Isaac Aley, Henry, Jacob T324.3.0
240. YATES, Thomas Sr. Adm. Thomas Jr. 2/21/89; widow, Thomas, Mary Brown, Elizabeth Maulane, Suzanna's heirs (Raphel Davis, Thomas Davis), Stephen, William, John, Ignatius T510.17.2
241. YATES, William. Adm. Joseph 10/12/90; widow 98.12.6; Sarah, Mary 66.4.2; Joseph, Joshua, William, Amos each 16.4.2 T295.17.6
242. YOUNG, George. Adm. Jacob Harry, George Nigh 6/29/05; widow, John, Samuel, Margaret T53.10.3/4
243. YOUNG, Lodwick. Adm. Jacob, Jacob Rench 6/4/99; Jacob, Marian Smith, Rebecca Rench, Isaac, Lodwick T1099.5.0

DISTRIBUTION OF ESTATE ACCOUNTS
Washington County, Maryland 1806 - 1816

1. ADAMS, John. Adm. Henry 10/3/10; Peter 1250.0.0; deduct advance 310.9.6; Henry, Jacob, John, Christian each 250.0.0; Mary 230.0.0; Christian Winebrenner 150.0.0; John, son of William 40.0.0; balance 425.15.1½ to 4 heirs T2785.5.7½
2. ALLEN, James. Adm. Martha K., Elisha Easton 10/12/15; widow, Archibald, Matilda Easton , Henry, James, Benjamin A.P. T431.10.1½
3. ALLENDER, Anna. Adm. William 2/2/11; Margaret Webb, Anna Webb, William, Thomas, Sarah Charlton, Euasilla Morgan, John D., Elizabeth Riley, Mary Webb's children (Anna and Mary) T10.3.0½
4. ANGLE, Henry. Adm. John, Jacob Adams 9/17/12; widow 600.0.0; David Stake, Daniel Stake, Susanna Stake each 400.0.0; old Brethren Society 75.0.0; amount of bond given by descendants Jacob 1100.0.0, deducted of interest 936.0.0; money received to pay future claims 37.10.0; balance 7835.1.2 in 8 shares each 979.7.8
5. ANKENEY, George. Adm. Henry Feiry, Catherine 4/20/11; widow, 7 children T1481.9.3
6. ANKENEY, George. Adm. Henry Steffey, Catherine 11/18/11; widow, 7 children T1164.10.11½
7. ANKENEY, George. Adm. Jacob Jones and Catherine his wife 3/29/16; widow, Michael Bova, George, John, Mary, Daniel, Samuel, Jacob T1018.36.0
8. ANKENEY, Jacob. Adm. Michael Bova, Jacob Jones 5/12/15; Catherine Jones, Elizabeth Bova, George, John, Mary, Daniel, Samuel T262.2.5 5/29/16 T $87.75
9. ANKENEY, Jacob. Adm. Henry 10/14/14; Susanna, Henry, David, Mary Miller, Sarah Healing, John, Margaret T601.17.7½
10. ARNSBERGER, Christopher. Adm. Christopher, George 9/22/12; Henry, Christopher, John, Frederick, Catherine, Mary Boon, Casandra Christian, Elizabeth, Michael, Esther, Jacob, George T539.4.9
11. ARTZ, Henry. Adm. Christian 12/15/08; widow, Abraham, Henry, Peter, Joseph, Elizabeth, Philip, John, Mary T215.5.9
12. BAKER, Nicholas. Adm. Sarah, Nicholas Fritz 3/23/14; widow, Peter, John, Jacob, Samuel, Lewis, Nicholas T1227.1.9½
13. BARNETT, Jacob. Adm. Henry, Jacob 4/25/12; Henry, Jacob, John Emil, Catherine McLaughlin, John, Susanna Emil, Casandra, David, Ann, Mary T1438.5.10
14. BARTOON, Jacob. Adm. Adam Hybarger 3/8/16; John, Adam Hybarger, Abraham Baker, John Cretzer each 49.9.7 3/4   T197.18.7
15. BAYER, Magdolena. Adm. Jacob 12/14/08; John, Christian T305.10.4
16. BEALL, Anthony. Adm. Andrew, Jacob, Conrad Mentzer 1/1/14; Andrew, John, Jacob, Frederick, David, George Liday, Conrad Mentzer T1571.3.8
17. BEARD, Nicholas. Adm. Christian Artz, n.d.; 9 heirs, interest from 5/3/07 T1576.4.6½
18. BEARD, Nicholas P. Adm. Joseph Kessinger 12/2/15; widow, 2 children T397.9.6; n.d.; widow, 5 heirs T159.0.7
19. BELCH, James. Adm. Susanna, William Simpkins 11/3/13; widow, 6 children T147.0.1
20. BETZ, Frederick. Adm. Catherine, Martin Rohrer 10/26/13; widow, Mary Davis, John, Frederick, Jacob, Sarah T252.3.5½
21. BETZ, William. Adm. Peter Palmer 1/9/08; widow, Jacob, Mary Ann, John, Catherine, Nancy T18.15.7½
22. BINKLEY, Catherine. Adm. Henry Shupe 10/16/09; 45 heirs T54.9.3
23. BINKLEY, Gutleib. Adm. Barbara 3/24/13; widow, 3 children T100.3.5; 7/17/13 T240.12.10
24. BOND, John. Adm. Edmund McCoy, Robert Chaney 12/22/09; Jealeur Chaney, Thomas, Mary McCoy, Luke, Elizabeth Chaney, John, Walter, James, Alexander T131.10.1½ 1/28/11 T28.12.9
25. BOOK, Catherine. Adm. George Shall 6/1/07; George Wagoner, Mary Wagner, Susanna Wagoner, John, Pricilla, Joseph each 2.17.11; Christian Hedrick 8.13.8½ T26.1.2½
26. BOTELER, Henry. Adm. Thomas,Lingan 4/24/16; Thomas, Lingan, Hezekiah, Henry, heirs of Mary Allen, Priscilla Clagett, Sarah Easton T $21,322.62
27. BOTELER, William. Adm. Christian Stonebreaker 2/23/16; Jane Stonebreaker, Eliza Linch, Hezekiah, Lingan, Alexander H. T121.5.2½

DISTRIBUTION OF ESTATE ACCOUNTS

28. BOUSER, Henry. Adm. George Nigh 12/16/07; Frederick, John, Barbara Binkley, Ann Richaback, Elizabeth Bayer, Magdalena Young T1861.17.4½
29. BOVEY, Michael. Adm. Barbara, Michael 7/26/06; widow, Magdolena Slagle, Michael, Daniel, Barbara Haine, Catherine, Mary T779.18.5
30. BOYER, Christian. Adm. John n.d.; Elenor, Nancy T157.8.1
31. BOYER, Magdolena. Adm. Christian 3/14/09; John, Christian, Eleanor, Nancy T6.13.10
32. BRANSTATER, John. Adm. Martin Ridenour 3/4/08; widow 1/3, plus 22.10.0; Elizabeth, Mary, Mary Ann T171.5.3 Interest from 12/7/05 to be paid to widow for support of children
33. BREWER, Daniel. Adm. Elizabeth after 6/10/02; widow, Jacob, Mary, John, Elizabeth, Margaret T267.19.0
34. BROADSTONE, Philip. Adm. Catherine 4/14/07; widow, Sophia, Catherine, Christina, Philip, Nicholas T94.1.6
35. CAPP, Michael. Adm. Samuel Hughes 12/2/07; widow, Jacob Earhart and wife, George Knode and wife, Michael T3523.23.0 Second distribution, n.d.; Michael received addition of 79.44.0; George Knode and wife reduced by 158.99.0
36. CARY, Robert T. Adm. Michael Hanner 6/30/14; George, James each $1364.99½; Cyrus, Eliza, William, Robert, John, Eleanor, each $454.83 T $5459.98
37. CHANEY, Jeremiah. Adm. David, John 12/2/15; legacy to Noamia Darby 25.0.0; Mary McCoy, Drusilla Lane, Noami Johnson, Elizabeth, Rebecca O'Neal T1540.16.9
38. CHAPLINE, Jeremiah. Adm. Elizabeth 8/27/11; widow, 8 children T535.16.16½
39. CLINE, Daniel. Adm. Harry Dillman 6/30/06; Catherine (line through name); 4 heirs T54.6.0
40. CLOM, Richard. Adm. John Hammond 2/21/07; widow, Mary, Rebecca, Sarah T95.1.9
41. CLOPPER, Henry. Adm. Mathias n.d.; Matthias, Henry Brim, Henry T149.19.10 10/16/09; T153.13.6 Received my proportion on above, signed Henry Brim
42. COMBS, Colman. Adm. John 2/23/10; widow, John, Sarah Douglas, Mary Edwards, Lewis's heirs, Thomas T801.17.8
43. COMBS, Lewis. Adm. Ruth, Stephen Bryan 3/28/08; widow, Mary, Nancy, Eliza T582.2.5½
44. CONRAD, Daniel. Adm. Jacob 8/14/07; widow, William, children of Venter each 71.10.0½ T214.10.1½
45. CONRAD, William. Adm. Adam Ott 12/9/06; widow, 5 children, plus interest from 7/10/91 T256.1.5 Second distribution, n.d.; 5 heirs T928.18.6
46. CRAMER, Godfred. Adm. Barnet Allan whose wife was Adm. 11/2/14; widow, John, Elizabeth T254.5.9 Share due when John and Elizabeth of age; Interest to date is allowance for support and maintenance of children
47. CROMWELL, William. Adm. George Grauff 4/10/11; widow, Maria Catherine, Richard, Constant Comfort, William T638.18.0½
48. CUSHWA, John. Adm. John, David n.d.; legacy to Margaret, Christian, Betsey, Sarah, Benjamin each 400.0.0; Catherine Eckelberger, John, Jacob, Jonathan, David, Margaret, Christian Speck, Sarah Bear, Elizabeth, Benjamin each 146.12.1½ T1870.0.3 4/20/08; T72.14.10 2/3
49. DAGAN, Jacob. Adm. Adam, Conrad Horine 3/6/08; Elizabeth Locher, Danise, Lewis Beall T54.9.1 3/4
50. DARLING, John. 5/13/12; Henry Downey received 0.17.5 from Darling estate; 5/18/12, 0.14.5 part of Mary Lowra's, estate of John Darling (not signed); 5/18/12, 0.14.0 part of Mary Lower's, estate of John Darling (not signed)
51. DAVIS, Mary. Adm. Samuel Miller. 7/2/16; heirs of Johan Caliour (William, Charles, _____, James) T $245.88 (Distribution crossed out in the book)
52. DAVIS, William. Adm. Samuel Miller 6/17/16; widow, William, James each 100.0.0; Stephen, Charles, Mary Cowan each 371.0.10½ T3692.3.10½
53. DEEDS, Adam. Adm. Adam Schnebly n.d.; Michael Miller, George Miller, Catherine wife of Abraham Hinkle, Susannah wife of Joseph Lantz, Margaret wife of Joseph Keel, Jacob Miller, Mary wife of Michael Gingler, Leonard Miller T360.17.7; 2/3 of 5/8 of above paid Michael Hinkle, Attorney for 5 of the heirs; fee power of attorney

1806 - 1816

54. DELLAHUNT, William. Adm. Philip Kreich (?), Nicholas Kriech (?) 1/31/11; Mary Bowles, amount deducted 30.16.1½; widow 55.6.4; Catherine 110.12.8; interest from 10/27/10 T196.15.1¼
55. DILLAHUNT, James. Adm. William, Thomas 2/7/07; John, Thomas, Richard Beck T38.7.9
56. DOWNEY, William. Adm. Susannah Gordon, Robert Downey 4/4/13; Susannah Gordon 2172.13.11; Robert, Samuel each 1086.6.11½; heirs of Elizabeth Blackburn 2172.13.4; T6518.1.9 4/3/16; Susannah Gordon, Hester Little, Ruth Wallace, William Baird T9068.16.16
57. DOYLE, Adam. Adm. George 5/7/13; widow, Representative of Henry, John, Doren, Margaret Karnes, George, Adam T283.19.9
58. EASON, William. Adm. Ruth, William, Elisha 8/13/06; legacy to John 22.10.0; William, Amelia; Elisha, Hesekiah, Elizabeth, John T429.13.0
59. EDWARDS, John. Adm. Thomas 12/16/07; 2/3 to widow 804.12.3; Benjamin, Thomas, Paregrine, Emmory, Owen, Editha T1208.8.4½ n.d.; 2/3 to widow, 6 children T1185.10.9 3/7/09; 2/3 to widow, 6 children T1486.8.0½ with interest from 8/3/06
60. EDWARDS, Mary. Adm. John Combs 6/12/11; Mary Combs, John Combs, Lewis Combs heirs, Rebecca Douglass, Thomas, Thomas Combs T1223.10.0
61. ELENBAUGH, Mary. Adm. Peter Conn 12/10/11; 7 heirs, names unknown T219.14.2
62. EMMERT, Leonard. Adm. Benjamin, Leonard, Michael 1/5/09; Benjamin's legacy 600.0.0 plus interest 105.0.0, for 4 years, 4 months, 21 days, T705.10.0, less cash 211.7.6, balance 494.2.6; Magdalena's legacy 600.0.0 less cash 279.7.8, balance 320.12.4; Michael, Joseph each 600.0.0; Catherine 600.0.0 less cash 178.12.4, balance 421.7.1; George, Daniel each 600.0.0; two desks for George 18.15.0; Benjamin, Leonard, Magdalena, John, Michael, Joseph, Catherine, George, Daniel each 342.14.10 3/4 T6739.10.11 3/4
63. EVERSOLE, Christian. Adm. Emanuel, Isaac Houser 2/15/10; Christian's legacy 1000.0.0; Emanuel 1400.0.0; Susannah Houser, Magdalena Peters, Catherine Furry, Hannah Middlecalf, Emanuel, Christian each 834.17.11; each of the above plus Elizabeth Baker received additional 1414.14.6 T17,312.9.4
64. FAUSNAUGHT, Henry. Adm. Jacob Root, John Hammond 4/29/08; 1/3 to widow 184.13.2½; Jacob, John, Abraham, Henry, Barbara, Catherine, Elizabeth, Susannah, Ulianna, Sarah each 36.18.7½ T553.19.8
65. FAUSNAUGHT, John. Adm. Julianna, Henry Shafer n.d.; widow 12.1.7; Conrad, Maria, Jacob, Dorathy, Catherine, George, John, Adam, Henry, Barbara, Susannah, Elizabeth, Eve, Barnett, Julianna each 1.12.2½; 4/3/10; widow, children T23.4.10½; received $76.66 each; received 1.18.4 each. Henry Shafer, Adm., received additional money from C_____ _____?, Eve and husband, Samuel Nunemocker, Peter Hessong and Susanna (each made their mark). n.d.; widow 1/3 to be placed in hands of the Trustee, the interest to be given the widow yearly T1624.2.2:
Fausnaught Notes in the Distribution Book:
- 5/4/10, Jacob received $20.45; John received same.
- Peter Hessong received by right of his wife Barbara, heir of John $124.50, signed his mark.
- estate of John.... (unreadable)
- 5/2/10, Samuel Noonemaker $57.24 from esatate of John.
- George Roads, 5/2/10 received $57.24 by right of wife Eve, heir of John.
- 5/2/10 received $124.54 full amount of Jacob, heir of John.
- John Shafer, guardian for 3 heirs of Henry, being their portion of estate of John, $51.39, 5/2/10
- John Shafer received $475.00 due Anna Maria, Susanna, from estate of father John 5/2/10
- Catherine, 5/10/10, received $20.45, heir of Henry, signed her mark
- Barbara, 5/10/10, received $20.45, heir of Henry, signed her mark
- 10/2/10, Henry received 35.9.4 from estate of John
- 6/24/13 $204.54, amount due Dorathy from estate of John, signed Peter Hessang, her mark
(Continued on next page)

DISTRIBUTION OF ESTATE ACCOUNTS

65. FAUSNAUGHT, John (Notes, Continued)
    - 4/24/10, Julianna received $44.28 from estate of John, signed her mark.
    - George Roads received $120.55.
    - Samuel Noonemocker received $124.55 for right of wife Elizabeth 4/27/10, signed her mark
    - 4/27/10 received $19.57, right of my wife Elizabeth, heir to Henry deceased, in full of all rent and final payment of the land of John deceased, signed Samuel Noonemaker, his mark
    - John, 5/11/10, received $204.04 from estate of John, signed his mark
    - 5/12/10, received of George Smootz $57.94 in full of my proportion of the estate of John Deceased in right of my wife Barbara. Peter Hesong (his mark) witness John Williams
66. FERROLL, Patrick. Adm. Patrick Quinan. n.d.; deducted for negro George who obtained freedom in Kentucky 47.10.0; deducted for negro Catey, Frank and Paris 120.0.0; to widow 1/3, 222.19.3, John, Peggy Dowelin, Francis each 148.12.10 T668.17.9 Second distribution: Adm. Patrick 4/8/06; widow relinquished will, received 1/3, 316.16.4½; 3 children 214.10.11 T950.9.½
67. FLORA, Conrad. Adm. Frederick Fishawk 3/31/15; Mary Karman, Catherine Hutcheson, Elizabeth McKain, John, Nancy T187.1.1
68. FLORA, John. Adm. Frederick Fishawk 9/14/11; specific legacy to Elizabeth 25.0.0; Mary Keirnan, Catherine Hutcheson, Elizabeth McKain, John, Nancy T718.3.6 Second distribution: Adm. Jacob Lambert n.d.; T54.5.5   3/31/12: Adm. Frederick Fishawk T186.6.1   3/29/13 T187.0.9   4/11/14 T184.3.6   2/28/16 T339.9.7
69. FOGLE, George. Adm. John, Robert Cowan 3/5/16; George's heirs, Jacob, Barbara Butts, John T $363.73
70. FOPLER, David. Adm. Mary 2/15/15; widow, Sarah T175.5.0
71. FORD, Abigail. Adm. William Blackmore n.d.; heirs of Th____ Jack, Esabelle Otto, Henry Houck, Esther Harlis, Mary Ellis, Sarah Blackmore, Joseph, Henry, the widow Ford T99.3.11
72. FORMAN, John. Adm. Mary 8/23/15; widow, Jacob I. T203.18.9
73. FOUTZ, Frederick. Adm. Susannah, Jacob, Jacob Alter n.d.; widow, Jacob, Henry, John, William, Frederick, David, George, Ann Thome?, Elizabeth Alter, Peggy, Charlotte T886.2.6
74. FRANTZ, Emanuel. Adm. Eve, Henry 4/26/16; widow, Frederick,Elizabeth, Julian, Leddia, Catherine, George, Nathaniel, Mary, Henry T $1116.11
75. FRYE, Abraham. Adm. Abraham Schmutz 3/19/14; widow received child's part; John, William, Joseph, Elizabeth Guchareah?, Frederick, Jacob, Catherine Schmutz, Wishore, Fanny Binkly T55.12.3
76. FUGATE, Mary. Adm. Thomas Charlton 12/3/08; specific legacy to negro Jeny 10.0.0; John, Mary Knowles, Ann Deltz, Ann Bayly, John Charlton, Joshua Charlton, Sarah Charlton, interest from 11/3/08   T195.8.9
77. FUNK, Henry. Adm. Martin, Henry n.d.; widow, 8 children T175.11.11½
78. FUNK, Henry of John Adm. John Rohrer of Martin 4/14/07; widow, John, Daniel, David, Mary T306.8.0
79. GALE, William. Adm. Catherine, John Combs 1/2/11; widow, James, Benjamin, Mary T64.14.11½
80. GARLOCK, John. Adm. Christian 12/21/10; widow, John, Christian, Elizabeth Besinger, Jacob T91.13.0 interest from 12/17/05
81. GARY, George. Adm. Jonas Hogmire, George Smith 11/23/14; specific legacy to Judith, Sarah, Susanna 700.0.0; to Elie Mott 100.0.0; to Mary, Eve each 800.0.0 T3800.0.0 Judith Eakle, Sarah Stebler, Susannah Mott, Mary, Eve Dunn each 6.10.0; Elie Mott 0.16.8 T33.6.8   12/2/14 Judith Eakle, Sarah Stebler, Susannah Mots, Mary, Eve, each 255.10.4½; Elie Mots 31.18.11½ T1309.10.9   2/20/16; Eve now Eve Davis T1313.19.11

1806 - 1816

82. GEETING, George A. Adm. Andrew Rinehart 7/20/13; Peter, Henry, Elizabeth Tanner, Barbara Core, Mary Clapper, Christian Bower, George, Jacob, Rosanna Houser, Simon T884.10.0
83. GEIGER, John. Adm. Susannah, John Harey 6/27/07; widow, Elizabeth, Ann Alieron?, Jacob H., Frances, Eleanor, Henrietta T8793.10.4
84. GEIGER, Peter. Adm. John 10/21/12; 5/6 to John, 1/6 to Catherine Fesler T507.4.0
85. GEIGER, Susannah. Adm. John, George Harry 4/18/10; Jacob, John, Eliza, George, Amelia, Frances, Jacob, Eleanora, Henrietta T1560.18.0 Interest from 11/3/09 till paid
86. GOOD, William. Adm. John 6/4/12; John, Josiah, William T203.12.2
87. GREY, Peter. Adm. John, Elizabeth 3/18/08; widow, John, Joseph, Susannah, Peter, Mary T366.1.9
88. GREY, Samuel. Adm. Jacob Runner 4/20/12; widow, Elizabeth, John, Samuel, George, Joseph T215.4.9½ Adm. Jacob Brunner 5/21/13; widow, John, Samuel, George, Joseph T87.9.6 8/4/14; widow, Elizabeth, John, Samuel, George, Joseph T90.17.8½ 4/8/15 T89.2.0 9/18/12 received $5.56 paid by Colloflower, part of legacy due children of Samuel Grey, signed Elizabeth Grey, her mark
89. GRIFFITH, Sylvanus. Adm. Elizabeth 12/7/14; widow, Eliza T473.13.5
90. GROUND, John. Adm. Joseph Smith 5/15/14; widow, Joseph, Sarah T368.16.3
91. GROUND, Philip. Adm. George 4/19/14; George, heirs of John, Elizabeth Rupall T3096.0.6 5/11/14, filled by George Smith for executor George Ground T249.2.0 4/28/15, George Smith, Atty. in fact for the estate; Adm. George Ground T782.16.0 5/6/16, Adm. George; George, John's heirs, Elizabeth T $4175.68
92. HALLER, John. Adm. Daniel 2/4/16; John, Elizabeth Wolgamot, Catherine Fogwell, Jacob, Mary Pottorf, Daniel, Susannah, Barbara, Samuel, George Miller T182.2.0
93. HAMMEL, John. Adm. Joseph, Isaac 3/16/11; specific legacy to Elizabeth 5.0.0; Joseph, Isaac, John, George, Elizabeth each 20.6.5 T106.12.3 Interest from 6/1/10
94. HARRY, Jacob. Adm. George I. Jr. 10/12/08; legacy left Elizabeth 100.0.0; widow, George I., Sarah, Elizabeth, Mary, John, Samuel, Hannah, Susannah T4014.19.1½ interest from 7/25/07 6/22/10 T711.12.0
95. HARRY, Martin. Adm. Jacob, Susannah Geiger 2/10/06; balance divided equally to widow and 2 heirs T5412.13.5
96. HARRY, Mary E. Adm. George I. 6/22/10; same heirs as Jacob Harry #94 T702.11.0
97. HECK, Andrew. Adm. Barbara, Henry 2/24/11; widow, Peter, Jacob, Henry, John, Barbara Hofmans children T257.16.1 4/18/12 Adm. Henry T4.6.6 4/28/13 balance due estate for 1812 T12.4.6
Heck Note: John Hoffman received 6/10/11, $15.75 due heirs of Barbara Hoffman who was heir of Andrew Heck. ____ Zuck received 6/30/11, 30.79.0½ due 5 children of Hoffman
98. HECKROTE, Henry. Adm. John Brumley, Eliza Brumley 5/10/06; widow, John 94.11.5. Children's expenses 48.12.7; 448.12.7 divided into 6 parts T993.0.0 n.d.; change in distribution, widow 253.12.10; each child 72.9.42 from 507.5.8 T760.18.6
99. HEFFLEY, Michael Sr. Adm. Frederick Alter 1/13/08; Charles, heirs of Michael, Catherine Wolford, Henry, Eve Miller T84.3.4 1/3
100. HELM, Thomas. Adm. John Asberry, Benjamin Yoe and wife 4/21/12; widow, Sp____, Meredith, Sarah, Margaret, Joseph T1631.16.3
101. HERSH, Jacob Adm. Fanny n.d.; widow, Elizabeth, Jacob, George, Henry, David T176.7.1½
102. HERSHEY, Isaac. Adm. John, Christian 9/16/13; specific legacy to Barbara wife of John and Joseph, each 900.0.0; Christian, Andrew, John, Barbara, Joseph, David, Isaac each 216.17.7 T3318.3.0
103. HERSHEY, John. Adm. Andrew, John 5/19/12; Andrew Shupe, Andrew, Magdalena Shelly, John, Christian, Barbara Miller, John, Joseph, David, Elizabeth Eby, Frany Avey each 600.0.0 Balance to be distributed, 3943.6.3; 11 heirs each 276.13.3½

DISTRIBUTION OF ESTATE ACCOUNTS

104. HESS, John. Adm. Henry Shafer 6/24/16; David, Samuel, John, Henry, Elizabeth, Susannah T $2678.66
105. HOFFMAN, John. Adm. Barbara n.d.; widow, John, Elizabeth Swingley T442.14.0 Second distribution: n.d. T395.3.7½
106. HOGMIRE, Daniel. Adm. Jacob Howell, Henry 2/16/12; widow, Henry T160.17.3
107. HOMLES, Conrad. Adm. Jacob, Conrad 2/14/07; 3 heirs T355.19.4½
108. HOOVER, Adam. Adm. William Andrews 8/11/09; Peter specific legacy 5.0.0; Elizabeth Andrews 30.6.3; Margaret and Jacob each 15.3.1 3/4 T65.12.7   Further receipts 4.0.2, ½ of which is 2.0.1, balance divided among the minors; Margaret and Jacob each 14.3.2¼ T28.6.4½; Washington County term 1/16/10 received of George Smoot, Register of Wills the above 14.3.2 for Jacob, signed Jacob Huyett. 8/26/11, 14.3.2 received by Margaret from estate of Adam, signed, her mark
109. HOOVER, John. Adm. Jacob Welty, Mathew Hoffman 3/6/16; John, Jacob Welty, Mathew Hoffman, Michael Sprinkle, John Wartz, Christopher, George Mentzer, heirs of Henry T1403.9.0
110. HORINE, Adam. Adm. John 3/6/17; widow, Nancy, Henry, Catherine, Daniel T295.15.10 9/18/13 T283.7.11   6/5/15; widow, Nancy, Henry, Daniel each 16.19.0 3/4, heirs of Elizabeth, to wit the widow, Nancy, Henry and Daniel 16.19.0 3/4 T101.14.5
111. HORINE, Catherine. Adm. Abel Williams 6/18/16; Catherine Williams (the mother), Nancy, Henry, Daniel each 25.17.10
112. HOUSEHOLDER, Adam. Adm. Jonathan Myers Jr. 3/13/07; Elizabeth, Eve Bayor, Margaret Bosart, Catherine Tyce, Mary T106.16.4
113. HOUSER, Abraham. Adm. Jacob, Jacob Huffer 8/5/14; specific legacy to Barbara Tetrick and Mary Grim 0.7.6 each; John, Elizabeth Garber, Jacob, Abraham, Henry, Christian, Barbara Deitrick's children, Mary Grim T1619.12.5   Second distribution 4/8/15; 8 heirs T20.9.2
114. HUGHES, James. Adm. Anthony, Samuel Jr. 5/21/11; amount in money $2834.28; amount in Negro property $1535.00; 1/3 to widow $1456.42; 3 children each $459.29; amount Negro property retained for children $1535.00 T$2834.28
115. HURST, Moses R. Adm. Jacques 3/22/15; Ann Jacques, Ruth Jacob, heirs of Morgan Hurst T85.1.10½   22.17.1 due estate of Joseph Hurst to be divided as above
116. HYLAND, Hugh. Adm. Elisha, John 3/20/09; specific legacy to Denmar 37.10.0; Elisha, John R., Mary Lowman T326.10.0   interest from 4/20/06
117. JACQUES, Thomas. Adm. Anthony 2/14/07; widow, one heir T150.16.3
118. JOHN, Daniel. Adm. Christian Beeler, Joseph Tenor 12/26/10; two bonds each 50.0.0 remain in the hands of the Adm.; Balance 30.7.6: Peter, Elizabeth. Thomas, Catherine Denor, John, Abraham, Susannah Beeler, Rachel Hoffman's children (Elizabeth, Susannah and Christine), Henry's child (Elizabeth), Margaret Beall's children (____, Catherine, Margaret, Elizabeth, Rachel, Daniel and John) T130.7.6
119. JOHN, Henry. Adm. Solomon Boyer n.d.; 1/3 to widow 68.15.4; one heir 137.10.8 T206.0.0
120. JOHNSON, Peter. Adm. John 1/24/14; Elizabeth Biles, Mary 9/7/14 T42.1.1½
121. JONES, John Adm. Elizabeth 4/8/06; widow, Anthony T46.9.8
122. KENNEDY, George. Adm. George French 3/22/11; widow, 2 children T1461.4.7
123. KEPLINGER, George. Adm. Jacob 4/21/10; specific legacy 18.15.0 and 50.0.0, balance 834.14.11½; Jacob, George T903.9.11½
124. KERSHNER, Elias. Adm. Anthony Howard 11/18/06; Adam Miller, Martin, Ann Howard, George, Joseph, heirs of Elizabeth Kendal T95.4.4
125. KNODE, George. Adm. George Nigh 5/22/09; Susannah the widow, Susannah, Mary, Jacob, George, Margaret, Elizabeth, Jonathan each 50.11.10 3/4 T404.15.2
126. KOALER, John. Adm. George 4/17/12; Jonathan, George, Catherine Culp, Christine Wentling's heirs, Esther Bowers T12.16.4½
127. KREPS, Sodwick. Adm. Christine 2/11/07; widow, 4 children T21.10.8

1806 - 1816

128. KYSER (KEYSER), Frederick. Adm. Michael, John Beard 2/6/07; Michael, Peter, Catherine Steffey, John Beard, Rosannah Heaver, Peggy Heaver, Hawn's heirs, each 17.3.10 Note: Column beside this indicates each 32.0.3, both entries crossed out. Possibly, the distribution was cancelled
129. LANTZ, Elizabeth. Adm. John Blecher 1/16/10; John Blecher, Catherine Meauck, Samuel Blecher, Henry Lance, Magdalena Smith, Henry T12.5.6
130. LANTZ, Frederick. Adm. Susanna Foutz, Jacob, Jacob Alter 3/31/13; widow, 10 heirs T2477.18.11
131. LANTZ, George. Adm. Christian 4/20/07; widow, 2 children T493.2.6
132. LANTZ, Jacob. Adm. Henry 3/11/11; Elizabeth Long, Barbara Keefauver, Henry, Magdalena Smith, Mary Poffenberger each 3.15.0
133. LECKROON, Simon. Adm. Jacob Jr., Jacob Sr. 6/3/15; Jacob, John, Samuel, Daniel, Ann, Mary, Elizabeth, Sarah, Margaret, Catherine, Susanna, Maria T1049.6.9
134. LEIGHTER, Peter. Adm. Peter Slickleather, Eve his wife 5/12/07; widow, Jacob, John interest from 2/9/94 T194.8.7
135. LOCHER, Frederick. Adm. Barbara, Frederick Grosh n.d.; widow 8.16.5; balance 17.12.10 to be placed at interest to the widow yearly for remainder of her life, and afterwards to be equally divided between John, Henry and Jacob T26.9.3
136. LONG, John. Adm. John, ____ Brumbaugh 2/7/16; widow, Elizabeth Brumbaugh, John, David, Susannah Martin, Samuel, Henry, Peter, Mary T1338.13.6
137. LONGANACRE, Christian. Adm. Philip Pry 8/15/14; 3 heirs T1.18.4½
138. LOSHBAUGH, Harmon. Adm. Michael Eckleberger 9/2/07; 1/3 to widow 147.6.6½; other allowances 157.14.1; Mary, John, Catherine, Margaret, William, George 21.5.5½ T441.19.8
139. LOWRA, Michael. Adm. Barbara, George 2/12/08; widow, Margaret, George, Elizabeth, Mary, Henry, John, Susannah T214.6.6
140. LYDAY, Adam. Adm. George Liday 9/2/06; widow, daughter, two others T224.13.6
141. McCLELAND, James. Adm. Alexander 6/25/07; widow, 11 children interest from 8/28/06 T46.1.10
142. McCOY, Archibald. Adm. James 6/6/11; 5 daughters T257.13.0
143. McLAUGHLIN, John. Adm. Susannah, Henry Barnett 11/?/10; Register fee 2.17.4; retained for William Gabriel 11.5.0; widow 97.3.11; Henry, John, Catherine Barnett, Susan Cromwell, heirs of Nancy Miller, Elizabeth Schnebley's heirs, each 32.7.11½ T305.14.1½
144. MALOTT, Peter. Adm. Peter, Michael, Daniel 9/15/07; widow, Thomas, Theodore, John, Joseph, William, Peter, Michael, Daniel, Hiram, Hannah South, Sarah Stuart T856.19.3
145. MARSTELLER, George. Adm. Elizabeth after 6/10/06; widow, Nicholas, Benjamin, Ann, Rebecca, John, Sarah, George, Polly T76.19.9
146. MARTIN, Anna. Adm. Jacob, Henry 3/14/09; heirs of Barbara Rohrer, Jacob Bare Jr. of Mary, Henry, Jacob, David, Peter Grey, Christian T902.16.4½
147. MAUCHLER, Christian. Adm. John Shafer 12/9/09; widow, Margaret T60.13.8
148. MILES, Charles. Adm. Easau Becknell 4/14/06; John, Sarah, William, Isaac, Charles, James T239.17.10
149. MILLER, John. Adm. Samuel 12/19/08; widow, Samuel, Sarah, Catherine, Elizabeth, Jacob, Magdalena, John T1161.13.1¼
150. MILLER, John. Adm. John Celler 5/27/14; specific legacy to John Light 300.0.0; to Harmon Wertz and John Shinefelt each 100.0.0; to Susanna Wertz 150.0.0; to Sarah, Hy____ Stonelling? each 30.0.0; balance ½ to John Light, ½ to Susanna Wertz, each 99.12.10½ T909.5.9½
151. MILLER, John. Adm. Jacob Schnebly 5/20/15; widow, Maria, George, Sally, Jacob T1165.12.6
152. MOYER, Abraham. Adm. Jacob Schnebly 5/7/12; widow, Nancy, Jacob, Betsy, Abraham, John, Peggy, Catherine Ross, Samuel T119.6.6
153. MUMMA, Henry. Adm. Jacob 3/30/11; 1/3 due estate 31.16.9; John, Barbara Warble, Henry, Joseph, Margaret, Jacob each 15.11.11 T125.7.4
154. MYERS, Michael. Adm. Adam 4/1/12; ½ to widow 83.7.4; Jacob, Adam, Frederick, Sarah Robinson, Magdalena Showman, Elizabeth Long, Barbara Middlecalf, heirs of Daniel Tinkle T166.14.8

DISTRIBUTION OF ESTATE ACCOUNTS

155. NEALL, Aquilla. Adm. William Copes and Esther his wife, the late Esther Neall who was adm. of Aquilla 2/13/09; widow, Rebecca, Sarah, Elizabeth, William, Curtis, St. Leger, Aquilla T458.2.4½ Above sum, interest from 10/19/06
156. NEALL, William. Adm. Elizabeth, St. Leger n.d.; widow, Mary, James, Sarah, St. Leger T1105.4.0   9/25/11, Adm. St. Leger T218.11.11   Notes: St. Leger to retain $37 out of the above borrowed of estate of Aquilla Neill to pay debts of William Neill estate: 10/11/11, received of George Smootz, Register of Wills, sum of $353.94, the amount St. Leger in his hands due me as Guardian of children of William Neill, signed Samuel Ringgold
157. NESBITT, Nathaniel. Adm. Nathaniel 4/10/16; Nathaniel, John, Peter's heirs, Jonathan, Jacob T $903.40
158. NEWSON, John. Adm. Jane, Joseph 2/13/15; widow, Mary, John, Alexander, Joseph, Rachel, Abraham T829.9.6
159. OHR, Nicholas. Adm. Margaret 10/19/10; Jacob, Elizabeth, Henry, Soloma T103.1.1
160. OSWALT, John. Adm. Eve, Benjamin 3/20/13; widow, 6 children T488.19.9
161. PETERY, Jacob. Adm. John, Christian Smith 3/23/13; 6 heirs T1747.5.0
Second distribution n.d.;John, Philip, Eve Binkley, Catherine, Barbara Arnold, Elizabeth Summers T2360.14.4   4/2/14 T437.12.11   4/6/15 T319.10.6
Note: wife of Jacob Petery, Elizabeth died 1811
162. PETERY, Sodwick. Adm. Christian Smith, Jacob Summers 2/18/13; widow, Elizabeth, Jacob, Catherine, Mary, Sodwick, Peter T269.0.5
163. PETTICORD, Hannah. Adm. Dennis Davis n.d.; William, Leakin, Alley, Rachel T306.5.10
164. PIPER, Jacob. Adm. Daniel 3/1/14; 1/3 to widow exclusive of advancement (354.5.4), 118.1.9; John, Elizabeth Kephart, Catherine Hammond, Margaret Eckhart, Jacob, Mary Stone, Barbara Johnson, Daniel, Rosannah Brown T1334.0.1
1/23/16, Adm. Jacob T92.9.5 (Pencil note: Jacob died 1813)
165. POFFENBERGER, John. Adm. Robert Smith, Henry 9/6/05; legacy to Adam and Polly, each 50.0.0; Adam, Valentine, Henry, John, Simon, Christian, Catherine, Polly T1898.4.3   5/16/12; Adam, Henry Eakle, Valentine, John, Henry, Christian, Simon, Philip Thame? T309.7.8
166. POFFENBERGER, Valentine. Adm. Henry Yeakle 1/14/13; widow, 6 children T387.11.0
167. POSTATER, Andrew. Adm. Jacob, David Long 6/15/08; John's legacy 140.0.0; Christine Shattley 0.15.0; Susanna Varner's legacy 100.0.0; children of Elizabeth 180.0.0; Catherine Snyder 187.0.0; Mary Tysher 200.0.0; Magdalena Grise 144.10.0; Rose Martin 188.0.0; Catherine Snyder, Susannah, Maria, Magdalena Grise, Rose Martin, children of Elizabeth each 200.0.0; John Grise 50.0.0; interest of 600.0.0 to widow; to be equally divided between Jacob, Catherine Snyder, Susannah Varner, Maria Tysher, Magdalena Grise, Rose Martin, each 19.13.3   T3127.18.0
168. POTTS, Jonathan. Adm. William Norris 2/10/07; widow, 9 children T74.12.5
169. POWLES, Jacob. Adm. John Cook 12/13/10; widow, Jacob, Margaret, Catherine, Daniel, Henry T177.14.6
170. PRATHER, Bazil. Adm. Samuel n.d.; Richard, Friend, Sarah, Bazil, Perry, Samuel, Ruth T108.13.7
171. PROTZMAN, John. Adm. Peter Heffley, David Harry 6/22/08; John, Henry, Kitty, John McKiernan son of Polly McKiernan T663.3.8; sum bears interest from 10/31/05
12/21/10; John, Elizabeth McKeirnan, Catherine, Henry T527.13.6   3/13/12; Michael McKeirnan, Catherine, John, Henry T235.0.9   4/8/14 (same as 1812) T367.0.7
172. REBB, Michael. Adm. Christian Lantz 3/3/12; Peter, Elizabeth Tailor, Rosannah Gainer, Christian, John, Eve Dick each 19.2.2 3/4
173. REEDER, John. Adm. Mary, Harmon 1/28/07; widow, Harmon, Kennllum, Frederick T534.2.7¼
174. RENCH, John. Adm. Jacob, John Schnebly, Jacob Zeller 5/17/06; Second and ____ 5707.0.3; Peter 3500.0.0; John 1969.10.0; Susannah Dunn 1476.0.0; Jacob, Peter, each 3259.16.0; John Schnebly, Jacob Zeller, John, Susannah Dunn each 2173.4.4 T15212.10.3   3/3/10; each above 183.4.1   2/23/16; Peter's heirs, Jacob's heirs, John's heirs, John Schnebly, Jacob Zeller, Susannah Dunn each 255.15.3 T1790.17.11

1806 - 1816

175. RENCH, Margaret. Adm. Christian Hager 1/20/08; John Schnebly 20.17.2; Jacob, Peter's heirs, John's heirs, Susanna Dunn, Catherine Schnebly's heirs, Elizabeth Zellers 97.18.4½ each T587.10.4
176. RENCH, William. Adm. Philip, John Jones 4/9/14; to widow 1/3 of personal estate 70.11.6½ and 1/3 of real estate to be paid annually 250.0.5½, total 320.12.0; Barbara, Henry, John, William, Philip, Margaret Houtzer, Catherine Facherhof, Barbara Jones each 80.3.0 T961.16.2   5/28/14; widow 70.19.8; Barnhart, Henry, John, William, Philip, Margaret Houtzer, Catherine Facherhoof, Barbara Jones each 17.14.11 T212.19.1 n.d.; Henry, John, William, Margaret Houtzer each 97.17.11 T391.11.8   By money paid Houtzer with interest, 77.5.0; balance 314.6.8 from office receipts given 5/28/14, Houtzers note in pocketbook, paid the parties 9/14/14; 9/15/14; widow, Barnhart, Henry, John, William, Philip, Margaret Houtzer, Catherine Teatherhoof, Barbara Jones T141.13.9   4/4/16 (same as 9/15/14) T $373.88
177. REYNOLDS, Danise. Adm. George Nigh, Mary 4/11/06; widow, Daniel, John, Peggy, Mary, Peter, George, Henry T57.12.3
178. REYNOLD, Peter. Adm. Daniel Hecrote, Peter n.d.; widow, Jacob, Mary Hoffer, Peter, Barbara Shank, Samuel T430.18.3
    5/7/16; Adm. Peter, D. Howell; widow, Jacob, Mary Steffey, Peter, Barbara Shank, Samuel T $60.83
179. RICE, Jacob. Adm. Jacob, Peter Newcomer, Jonathan Newcomer n.d.; widow, 6 children plus interest from 10/19/04 T696.16.1
180. RICHART, Jacob. Adm. Jacob, Daniel 4/20/12; specific legacy to Marice Bucks heirs, Eliza Holsinger, Catherine Long, Barbara, Christian, Jacob, Jacob (listed twice) each 100.0.0; Eve 500.0.0; to Buck heirs, Holsinger, Isaac Long, Barbara each 100.0.0; in the hands of the estate 41.15.6 T1641.15.6   2/22/14; specific legacy to _____ 50.0.0; Elizabeth Holzinger, Catherine Long, heirs of Buck, Barbara, Christian, Jacob, Daniel, John each 93.13.7 T745.15.11   5/27/14; Elizabeth Holtzinger, Catherine Long, heirs of Frederick Rench, Barbara, Christian, Jacob, Daniel, John each 22.7.8 T179.1.4
181. RIDENOUR, Charles. Adm. Mary, Adam 3/14/16; widow, Daniel, Anne, Mary T $2609.51
182. RIDENOUR, David. Adm. Samuel 2/12/07; two bonds due estate from Balzer Goll, 368.6.8; one bond from Middlekauf children, 175.0.0; and the Register (of wills?) 4.3.3; distributed to widow, 8 heirs T681.18.8½   12/11/11; Samuel, Susannah Markle, Catherine Miller, Jacob, Conrad, Sarah Foster, Milly Kealhoofer, Mary each 201.14.5½
183. RIDENOUR, Eve. Adm. Gerard Stonebraker 1/10/15; Amelia, Nancy T77.6.4½
184. RIDENOUR, George. Adm. Conrad Flora 4/8/08; George 5.0.0; Catherine Johnston 5.0.0; heirs of Henry each 15.0.0; Margaret Flora, Sarah Small, heirs of George, heirs of Henry, heirs of Magdalena Singer, Eve each 81.3.8   4/14/09; Flora, Sarah Small, heirs of George, heirs of Henry, heirs of Magdalena Singer, Eve T117.18.11 (Note: the remaining distributions follow that of 4/14/09)   4/13/10 T89.5.4 4/16/11 T85.5.4   4/28/12 T89.5.4   4/26/13 T89.5.4   5/28/14 T89.5.4 4/18/15 T455.3.2   4/22/16 T89.5.4
185. RITCHIE, John. Adm. Jonas McPherson, Atty. in fact for Esther 9/6/11; 1/3 to the devisee of Esther, deceased 430.5.6 3/4; Archibald heir of the deceased 860.11.1½ T1290.16.8½
186. RITTER, Jacob. Adm. Christian Lantz n.d.; Ann Smith, Jacob Harter (of his late wife Elizabeth), John, Philip Willson's heirs, Rebecca Ribble, Henry Clapper, Elias, each 73.2.8 3/4, add 4.14.10 given to each of 8 heirs T585.2.10 plus 37.18.7/12   n.d.; 8 heirs entitled to 10.11.0 each T84.8.3
187. ROBEY, Susannah. Adm. William, Owen 4/4/15; William, Mary Rigges, Ann Moreland, Deborah Parroll, Statea Angle, Elizabeth Rigges, Owen, Isaac, Susanna Witten T839.13.0½ (This distribution crossed out and rewritten on the next page) Rewritten 4/7/15; specific legacy Deborah 50.0.0 less 36.0.7, 13.19.5; Statea 50.0.0, less 35.7.7½, 14.12.4½; Susannah Witten 50.0.0 less 25.4.4½, 24.15.7½;

DISTRIBUTION OF ESTATE ACCOUNTS

187. ROBEY, Susannah (Continued): Owen 50.0.0 less 20.8.9, 29.11.5; Isaac 50.0.0, less 24.0.5, 25.19.7; Edmund Rigges 50.0.0; balance divided among all the children; William, Mary Rigges, Ann Moreland, Deborah Parroll, Statea Angle, Elizabeth Rigges, Owen, Isaac, Susannah Witten T838.2.10½
188. ROHRER, Christian. Adm. Samuel 6/14/14; Samuel, Christian, Jacob, Daniel, Mary Troxell, Ann Miller, Barbara Bragonier, each 81.8.11
189. ROHRER, Jacob. Adm. Mathias Kepler, Frederick 3/31/10; John, Jacob, Frederick, Samuel, Mary Orendorff, Catherine Crumbaugh T464.9.1 4/26/11; Adm. Mathias Kepler T43.18.6
190. ROOT, Barbara. Adm. Jacob 8/13/13; Anna Fausnaught, Barbara Fausnaught, Motlena Fausnaught, Susannah Fausnaught, Elizabeth, Jacob, Esther, Mary Herr T26.9.7
191. ROOT, Jacob. Adm. Jacob n.d.; Jacob's legacy 100.0.0; Mary's legacy 25.0.0; Balance 98.17.0; widow, 8 children T223.17.0 3/11/12; widow, 8 children T41.10.6
192. ROWLAND, Christian. Adm. Christian, Christian Hauer 3/2/15; widow, Christian, Emanuel, Jacob, Jonathan, Rosannah each 121.8.10 3/4
193. SCHNEBLY, Leonard. Adm. David 2/16/07; Henry, James, John, Ann T652.2.6½
194. SHAFFER, Barbara. Adm. Jacob Seibert 10/27/07; Peter Jones and wife legacy, 32.0.0; Mary Stuckey, legacy 20.0.0; Daniel Miller and wife 5.0.0; Abraham Stuckey, Simon Stuckey, Daniel Stuckey, Mary Stuckey, Jacob Stuckey, Samuel Stuckey, George Benner and wife Susannah T240.13.8
195. SHAFER, George. Adm. Christian Ankeney 4/2/12; specific legacy to Henry 200.0.0; Christian Ankeney, Jacob Lower, Simon Hayes, Henry, heirs of Peter T5166.13.6
196. SHEARER, John. Adm. Jacob F. Towson 12/5/15; widow, Henry T706.1.0
197. SHELLER, Daniel. Adm. Christian, Christian Palmer 6/10/09; William, Elizabeth Welty, Daniel, Henry, Christian, Nancy Welty, Adam each 120.19.0½
198. SHONEFELT, Henry. Adm. Peter Sailor 3/18/14; widow, Peter, Sarah, Susannah, Elizabeth, Henry T848.4.1
199. SHONEFELT, William. Adm. Andrew, Jacob Leckron 6/20/15; widow 450.0.0; specific legacy to Jacob 7.10.0 and to William 15.0.0; Margaret Leckroon, Susannah Boon, Catherine Avey, Jacob, John, Henry, William, Andrew each 20.17.6 T639.10.1 1/3
200. SHOOK, Susannah. Adm. John Fogle 3/5/16; Barbara Butts, John, Elizabeth T29.14.5
201. SHORT, Jane. Adm. Richard Pindell 8/15/11; Alexander Kennedy, heirs of George Kennedy, Elizabeth Dorsey, interest from 1/23/08 T905/17/4½
202. SHULL, Jacob. Adm. Theobald Eckleberger 1/25/16; due Stephen $161.33; widow, 4 children T $1115.76
203. SHUPE, Jacob. Adm. David Harry, Peter Woltz 8/2 or 12?/07; widow, Frederick, John, Henry, Elizabeth, David, Daniel, Jonathan, Samuel, Susanna, Simon, Ann each 3.8.10 3/4 T41.6.9
204. SIBERT, Jacob. Adm. John Cushwa, Henry 10/1/11; Bond due estate of Henry Ankey 200.20.0; widow, Catherine Cushwa, Jacob, Peter, Henry, Elizabeth, Michael T1240.7.6
205. SIBERT, John. Adm. Peter, Delores Now? n.d.; widow 131.1.0; 10 children, add monies received from 1797 through 1806; 427.5.1 equally divided among 10 children T796.55.0 plus 427.5.11
206. SILER (SILOR), Daniel. Adm. Thomas Mainer 1/23/07; widow, John, Elizabeth, George, Mary T257.9.7
207. SLIFER, Stephen. Adm. Jacob Bova 12/9/07; heirs of Philip, Catherine Causett each 89.5.8; ½ to brothers and sisters of Mary (1 brother, 5 sisters), each 25.10.2¼ (1 sister being dead) T357.2.8
208. SMALLENBERGER, Francis. Adm. Henry Schlenker 3/4/09; Henry, Peter, Anna Allilia, heirs of Michael T39.12.3½ Interest from 10/18/07
209. SMELTZER, George C. Adm. David Ludy n.d.; Catherine and Elizabeth each 52.0.8
210. SMITH, Alexander. Adm. Joseph, Margaret 7/7/07; widow, 3 children T553.17.11
211. SMITH, Nicholas. Adm. George Keller, Benjamin Swingley 5/13/15; Benjamin Swingley, Jacob Wagoner, Frederick Raimer, George Keller, Catherine Smith T394.0.3
212. SNAVELY, Jacob. Adm. John Huffert, David Funk 4/5/15; widow, John, George, Catherine, Jacob, Joshua T597.17.4

1806 - 1816

213. SNYDER, Casper. Adm. Mary, George 5/9/07; 1/3 of 748.18.6, balance of personal estate together with real estate amounts to 2008.7.4, to be divided; George, John, Jonathan, Catherine, Jacob, Susannah, Peter, David, Henry, Leonard T2258.0.2
214. SNYDER, Henry. Adm. George Nigh, Samuel Hogmire n.d.; specific legacy Henry 50.0.0; Henry Howell 40.0.0; Catherine Tyler, Elizabeth Grail?, Mary, Margaret, Jacob, Henry, George, Michael each 110.4.1¼ T971.12.11
215. SNYDER, Margaret. Adm. Jacob Howell, Daniel Howell 2/18/14; 10 heirs each 7.7.1½ T73.11.1 NOTES:
    - Samuel Newcomer received $40.92 as guardian of children
    - 8/14, 7.7.1½ distribution share of estate of Margaret. Hilland G____, witness Jacob Huyett
    - Jacob Huyett received 2/18/11, 7.7.0½ from my father Sodwick Hewett and of the hair of Margaret Snyder
    - 5/5/12, 7.7.0½ from Margaret Snyder estate by Philip Hiwit
    - Received 5/23/14, 7.7.0½ from estate of Margaret Snyder, Catherine Shafer by George Hoopingardner
    - 3/10/12, Catherine Mong received 7.7.0½ from Margaret Snyder estate
216. SNYDER, Martin. Adm. Jacob 4/7/15; Jacob, Michael, John, Adam, Motlena, George, Catherine, Martin, Elizabeth, heirs of Mary Baker T382.12.6
217. SNYDER, Michael. Adm. Henry Shafer 4/2/14; widow 400.0.0; widow, John, Michael's heirs, Martin each 693.14.0½ T2481.2.1½
218. SNYDER, Peter. Adm. David Westenberger, Daniel Welty 4/20/15; Peter, John, Sarah, Jacob T852.0.4
219. SOUTH, Benjamin. Adm. Gara 10/20/09; widow, 9 heirs T53.7.6   6/5/11 T12.4.7
220. SPEILMAN, Michael. Adm. Valentine Nichodemus 4/14/15; Jacob, John, Aquilla Bennet, Valentine Nichodemus T117.13.0
221. STEFFEY, Elizabeth. Adm. Nicholas 1/22/11; Andrew, George, Catherine, Peter, Elizabeth, Nicholas T48.17.2
222. STEFFEY, George. Adm. Francis Protzman 4/29/06; widow, 2 children T499.18.0 Second distribution: n.d.; widow, 2 children T469.14.6
223. STERRETT, James. Adm. Jacob L. Lawson, William McClelan 8/8/13; specific legacy to John W. 100.0.0; Mrs. Luckett widow of deceased to have childs part 205.0.2; Maria Edwards, Nancy, James, Joseph W. each 205.10.2 T1125.0.9
224. STINE, Henry. Adm. E., William Kreps 1/25/16; widow, John, Samuel, Elizabeth, Polly, Susanna, Julianna, Margaret T $437.40, sum bears interest from 8/11/14
225. STONER, John. Adm. Christian Good 1/30/11; widow, 9 children T644.2.10½ 12/12/12; Adm. Christian Good, Jacob Beam; widow, 9 children T8.5.4
226. STOVER, Jacob. Adm. Margaret, Christian 9/11/11; 1/3 to widow exclude advance 43.2.4; Ann Troup, Jacob, Christian, Elizabeth Rowland, Barbara Hoover, Mary Ridenour, John, David, each 20.6.6½ T205.14.8
227. STOWTER, Mary. Adm. Philip 1/2/11; Philip, Charlotte Strohe, Mary Zuckman, Catherine Coon T16.11.11
228. STULL, Daniel. Adm. Elie Beatty 8/11/13; Maria Goll, Sarah Moore, Emily, Eliza T1191.3.8½
229. STUTOR, Philip. Adm. George Nigh 4/14/06; Philip, Charlotte, Mary Ditnzman, Mary, heirs of Catherine Coon T88.11.6¾
230. SUMMERS, John. Adm. Jacob 2/25/09; specific legacy Elizabeth Petre and Mary each 100.0.0; Jacob 50.0.0; Mary, Peter, Elizabeth Petre, Jacob, each 102.13.2 T660.12.8   2/3 paid now, other 1/3 after death of widow
231. SWEIGHER, John. Adm. John 10/31/09; widow, Elizabeth Tooler?, Doratha Winder, heirs of Isabella Ward, Catherine Gush, John, Mary Leonard T124.1.7½
232. SWEIGHER, Mary. Adm. John 1/8/10; Esther Tooler?, Dorathy Winders, Simon Ward, Catherine Grush, John, Mary Leopard T56.13.3
233. SWINGLEY, Barbara. Adm. John Whiteman, B. Kershner n.d.; Christine legacy 25.0.0; Barbara Scouther?, Jacob Whiteman, John Whiteman, Philip Whitman, Elizabeth Whiteman each 7.5.10½; Barbara Whitman alias Kendal 36.9.3; Mary Ann Kershner 36.9.3; Mary Scoither?, Philip, John each 12.3.1; Christine 36.9.3 T243.15.6

DISTRIBUTION OF ESTATE ACCOUNTS

234. SWINGLEY, Philip. Adm. Benjamin, Peter Light 4/12/08; ¼ to Barbara 96.4.0¼; 3/4 to Samuel 288.12.1½ T384.16.2, interest from 1/17/07 paid widow 5/8/10; 1/3 to widow 51.4.4; specific legacy to Barbara 50.0.0; ¼ balance paid Barbara; Balance to Samuel
235. SWOOPE, Peter. Adm. Catherine, Daniel Griffith 5/19/14; Catherine 737.19.11; Catherine Sibert, Christine Davis, Susannah Yontz, Sarah Griffith, Rosanna Crouse, Elizabeth, Jacob, Magdalena each 184.10.0 T2213.19.11
236. TAYLOR, Michael. Adm. John Ringer 3/1/07; widow, Peter, Elizabeth, John, Polly, Catherine, Barbara, David T499.2.8½   Note: Above bears interest from 2/25/06
237. THALLS, Joseph. Adm. Richard 1/28/11; widow, Rebecca, Rachel Brown, Richard, Sophia, Mary, Samuel T47.1.0
238. THOMAS, Jacob. Adm. Jacob, Christine Core 8/13/12; specific legacy to Henry 700.0.0; to George and Michael each 500.0.0; to George, Michael, Sodwick, Abraham each 65.12.6; Jacob, Henry, Sodwick, Thomas, Abraham, George, Michael, Christine Stull, Eliza Core, Magdalena Core, Catherine Doup, Susanna Fry each 146.1.7 T1606.17.6
239. THOMAS, Peter. Adm. Margaret 4/14/08; names included Mary, David, Sarah, Mary, John, Susanna, Nancy....(distribution cancelled): Second entry: distribution legacy: the distribution of Peter in right of first wife 110.1.7 minus 63.19.1 and 1/3 to widow 21.6.4; Michael, Margaret, Catherine, Elizabeth, David, Rosanna, Polly, Sarah, Mary, Peter, John, Susanna, Nancy each 3.5.8 T174.0.8
240. THUMB, Baltzer. Adm. Ann, Jacob Foutz 3/1/13; Elizabeth Wachtel, David, William, Susannah, George T44.13.6
241. TICE, Henry. Adm. Michael 7/1/07; widow 600.0.0; 13 children each 112.17.6½ T2067.8.3   8/1/07; 13 children T20.9.0
242. TICE, Peter. Adm. Daniel Harry and Esther his wife, Esther 3/13/06; widow, 6 children T118.19.0
243. TYLER, Daniel. Adm. Thomas Mains 3/24/13; widow, 4 children T41.6.0
244. TYSHER, Peter. Adm. John Tisher n.d.; Peter Ridenour, Joseph Ridenour, Susanna Pottorff, Dorotha T710.13.5   4/5/11 T248.5.4   4/13/10 T248.5.4   5/22/12 T243.7.5
245. TYSON, Benjamin. Adm. George Heddrick 10/21/13; 1/3 to widow $2391.30; George Heddrick same; children of P. Ham $2391.30 (Note: the number 4 followed P. Ham, possibly there were 4 children)
246. VANBUSKIRK, Daniel. Adm. Catherine 12/7/15; widow, Mary, Lawrence, Daniel T168.4.4½
247. VERPIL, John. Adm. John, John L. Hovermail 1/4/12; his children each 28.7.1½ T170.2.9½ (divided out, the figures suggest 6 children)
248. VOLTZ, Elizabeth. Adm. John Smith, Daniel Boerstler 11/1/15; Jacob Oshitz (Ashitz?), Michael Wolfinger, Jacob Flocker, John Smith, Joseph Beckman, Ulianna, Maria T231.15.4
249. VOUSSEN, Henry. Adm. Cosin, Henry 8/30/10; Cosin, Henry, Peter, Nancy T6.10.10
250. WACHTEL, John. Adm. Edward, Jacob Kershner 3/6/12; widow, 11 children T66.5.10
251. WARNER, Margaret. Adm. Jacob Lambert 2/6/16; Elizabeth Spitznogle, Christian Ropp, George's child, Mary Hahn, Jacob T61.19.4
252. WELLS, Jeremiah. Adm. Rezin, Frederick Shaw 4/9/11; Rezin, Keziah Brand, Aron, Eleanor Shaw, Arlimacy Bayly's child, Mary Jones, Melly Jones T1301.17.7
253. WELLS, Rezin. Adm. Elizabeth, Jacob F. Towson n.d.; widow, Polly, Thomas, Isaac, Ann, Susanna, Elijah, Rachel T1102.6.2
254. WELTY, Frederick. Adm. Christian Snyder, John 11/6/15; widow, Elizabeth Snyder, John, Jacob, Samuel, Mary, George, Susannah, Henry, Christian T692.16.10½ Second distribution: n.d.; T$147.67 (Note: 2d dist. lists Christian as Christine)
255. WELTY, Jacob. Adm. Henry 3/9/10; widow, Henry, Elizabeth Garber, Jacob, Susanna, N. Mayes, Barbara T769.16.8
256. WESTENBERGER, Paul. Adm. John 5/17/11; John, Paul, David, Mary, Susanna, Motlena T33.4.9

1806 - 1816

257. WHITEMAN, Jacob. Adm. Jacob 6/24/09; Jacob, Barbara, Philip, Elizabeth T455.16.9½
258. WINTER, Ann. Adm. John Hoover 5/4/15; John, Daniel, Andrew, John Harbaugh, Conrad Flora, Charles Ridenour heirs, Susanna, Catherine, Margaret Hoover each 70.10.10 3/4
259. WINTER, George. Adm. John, Martin Ridenour n.d.; 1/11 to widow 5.9.8½; each child 5.9.8½ T60.7.0   5/1/07; 1/11 to widow 5.14.9½, each child 5.4.9½ T63.2.9 4/28/08; 1/11 to widow 5.14.9½, 10 children each 5.14.9½ T63.2.9   5/1/09; 1/11 to widow, 10 children each 5.14.9½ T63.2.9
260. WOLTZ, George. Adm. George Brumbaugh 1/19/15; widow, Elizabeth Little, Mary Reynolds, Catherine Lane, George, William, Elie, John T21.7.9
261. WOLTZ, Samuel. Adm. Catherine n.d.; widow, George, Mary T $2276.07
262. WOODALL, John. Adm. Josiah Rieley 4/5/15; 2 heirs T124.7.0
263. WOOLF, Daniel. Adm. Jacob, Ludwick n.d.; widow, Catherine Kemmell, Elizabeth Hawn, Christine Powles, Jacob, Frederick T669.1.11
264. WORLEY, Evan. Adm. John 1/17/07; John, Catherine Boyer, Jacob, Stephen T131.13.9
265. WYAND, Christian. Adm. Jacob Snyder, Jacob Snavely 3/20/13; widow, Elizabeth, Mary, Lena T431.12.4
266. YEAKLE, Jacob. Adm. Elizabeth, Henry 3/28/10; widow, Catherine, Jacob T318.7.3
267. YOUNG, George. Adm. Jacob Hargrave, George Nigh 6/10/12; deduct amount of personal estate, making distribution 1596.14.8; widow 339.3.8; John, Samuel, Margaret each 399.3.8 T1596.14.8
268. YOUNG, Jacob. Adm. Jacob, Jacob Hershey 12/26/15; Margaret Hershey, Eliza Pence, Jacob, Lewis, Magdalena, Martin, Catherine, Sarah T313.15.4
269. YOUNG, Lodwick. Adm. Jacob, Jacob Rench 6/26/09; Jacob, Isaac, Lodwick, Mary Ann Smith, Margaret Rench T21.5.10
270. YOST, George. Adm. Susanna 12/15/10; ½ to widow 301.4.4½; Catherine Hously 301.4.4½ T602.8.9
271. YOUNTZ, William. Adm. Peter Swoops 8/26/06; widow, 2 children T510.14.10½
272. ZUCK, Michael. Adm. Joseph Wolf, Nellie his wife, Jacob 3/7/11; Joseph Woolf in right of his wife 309.1.0 3/4; Jacob 309.1.0 3/4 T618.2.1½

DISTRIBUTION OF ESTATE ACCOUNTS
Washington County, Maryland 1817 - 1828

1. ADAMS, James. Adm. Margaret 8/14/27; widow, Martha, Mata, Amos, Martin A., Helena   T $138.05
2. ALTER, Samuel. Adm. John Troxell, Mary his wife 4/9/17; widow, Catherine Kealhoofer, Mary Ott, Margaret Bender, Magdalena Heffley, George, David, Susanna (mother)   T $1,251.21
3. ANKENY, George. Adm. Catherine, Henry _____ 11/18/21; widow, 7 children T110.18.1½
4. ANKENY, John. Adm. George 11/13/23; Catherine Jones, Michael Bova, George, Mary, Daniel, Samuel T $2,043.81
5. ANKENY, Susanna. Adm. Henry 8/30/22; deed a negro woman $180.00, 6 heirs T $2064.15
6. ARNSBERGER, Christopher. Adm. Christopher, George 2/14/21; widow, Henry, Christopher, John, Frederick's heirs, George, Michael, Catherine Brantner, Mary Boon, Christine Christian, Elizabeth Spong, Esther Carter, Jacob   T $2,935.91
7. ARTZ, Henry. Adm. Christian 4/19/26;   widow, Abraham, Henry, Peter, Elizabeth, Philip, John, Mary T $182.16
8. ASHBERRY, John. Adm. John Harry 3/18/26; widow, 10 children T $1,781.05
9. BACHTEL, Samuel. Adm. Martin 10/1/23; 9 children T $1,617.26   11/3/24 T $1,077.52   8/8/25 T $1,200.65   5/10/26 T $998.80
10. BAKER, David. Adm. Frederick 11/15/24; widow, Amos, Sarah, Susanna, David each $450.90¼; deduct 50¢ from each and $1 from widow for release   1/28/25; widow, $28.92; Ames, Sarah, Susanna, David each $14.46
11. BAKER, Peter. Adm. John, Jacob Price 12/17/19; Susanna Price, John, Elizabeth Long, Catherine Long, Peter, Mary King, Abraham T1192.10.3
12. BAKER, Samuel. Adm. Frederick, Jacob 9/14/20; specific legacy to Mary Long, Magdalena Cost, Rosanna Betebenner, Rebecca, David, Samuel, Elizabeth Doner, Christine Core, Frederick each $266.66. In addition each received $727.43 T $5,819.44 Deduct $1 from each child for release
  Second distribution: Adm. Jacob n.d.; 8 heirs T $1,512.70
13. BAKER, Samuel Jr. Adm. Jacob, Frederick 1/28/25; Elizabeth Donner, Mary Long, Magdalena Cost, Rosanna Betebenner, Rebecca, Lemuel, Frederick, David T $129.40
  Second distribution: land willed from Samuel Baker Sr. $183.09; reserved for tombstone $15; 8 heirs   T $1,128.13
14. BARKMAN, Michael. Adm. Eve, Jacob 4/18/20; Michael, Jacob, Catherine Smith, Eve, Dolly, Susanna T $2,196.78   12/8/25; Michael, Catherine Smith, Eve, Dolly Hellery, Susanna Moyer T $982.66
15. BARKS, John. Adm. Jacob, David Otto 1/15/23; 4 children T $2,199.83
16. BARKS, John. Adm. Jacob 6/23; reserved for widow $1,000.00; for Margaret Myers $800.00; 4 children each $1,235.28 T $6,741.72
17. BARNETT, Jacob. Adm. Henry, Jacob 4/25/17; Henry, Jacob, John Emil, Catherine McLaughlin, John, Sarah Emil, Casandra, David, Ann, Mary T1438.5.10   Due the ward 134.6.3
18. BARRICKMAN, Frederick. Adm. Henry 12/10/17; 9 children T $1,111.74
19. BEECHER, Samuel. Adm. Jacob 6/1/25; widow $165.72; Mary Short received $300.00; Elizabeth Lower received $400.00; balance between remaining children: Sarah Fechtig, Jacob, William W., each $110.48 1/3 T $497.17   Note: in cancelled distribution, John Short and wife are named in place of Mary Short
20. BELL, Leonard. Adm. Henry Schleigh 9/7/25; Catherine Kretzer, Betsey Coleman, Rachel Sheetz's heirs $257.00 plus $14.89; Peggy, Daniel, John $300.00 plus $17.38 T $96.82   Note: the total does not seem to relate to amounts in the distribution
21. BELL, Thomas. Adm. Daniel Sprigg 12/5/26; Sarah Boone _____, to Shroeder, Daniel Sprigg T $1,973.49
22. BENNER, John. Adm. Jacob, Christian 11/29/26; Henry, John, Elizabeth Bowers, Catherine Cooke T $114.90
23. BETT, Thomas. Adm. D. Sprigg 4/15/25; Levin, Lloyd, Josiah's heirs   T $686.70   4/15/26; Levin, Lloyd, Sarah's heirs each $229.23 1/3   5/27/24; Levin, Lloyd, Josiah T $1,367.44

24

1817 - 1828

24. BETZ, Jacob. Adm. Joseph Woolf 4/21/24; 4 heirs including mother each $12.58 T $58.97 4/1/25; 4 heirs T $23.90 4/1/26; 4 heirs T $23.90
25. BETZ, Mary. Adm. Joseph Woolf 4/9/24; Christian, John, Frederick's heirs except Mary, William's heirs except Mary, Ann, Mary T $1,769.23 4/1/25; Christian, John, Frederick's heirs, William's heirs, Ann, Mary T $801.90 4/1/26; John, Christian, Frederick's heirs, William, Ann, Mary T $801.90
26. BETZ, Sarah. Adm. Joseph Woolf 4/21/24; 4 heirs including mother each $12.58 T $58.97 4/1/25; 4 heirs T $23.90 4/1/26; 4 heirs T $23.90
27. BEVINS, Leonard. Adm. John Adams, Leonard 9/22/17; widow, Mary McCoy, Basil's heirs, Martha Moore, Jane McElhenny, Thomas, Leonard, Ann Doyle, Margaret Quigley, Elizabeth Moore, Susanna Murray T $510.11
28. BLAIR, Andrew. Adm. Sarah 7/28/25; widow, Joseph, Charity T $261.34 Interest from 10/21/21
29. BOTELAR, Edward. Adm. Martha 2/4/24; widow, Casandra McLin, Henry, Priscilla Morrison T $3,208.28 Deducted $30 for latent claim 3/25/25 T $2,326.90
30. BOTELAR, Alexander H. Adm. Christian Stonebraker 4/30/24; 4 children T $1,677.50
31. BOVEY, Catherine. Adm. Henry, Daniel 2/8/25; 10 heirs T $374.01
32. BOVEY, Jacob. Adm. George, Henry, Daniel 4/15/18; Interest of sum to the widow paid annually $11,066.66; Jacob, Catherine, John, George, Henry, Elizabeth, Mary, Magdalena, Daniel, Christine, Susanna each $169.07 T $2,926.45 4/14/20; Adm. George, Daniel T $237.34 2/8/25; Adm. George, Henry, Daniel T $2,541.12
33. BOWERS, George. Adm. Ludwick Protzman 6/9/25; widow, Jacob, George, Mary D., Elizabeth, Barbara, Sarah Ann T $866.87
34. BOWIE, Thomas. Adm. John Kennedy 12/15/19; Jane, Charity T $121.74
35. BOWMAN, Frederick. Adm. Jacob Ridenour 10/17/18; widow, John, Elizabeth, Peter, Jacob T $73.54
36. BOYER, Jacob. Adm. John 10/17/25; widow, 7 heirs T $135.84½
37. BRAGONIER, David. Adm. Samuel, John Harry 2/14/20; Samuel, David, Jacob, Daniel, Elizabeth T $589.59
38. BRANSTATER, Andrew. Adm. Daniel, George Barkdoll 6/17/18; widow, Daniel, John's heirs, Susanna Barkdoll, Elizabeth Latshaw? T $1,729.93
39. BRANTNER, George. Adm. John, Jacob 5/31/17; widow, George, Mary Poffenberger, Jacob, Michael, Samuel, Henry, Andrew, one whose name is unknown, Eliza T $1,832.68
40. BRANTNER, John. Adm. Henry Nyman, Michael 8/25/19; $2,000.00 left widow to be placed in hands of George Brantner, the interest to be paid annually; specific legacy to John $200.00; Michael, George, John, Jacob, Samuel, Susanna Nyman, Elizabeth, D____, each $1,111.93 T $10,025.56 2/18/24; 7 heirs T $3,594.93 8/6/26; 7 heirs T $288.40 6/25/27, 7 heirs T $225.91 11/20/27; 7 heirs T $106.59
41. BREAKBELL, John. Adm. John N. Swearinger 9/3/24; widow, 8 heirs T $102.45
42. BREWER, Gustavius. Adm. John 8/20/16; specific legacy to Jacob and John, each $66.66 1/3; Peter, John, Jacob, Mary, Ann Kershner, Mary Light, Susanne Flenner, each $913.34 T $5,619.39
43. BREWER, John. Name entry, no information.
44. BROWN, Benjamin. Adm. William C. Downy 2/10/26; Barbara, Lewis, Hanson, Ignatius, George Wilmouth and wife, Samuel Burch and wife, Margaret McClain T $2,061.51
45. BROWN, George. Adm. Samuel Slifer 5/10/19; widow, 5 children T $1,867.30 1/20/20 T $274.54
46. BRUMBAUGH, Daniel. Adm. George 12/16/25; widow, Susanna, Elizabeth, Daniel, Maria, Louisa, Joshua, Samuel, Isabella, Caroline T $737.87
47. BRUMBAUGH, Jacob. Adm. Daniel Schnebly 1/8/17; widow, Joseph, John, Jacob, Margaret, David each $292.42 4/22/20; Adm. Joseph, Catherine the mother; Joseph, Margaret Angle, David, each $14.10 T $70.53 Deduct 20¢ from each for release
48. CARNACUM, Jacob. Adm. Jacob Hershey 6/2/26; widow, 4 children $260.85

DISTRIBUTION OF ESTATE ACCOUNTS

49. CHAPLINE, Joseph. Adm. Elizabeth 4/11/17; 8 heirs, the mother included each $14.21 T $113.71
50. CHARLTON, Thomas. Adm. Stephen Barton, Susanna Barton 4/18/23; specific legacy to Sarah $100.00; Andrew Bayley, John, Thomas each $1.00; Jonathan, Adam and Mary his wife, L. Snyder and Margaret his wife, William, James each $408.37 T $2,041.87 $3.50 deducted from each share   5/6/24; Jonathan, Otho Adams and wife, Leonard Snyder and wife, William, James T $1,415.72   4/13/26; 5 heirs T $1,433.72   12/26/27; 5 heirs T $1,656.89
51. CLAGGETT, Zachariah. Adm. Robert, Haratio, Alfred 6/20/26; Robert, Mary Ann Garrett, Sarah Boteler, Eliza, Elizabeth Gray, Martin, Aleatha Boteler T $10,771.13 7/17/27 T $386.19   1/9/27 T $2,241.97
52. CONN, Peter. Adm. Peter Funk 6/6/20; Susanna Funk, Peter Funk, Michael Funk, David Brookhart T $9,209.01
53. CRAIG, John. Adm. Elias Stillwell, Sarah his wife 10/10/20; widow, 5 children T $277.22
54. CRAMPTON, Ann Mary M. Adm. Elie 5/18/26; specific legacy Elizabeth Keller $100; Elias, Ruth Jackson, Mary Wood, Elizabeth Keller, John, each $623.54; one share to child of Josiah after deducting debts due by said Josiah; Elias $304.27, John $244.00, Isaac S. White $19.52; total debt $567.99; due child $55.75 T $3,741.24
55. CRAMPTON, Elias. Adm. John, Elie 8/14/26; widow, John, Elie, Elizabeth Rohrer, Thomas H. T $3,628.16
56. CRAMPTON, Thomas. Adm. Elias 8/22/22; widow, Elias, Ruth Jackson, John, Josiah, Mary Wood, Elizabeth Keller, heirs of Thomas (8 each $271.93) T $22,842.65 4/1/24; widow, 7 heirs T $798.65
57. DAVIS, Charles. Adm. Samuel 3/28/17; Mary Dugan, John, William, James, Kitty, Elizabeth T $172.96
58. DAVIS, George W. 8/13/22 (Note: nothing entered)
59. DAVIS, Mary. Adm. Samuel Miller 8/15/16; William, Charles, Stephen, James, heirs of John Colevin T $1,921.80
60. DAVIS, Sophia. n.d.; 4 heirs not named (Note: entry crossed out)
61. DELLAHUNT, Mordica. Adm. Mary 9/6/20; widow, Mary Ann, John T $1,292.88   A first entry, crossed out, T$1,709.22
62. DEMOND, Barnabas. Adm. Christopher Florey 12/16/16; 1/3 to ____, John, Nancy T $68.94
63. DENOR, Yost. Adm. Christian, Frederick Baker 11/23/22; specific legacy to Christian $100; widow, Susanna Snyder, Catherine Baker, Sophia Rohrer, Rachel Rohrer, Polly Baker, Samuel T $1,950.24
64. DIEDIE, Solomon. Adm. Jacob Mumma, John Beard 8/21/17; widow, Mary Ann Wade, Kessiah Showman, Henry T $1,324.84
    Second distribution: n.d.; 1/3 of whole $13,661.06, interest to be paid widow annually, some having been received in manner following ½ in hand and balance in three payments annually without interest equal upon calculation to the sum of $12,887.78; 1/3 of which is $4,295.91; 1/3 of rent to widow, $118.33; specific legacy to Henry, $1,000; Kesiah Showman, Mary Ann Wade, Henry each $437.11 T $6,725.57   Deduct $425.24 from the widow's share, the interest of which she is entitled during her life agreeable to will of deceased. Remaining distributions to Mary Ann Wade, Kesiah Showman, Henry: 4/6/19 T $2,156.15   4/11/20 T $2,160.52   9/4/23 T $903.13
65. DUNDORE, John. Adm. Peter Humrichouse 6/1/25; widow, 6 children T $110.25
66. EAKLE, Amos. Adm. Christian 6/9/26; widow, 7 children T $686.21
67. EASTON, William. Adm. William 5/29/27; Elisha, Heziakiah, William, John, Elizabeth Botelar T $781.31
68. ECKLE, Linny. Adm. David Grove 9/27/23; John, Peggy, Sally, Polly T $59.61

1817 - 1828

69. ECKLEBERGER, John. Adm. Jacob 4/25/23; widow, 6 heirs T $290.92;. Two other distributions: n.d.; T $12.38; Stock in Turnpike, $40.00; T $26.66
70. ELINBAUGH, Mary. Adm. Peter Conn 12/10/11; 7 heirs, names unknown T219.14.2
71. ENSMINGER, Christian. Adm. Michael Roney and Margaret his wife 4/22/18; Michael Finley's claim $31.19, E.G. Williams $7, Martin $20.99; Balance: widow, Margaret, Christian, David, Eve, Catherine, Martin, Sodwick, Mary T $1,769.88
72. ENSMINGER, Philip. Adm. Elizabeth 4/17/23; widow, 4 children T $173.56
73. EVERSOLE, Christian. Adm. Emanuel, Isaac Hamer, Peter Middlekauff 6/2/19; Christian, Emanuel, Susanna Hamer, Magdalena Petres, Catherine Feiry, Hannah Middlekauf, Elizabeth Baker T $9,006.36
74. FAUSNAUGHT, ____. Adm. Henry Shafer 2/13/18; 15 heirs T $1,547.15
75. FEIRY, John. Adm. John Troup, Joseph Brewer 5/9/27; widow, Joseph Brewer and wife, John Brewer and wife, Joseph, Solomon T $1,734.90
76. FESSLER, Mary. Adm. John Welty, Elizabeth 8/20/24; 4 heirs T $2,025.92 9/13/25; 4 heirs T $360.01
77. FIGALY, William. Adm. David Artz 10/16/26; widow, 6 children T $92.77   Interest from 9/20/25
78. FIREY, John. Adm. John Troup, Joseph Brewer 3/11/26; widow, Joseph Brewer and wife, Jonathan Brewer and wife, Joseph, Solomon T $6,698.38
79. FLORA, Adam. Adm. Frederick Fishawk 3/31/12; heirs received 37.5.2½
80. FLORA, John. Adm. Frederick Fishawk 9/14/11; specific legacy to Elizabeth 25.0.0; Mary Kainan, Catherine Hutcheson, Elizabeth McKain, John, Nancy each 138.12.8 T718.3.6   Second distribution: n.d.; T 54.5.5
81. FLORA, John. Adm. Christopher 1/23/26; widow, 8 children T $455.79 6/6/26 T $96.28
82. FORD, Abigail. Adm. William Blackmore n.d.; heirs of Freelove? Jack, Esabella Otto, Henry Houck, Esther Harlin, Mary Ellis, Sarah Blackmore, Joseph, Henry, the widow Ford T99.3.11
83. FOSSLER, Mary. Adm. John Welty, Elizabeth 1/29/23; 4 heirs T $680.34
84. FULTZ, John. Adm. John, Henry 2/22/19; widow, Nancy Lowman, Barbara Groff, Elizabeth Mong, E. Huffer, Mary Line, John, George, Catherine, Motelena, Susanna, Jacob T $2,120.90
85. FUNK, Ann. Adm. David 5/18/25; David, Elizabeth Siderstick, Henry, Jacob, Nancy, Hannah T $315.62   Adm. John 6/14/27; Henry, John, Elizabeth Newcomer, Susanna Rohrer, Catherine Newcomer, heirs of Martin T $1,049.36 1/3
86. FUNK, Susannah. Adm. Daniel Richard 4/4/26; specific legacy Joseph Rohrer $600; Susannah Gehr $1,000; Margaret Gehr, Susanna Mong, Elizabeth Rohrer, each $1,239.43 1/3 T $5,318.30
87. FURRY, Catherine. Adm. Jacob F. Miller 8/3/24; 2 heirs T $42.01
88. FURRY, David. Adm. John Keedy, Daniel Keedy 3/9/24; Martin, Elizabeth each $933.33½; Mary Keedy, Elizabeth Hile (Hill), Magdalena Keedy, Catherine's heirs, Barbara Bleecher, Nancy Neikirk, each $84.18 T $2,371.78   7/12/25; each $78.72 T $422.32   Third distribution: n.d.; each $77.23 T $443.39
89. FURRY, John. Adm. Jacob F. Miller 8/13/22; widow, 4 heirs T $290.52   12/16/23 T $281.71
90. GANTZ, Nicholas Sr. Adm. David Martin 7/27/27; latent claim $533.33; $1,333.33 remains in hands of executor, interest to be paid widow annually; 9 children each $500.24 T $6,368.00
91. GANTZ, Nicholas Jr. Adm. David Martin n.d.; widow, 8 children each $29.86 T$268.72
92. GARY, George. Adm. Jonas Hogmire, George Smith 8/20/17; Judith Eakle, Sarah Stebler, Susanna Mots, Mary, Eve Davis T $3,712.56 (Deduct $90.44 for Eli Mots before distribution)
93. GEARHART, Christian. Adm. William Simpkins, Catherine n.d.;widow 224.7.6; Daniel, Mary, Jonas each 44.17.4; 9/24/18; widow 133.4.7; Daniel, Mary, Jonas, Elizabeth, Henry, Susanna, John, Christian, Catherine each 29.12.1½ T614.0.0

DISTRIBUTION OF ESTATE ACCOUNTS

94. GEARHART, Sophia. Adm. Jacob Lambert 9/9/18; Jacob's heirs, Mary Mowen, Elizabeth Lambert, Betsey Hewett, Henry, Christian's heirs, Catherine Beltzhoover, Sophia Taylor, Daniel, Susanna Firestone, Sophia Hannah, John T $569.14
95. GEHR, David. Adm. Daniel, Catherine 7/19/25; George, Daniel, Andrew, Samuel, Isaac, Mary Welty, Catherine Price, Sarah Beard, Eliza Mumma, T $7654.20
    Second distribution: each boy $248.25; each girl $206.87 T $2,068.76
96. GEIGER, John. (Note: the following entry was crossed out) In consequence of an advancement to Amos Allison by the deceased in his life time of more money than he is entitled to and the said Amos dying insolvent, is entitled to no part of the personal estate, 4/15/18   Adm. John Harry Jr. 6/2/18; widow, Elizabeth, Jacob H., Francis, Eleanora, Henrietta T $6,632.60
97. GEISER, Michael. Adm. Benjamin Oswald, John 10/4/27; widow, Daniel Branstater and wife, Abraham Snyder and wife, Mary Beard, Jonas Liezer and wife, David Bachtel and wife, Benjamin Oswald and wife, Frederick, Martin, Peter, John T $1,048.63
98. GELWICKS, Charles. T $10,065.09   Entry crossed out. Second entry: Adm. George Brumbaugh, George 5/1/20; Frederick, George C., heirs of Da____, heirs of Barbara Slagle, John Slagle, George Brumbaugh, John, Elizabeth, heirs of Mary Betzel T $10,320.52   Deduct from each $59.95
99. GILBERT, Wendel. Adm. Alexander Neill 7/12/23; ½ to widow, $344.79; Jacob B., Peter, John Leasure, Michael Leasure, Magdalena Metz, John Smith and Mary his wife, John Shaneberger's representative, Elizabeth Gaylord's representative each $49.25 T $689.59
100. GITTINGER, John. Adm. Jacob Woolf 2/28/17; widow, John, Jacob, Samuel, Susanna, Elizabeth Woolf, Sarah each $54.83
101. GLECKNER, Jacob. Adm. Philip Studer, Elizabeth his wife 3/14/25; widow, Catherine Henshaw, Margaret Richardson, Jacob, Mary Long, Susanna, Elizabeth, Joseph, Rosanna T $629.69
102. GLECKNER, Devolt. Adm. Elizabeth, Jacob 5/1/20; widow, Catherine Henshaw, Margaret Richardson, Jacob, Mary Long, Susanna, Elizabeth, Joseph, Rosanna T $933.67 (This entry not in original book index)
103. GONCE, Nicholas. (No entry, name crossed out)
104. GOOD, Christian. Adm. Christian, Stephen Martin 5/16/25; Peter, Christian, Elizabeth Funk, John, Barbara Martin, Jacob, David, Abraham, Nancy Newcomer T$12,220.52
105. GOOD, William. Adm. John 6/4/12; John, Joseph, William T 203.12.2
106. GREY, Catherine. Adm. George Colleflower 3/23/21; 5 children T $31.90
107. GREY, John. Adm. John Fultz 8/12/23; Elizabeth, Catherine Fultz, Anna T$2,747.31 4/14/27 (Anna now Anna Brumbaugh) T $360.99
108. GREY, Samuel. Adm. Jacob Brunner 4/20/12; widow, Elizabeth, John, Samuel, George, Joseph T 215.4.9½
109. GRIM, Abraham. Adm. Barbara, settled by B. Grim 4/17/24; 1/3 to widow after advance, $1,076.27; 12 children each $185.71 T $3,304.81
110. GRIM, Barbara. Adm. Benjamin 8/21/24; 12 heirs T $666.71   12/6/24 T $100.26
111. GROUND, Philip. Adm. George 4/24/18; George, heirs of John, Elizabeth Rusell T $5,208.33
112. GROVE, Jacob. T $1,698.27 (entry crossed out). Second entry: Adm. Philip 12/5/21; Elizabeth Wolf, John's heirs, Jacob, Henry, Peter's heirs, Stephen's heirs, Catherine Smith, Philip, Paul T $1,923.69
113. GUNDERMAN, C.L.D. Adm. John P. Herr 3/4/23; 3 heirs T $721.48
114. HAHN, Henry. Adm. Jacob Lambert 11/22/16; widow, Henry, George, David, Margaret, Christine, John T $279.60
115. HAINES, Jacob. Adm. Adam 12/2/22; Jacob, Elizabeth Brunner, John, Mary, David, Catherine Garlock, Adam, T$8,185.28   6/13/23 T $275.50
116. HAMMACKER, Samuel. Adm. Peter 1/26/27; Peter, Elizabeth, Susanna, Samuel, Adam, Daniel, Mariah, Rebecca T $47.78¼

1817 - 1828

117. HAMMOND, Paul. Adm. John, Jacob M. Knode 11/2/22; Peter, Philip, Michael, Jacob, John, Susanna Shup, Elizabeth Knode, Mary Gontz T $1,041.18   4/20/24 each $42.68
118. HANER, Jacob. Adm. ___ 1/12/25; 7 children T $289.81
119. HARTER, Jacob. Adm. David 2/21/26; 1/3 personal estate to widow after deducting $15.14; $100 of real estate to widow; specific legacy to David $30; Jacob, George, John, David, Judith each $74.24 T $556.33   3/31/27; 5 heirs T $113.59
120. HAWKEN, George. Adm. Alexander Neill 10/3/22; widow $1,466.91; John's heirs, Margaret Miller's heirs, George, Jacob, Samuel, William, Christian, Nancy each $366.73   Second distribution: n.d.; heirs above (omitting Christian) each $42.83 T $342.68   Third distribution: n.d.; widow $443.74; heirs above (Christian deceased, Nancy now Nancy Lewis) each $110.93 T $1,331.18   Fourth distribution: n.d.; each $12.94 T $103.52
121. HAYES, Jeremiah. Adm. John West 1/13/19; widow $433.45; specific legacy $1,000; due the executor and settled in the estate of P. Hayes, $123.10 T $1,310.35
122. HECK, Andrew. Adm. Henry 4/18/12;   widow; 5 children T4.6.6
123. HECKMAN, Mathias. Adm. William Collier 9/4/16; Catherine Whitnight, Mary Cadderman, Elizabeth Collier, Susanna Emreck T $105.25
124. HEFFLEICH, John. Adm. Magdalena 7/28/18; widow, Ann Maria, Amelia L., Elizabeth, Matilda T $369.46
125. HEISTER, Rosanna. Adm. Christian Hager, Philip Wingert 4/2/23; specific legacy Philip Wingert $3851.24; Rosanna Hager Kershner, Rosanna Henrietta Hower, Maria Rosanna Baer, Alexander Swann, each $26.67; balance to Magdalena Hager, John Hager, Christian Hager, Elizabeth Rosanna, each $468.97
126. HEISTER, William. Adm. Henry Lowry 12/29/27; William, Isaac, Daniel J., John P., William Eckert and Rebecca his wife, Edward Clymer and Maria his wife, Catherine, Juliana Miller T $1,115.40
127. HELM, Sarah. Adm. Benjamin Yoe 1/7/18; Mrs. Yoe the mother, Sophia Martin, Margaret, Meredith, Joseph T $1,379.23
128. HELM, Thomas. Adm. Benjamin Yoe, John Ashberry 12/24/17; Benjamin Yoe 889.5.1; Sophia, Meredith, Sarah, Margaret, Joseph each 355.14.0½ T2667.15.3   4/21/12; Adm. Benjamin Yoe and wife, John Ashberry; widow 543.18.9; Sophia, Meredith, Sarah, Margaret, Joseph each 217.11.6
129. HERR, Rudolph. Adm. Joseph Charles Jr., Rudolph 5/14/27; Rudolph, Henry, Joseph, Anna Brewer, Fanny Kreps, Elizabeth Lutz, Mary M. Steaman, Easter Baughman's heirs, Susanna Kauffman T $1,316.38
130. HERSHEY, John. Adm. Andrew, John 5/19/12; Ann Shup, Andrew, Magdalena Shelly, John, Christian, Barbara Miller, Jacob, David, Joseph, Elizabeth Eby, Frany Avey, each 600.0.0   Second distribution: n.d.; T9643.6.3
131. HILL, Valentine. Adm. John Clopper 8/22/16; 1/3 to widow (advance deducted), $200.38; John $1; Jacob, Daniel, Abraham, Joseph, Jonathan, ___, Elizabeth Roebeck's (Rohrback?) heirs, Barbara, Peter each $71.50 T $844.90 (Jacob Barks' name here but crossed out)   Second distribution: n.d.; Jacob Barks' name added T $107.25   6/15/18 T $117.76   6/18/19; widow, heirs T $117.76   6/17/20; widow, heirs $117.76   6/12/24 T $117.76   10/10/25; 10 children $117.76 9/21/26; 10 children T $117.76   12/22/27; 10 children T $117.76
132. HILLIARD, Christopher. (First distribution crossed out) Second distribution: Adm. Jane, John Hershey 5/26/25; widow, 7 children T $759.49
133. HOGMIRE, Daniel. Adm. Jacob Howell, Henry 2/16/12; widow, Henry T100.17.3
134. HOOPER, John. Adm. Kellurah 2/9/25; widow, Mary Ann $104.57
135. HOOVER, Christian. Adm. Hester, John Welty 9/26/26; John, Jacob, Hester, Mary, Leah, Susanna T $1,106.51 Note: Samuel Gehr, husband of Anne received advance of $400, the heirs of Anna not entitled to any part of this distribution
136. HOOVER, John. Adm. John Barr 10/25/24; widow, 7 children T $53.56

DISTRIBUTION OF ESTATE ACCOUNTS

137. HOOVER, John. Adm. Jacob Welty, Mathias Hoffman 6/8/26; John's heirs, Jacob Welty, Mathias Hoffman, Michael Sprinkle, John Wertz, Christopher's heirs, George Mentzer, Henry's heirs T $613.32
138. HOOVERMAIL, Lodwick. Adm. Margaret Hoovermaile, George Smith 8/19/16; widow, Sarah Watson, John, Judith, Elizabeth, Peter, Daniel, Susannah, Joseph T $1,742.65
139. HOSE, Geroge. Adm. David Harry 10/19/25; 7 heirs T $64.71
140. HOUCK (HOUK), John. Adm. Joseph Feiry 4/7/18; Mary Sprecher, Catherine, Jacob T $535.50
141. HOWER, George (settled by John Hower said Adm. of Jacob Hower). Adm. Jacob 1/2/27; widow, Elizabeth, Maria, David, Sarah T $248.62 (above crossed out) 3/24/27; widow, 4 children T $249.24
142. HOWER, Jacob. Adm. John 3/24/27; John, Susanna Ridenour, Jacob, Mary Smith each $610.27
143. HUNT, Job. Adm. Ann, David Boyd 6/22/26; widow, 6 children T $342.08
144. HYLAND, John R. Adm. Charlotte, Andrew Kershner 12/17/25; widow, Mary Ann, Hugh, Ann, Joshua T $1,330.89
145. IRVIN, John. Adm. Jacob T. Towson 7/6/27; widow, Rachel Sterrett, Nancy Sterrett, John Hogg, Sarah Craig, William Hogg T $351.21
146. JAMES, Walter. Adm. Mathias 4/1/23; Walter $206.72; Rachel $103.36 T$310.08
147. JOHN, Henry. Adm. Solomon Boyer 9/13/16; widow, Elizabeth T $599.77
148. JULIUS, John. Adm. Joseph Groff 8/31/25; retain by administrator for latent purposes $122.80; widow, 7 children T $2622.80
149. KEESACRE, Simon. Adm. Jacob, Henry Shafer 3/27/24; 3 heirs T $90.05
150. KELLER, Elizabeth. Adm. Elie Crampton 11/7/27; Ann. M. $851.72½, property retained for her by administrator $333.25; Alfred $996.47½, property retained for him by administrator $188.50 T $2,369.95
151. KELLER, Joseph C. Adm. Isaac S. White 12/3/27; widow, Ann Marie, Alfred T $333.50
152. KERSHNER, Jonathan. Adm. George Gacharia 3/25/18; 6 children T $380.16
153. KERSHNER, Martin. Adm. Andrew 12/26/22; Jacob Bachtel, Barbara's heirs, Elizabeth's heirs, Solomon, John Dunn, John Ankeny's heirs, Susanna Schnebly, Jacob Dunn T $21,516.00 10/15/23 T $3,229.25 12/17/25; Catherine Bachtel, Barbara's heirs, Elizabeth Rockafield's heirs, Solomon, John Dunn, Ann Ankeny's heirs, Susanna Schnebly, Jacob Dunn T $1,892.06
154. KINKLE, Jacob. Adm. Jacob 10/3/23; Jacob, Henry, Adam, Elizabeth T $710.72
155. KNEEDY, Elizabeth. Adm. John Frener 9/8/24; 8 heirs T $14.40
156. KNODLE, George. Adm. George, Benjamin Cushwa 1/13/20; widow, Leonard, Catherine Light, George, Jacob T $2,033.56
157. KOALER, John. Adm. George 4/7/27; Jonathan, George, Catherine Culp, Christian Wentling's heirs, Esther Bowers T12.16.4½
158. KREIGH, Andrew. Adm. William 3/28/27; mother, 8 brothers and sisters equal shares T $303.00
159. KREIGH, Philip. Adm. Andrew Kline, William, Philip 4/5/23; widow, 9 children T $2,922.10
160. KREPS, John. Adm. Jacob 11/8/26; Christine the mother $47.42; Jacob $47.42; 4 children of Elizabeth Brewer each $11.85½ T $142.26
161. KRETZER, Leonard. Adm. Henry, John 4/16/23; specific legacy to Adam $300, David $200, Christian $50; 8 heirs each $176.64 5/24/26; 8 children T $3,648.96 (this crossed out and the following entered): 8 children T $3,613.84
162. KRETZINGER, Lodwick. Adm. William Cost 7/29/19; widow, George, John, William Cost, Henry Rinehart, Samuel Sprecher, Lodwick, Charlotte, Susanna, Nancy T $65.78
163. LAMBERT, Jonas. Adm. George H. 3/27/26; widow, 5 children T $276.13 interest from 11/19/23
164. LANE, Catherine. Adm. Christian G. 3/16/26; retained by administrator for latent purposes $10.02; 7 children each $107.01 T $749.09

1817 - 1828

165. LAWVER, John, Guardian to child Colier? Lee; distribution of Mrs. Davis' estate; Eve Allen born 1/2/02, Walter Boyd, guardian. (This note found inside cover of Distribution Book III)
166. LEARY, Edward. Adm. Edward 1/12/24; widow, Margaret Brown, Elener, Edward, Joshua T $109.64
167. LEASURE, Elijah. Adm. John Miller 7/14/23; widow, Christian, Susan, Elizabeth T $1,784.26
168. LECKROON, Isaac. Adm. Jacob Bayer 11/17/19; widow, Jacob T $497.12 Interest from 11/24/15
169. LECKROON, John. Adm. John Woolfersberger 11/1/24; widow, Elizabeth, Rebecca, Catherine, Maria, John T $1252.74
170. LEFEVER, David. Adm. George 4/7/24; 5 children T $627.09 1/17/25; George, Henry T $387.91
171. LEFEVER, John. Adm. George 2/11/17; widow, Mary, Elizabeth, Isaac, Henry, Sarah, John, Mariah, Samuel T $2,617.10
172. LEFEVER, Sarah. Adm. Christine 4/19/27; Christine the mother, Isaac, Henry, John, Maria, Samuel, Thomas C. Thornburgh T $1,340.87
173. LEIDER, Abraham. Adm. George Shenk 4/16/19; Susanna Moler, Judith Morgan, Catherine Shenk, Elizabeth _____ wall, Julianna Shenk, Eve Bowart, John T $1,248.47 4/14/20 T $356.17 (Elizabeth's name appears to be Ollawall or Ottowall)
174. LEITER, Jacob Sr. Adm. Lewis Zeigler 3/26/25; Elizabeth legacy $40; Elizabeth, Andrew (George Lambert?), Jacob (David), John, Abraham, Susan wife of S. Houser, Samuel, Catherine wife of Jacob Houser, Fudid wife of B. Hartman, Julia wife of Peter Bell, each $48.24½ T $682.46
175. LEITER, John. Adm. Daniel Lowman, Catherine his wife, the late Catherine Leiter 5/23/26; Sum retained by administrator for latent claims $200; widow, Henry, Peter, Jonas T $533.70
176. LINE, Jacob (1st crossed out) 2nd entry: Adm. George, David Fuah 3/9/24; 7 heirs T $766.80
177. LONG, David. Adm. Daniel 9/4/19; 1/3 personal estate to the widow, 1/3 real estate held by executor to be paid widow annually $1,168.75; John's heirs, Rosanna Bond's heirs, Catherine Leidy's heirs, Margaret Study's heirs, Susanna Custard's heirs, Nancy Finecy's heirs, each $149.89 T $2,068.14
178. LONG, John. Adm. Catherine 9/2/22; widow, 6 heirs T $3,475.80
179. LOWMAN, John. Adm. John V. Swearingen 9/13/25; widow, Henry, Jacob, Catherine Artz, Levie Housely T $296.72
180. McCAFFERTY, Dennis. Adm. Zebina Smith 5/2/26; widow, Robert, Elizabeth, John T $319.39
181. McCLAIN, James. Adm. Margaret, John 8/6/25; widow $592.87; John specific legacy $500; 14 heirs each $48.98 T $1,178.63 (Note: see equity No. 798 liber 3 folio 575)
182. McCOY, Joseph. Adm. John Witmer 12/8/19; 33 grandchildren each $101.44 T $3,347.74 4/2/20; the goods and chattles paid to Martha M. Ford and Thomas Ford $1,170.39; Thomas and Martha M. each $105.32 T $1,381.04 12/11/20; 33 heirs each $51.69 T $1,705.84
183. McCREA, John. Adm. John Witman (mer) 9/6/20; widow, Adam, Rebecca, John, Michael, Samuel, Martha, Mary Ann T $1,789.42
184. McDILL, Catherine. Adm. Jacob Sturr, John Noble, Jacob Sturr named as heirs (crossed out) 3/8/25; John, John Sweyer?, Henry Duble each $184.18 T $552.54 $58.14 divided and deducted from each for amount of inventory
185. MALONE, James. Adm. James, Jacob Dean 9/15/17; widow, Richard, John, James, Benjamin, Lidna Dean, Rebecca Erickson, Jane Powell, Elias, Elizabeth Usherman T $2,278.99
186. MALONE, John. Adm. John Brien 6/11/17; heirs of Edward, heirs of Thomas, Mary, Bryan, John, heirs of Daniel, James, Susanna (m. John Miles), Grace (m. John Long) T $1,016.83 6/15/20 T $926.12
187. MALOTT, Benjamin. Adm. Theodore, Benjamin 9/10/16; specific legacy to James Gole, Benjamin Gole each $80.00; Mary Ann $160.00; Theodore, Elias, Elizabeth Newell (Nowell), Rebecca Snell, Catherine Gole each $556.19 T $3,180.97 5/19/17; each $1,390.12 T $6,950.00

DISTRIBUTION OF ESTATE ACCOUNTS

188. MALOTT, John. Adm. Theodore 11/12/16; widow, Mary Ann T $5,067.18
189. MALOTT, Kitty. Adm. Jonas Hogmire 3/28/26; mother of deceased $66.21; Hiram $66.21 T $132.42
190. MALOTT, Michael. Adm. Daniel, Catherine 9/24/19; widow, Thomas, Theodore, John, Joseph, William, Peter's heirs, Daniel, Hiram, Hannah, Sarah Steward T $1,153.15 $151.33 reserved for Susanna Price
191. MALOTT, Peter. Adm. Daniel 3/28/17; widow, Hiram, Kitty T $598.93
192. MANTESBAUGH, William. Adm. John Wagoner, Jacob 2/5/24; money paid guardian of child of Beeler $492.47; specific legacy Jacob Beeler $40; 6 children each $118.96 T $1,246.22
193. MASON, John. Adm. Elizabeth 8/25/27; widow, Elizabeth A.T., Mary B., Abraham B., Melchor B., John T., Thompson, Virginia T $16,978.28
194. MEAD, Benjamin. Adm. Samuel Lynch Jr. 4/21/20; agreeable to the will, agreeable to the specific devisee of Negro property; Jeremiah $1,220.60; Benjamin $1.179.80; Samuel $1,052.91 T $3,453.31
195. MELTON, Philip. Adm. Thomas McCardell 4/20/18; widow, Philip, Ann, Thomas, each $332.98 T $1,498.40 9/25/18; widow, Philip, Ann T $23.86 6/8/27; widow, Philip, Ann T $116.85 3/4
196. MELTON, Thomas. Adm. Thomas McCardell 4/20/18; the mother, Philip, Ann each $106.79 T $320.37
197. MENTZER, John. Adm. John, Catherine 4/13/24; widow $1,844.14; Margaret Gilbert, John, Elizabeth Strite, Catherine, Samuel each $737.86 2/13/26; each $154.69 T $1,160.22
198. MILLER, George. Adm. Jacob Schnebly 4/21/17; the mother, Maria, Sally, Jacob each $105.36 T $421.47
199. MILLER, Mason. Adm. Levin 4/24/20; Elizabeth, Samuel, Ann Filligrin, William, Sophia Hafter, John Hall, William H.,John, Levin T$607.14
200. MILLER, Peter. Adm. Daniel, George Gehr 4/30/23; $675.13 payment of bond; 8 heirs each $35.41 T $958.48 6/13/26; specific legacy Daniel $740; John, Daniel, Sarah Otto, Rebecca Renner, Mary, Anna Otto, Elias, Peter each $2,986.15 T $23,889.21
201. MILLER, William. Adm. Levin Mills 3/30/20; widow, John Hull, William H., John, Mason T $4,503.57 Hall's $26.16, Shup $2.00, 22.76; 1/3 or $7.58 deducted from widow's share, $3.79 deducted from each child's share
202. MONG, Jacob, Adm. Jacob B., Barbara 3/17/20; widow, Jacob B., John, George, Peter, Elizabeth, Margaret, Mary, Amelia T $4,690.18
203. MOYER, Abraham.Adm.Jacob Schnebly 5/7/12;widow, Nancy, Jacob, Betsey, Abraham, John, Peggy, Catherine, Rose, Samuel T119.6.6
204. MOYER, Elizabeth. Adm. Henry Hershey 9/18/18; Nancy, Jacob, Elizabeth, Abraham, John, Margaret, Catherine, Samuel, Rose T $48.69
205. MOYER, John. Adm. Christian, John 1/10/27; Jacob, Elizabeth Dusing, Samuel, Barbara, Mary Abracht, Susanna Hose, Henry, Christian, Isaac, John, Esther Ridenour, Nancy T $7,468.24
206. MOYER, Michael. Adm. Joseph Graff 12/5/16; sum received for latent claim $60; Christopher, Margaret Stine, Mary Turner, Susanna Humphreyville, George Lewis, Catherine Stephens, Mary Ledely each $10.37½ T $83.00
207. MUIR, James. Adm. Peggy 1/7/23; widow $476.95; Negro property for benefit of children $420; 4 children each $133.47 T $1,430.85
208. MYERS, Jacob. Adm. John Beard, Adam 1/22/24; Elizabeth Hoskins $2,372.18, advance $1,146.33; her 6 children $200 each; John Myers $2,372.18, Advance $2,258.52; to his 4 children each $28.41½; Jacob, Susanna Hoffman, Frederick, each $2,372.18; Mary $4,744.36 T $16,603.28
209. MYERS, Michael. Adm. Adam 4/1/12; ½ to widow 83.7.4; Jacob, Adam, Frederick, Sarah Robinson, Magdalena Showman, Elizabeth Long, Barbara Middlecalf, Daniel Tinkle's heirs, each 10.8.5 T166.14.8

1817 - 1828

210. MYERS, Peter. Adm. John Beard 8/15/18; specific legacy of all debts to widow $2,666.04; interest on farm $230.45; specific legacy to Rosanna $60; 1/3 to widow $383.51; John, heirs of Jacob, Henry, Elizabeth, Polly Kingery, Sarah, Peter, Rosanna each $95.88 T $1,150.55
211. NAVE, David. Adm. John Geiger, John Newcomer 2/15/26; widow, Catherine Newcomer T $2,117.88   2/22/26   T $14.37
212. NEFF, John. Adm. Jacob 8/26/19; Henry's child, Jacob's child, Margaret's child, Adam, Catherine, Esther T $2,165.49
213. NEALE, William. Adm. St. Leger 9/25/11; widow, Mary, James, Sarah, St. Leger T218.11.11; St. Leger to retain $37 from above sum borrowed of the estate of Acquilla to pay debt and by the estate of William and for which the estate of William hath been credited Balance 204.14.5
214. NEWCOMER, Elizabeth. Adm. John Witmer, Peter 12/22/19; Nancy, Mary Swingley, Samuel, Jacob, Catherine, Susanna, Joel, Isaac, Thomas, Joshua, Henry T $1,411.00
215. NEWCOMER, John. Adm. Christian, Peter 12/28/25; Peter received advance of $1,000 receives no part of this distribution; Christian, Magdalena Welty, Elizabeth Stouffer, Fanny Stoner, Nancy Hoffman, John, Andrew, Jacob T $1,015.25   3/18/26   T $187.76   4/4/27   T $187.76
216. NEWCOMER, Samuel. Adm. Peter, John Witmer 12/22/19; deduct legacy left to 6 guardian children of the deceased by Jacob Hufford with interest $2,940.41; specific legacy to above children $1,333.33; Nancy, Elizabeth, Mary Swingley, Samuel, Jacob, Catherine, Susanna, Joel, Isaac, Joshua, Henry each $811.33 T $13,198.93
217. NEWSON, John. Adm. Jane 5/13/24; to mother, Alexander, Joseph, Rachel, Abraham, each $42.80 T $214.03 (Distribution crossed out)   Second entry; each $35.67 T $214.03
218. ODERFER, John. Adm. Henry Butterbaugh 4/15/18; Elizabeth, Henry, Barbara, Mary, John, Esther, Sarah, Margaret T $387.91   interest from 3/21/17
219. OSWALD, Margaret. Adm. Benjamin 11/29/23; Catherine Elbzrote, John's heirs (each $47.71), Adam, Benjamin, Elizabeth Flory, each $286.27 T $1,431.35
220. OTTO, Isabella. Adm. Jacob Dunn 4/13/26; Jeremiah, Jack and wife, Mathias, Samuel Silver and wife, Henry T$1,068.68
221. PALMORE, Peter. Adm. Christian Middlecauff 4/4/17; when of age, John $106, Christian $93.33, Peter $13.33, Jacob $53.33, Joseph $146.66, Jonathan $226.66, David $80; also Christian, John, Peter, Jacob, Joseph, Jonathan, David, Elizabeth Betz, Barbara Knocatee, Catherine, Anna Coffman, Mary King's children each $133.33 1/3; 14 children each entitled to $1,160.83 T $18,571.59
222. PERRIN, Debra. Adm. John Ingram 3/20/27; 11 children of Joseph and Rachel Ingram, each $2.30 T $25.29
223. PETERY, Elizabeth. Adm. John Shafer 4/25/20; 5 heirs T $430.70
224. PETERY, Jacob. Adm. Christian Smith, John 4/10/18; John, Philip, Eve Binkley, Christian Smith, Rebecca Arnold, Elizabeth Summers T $5,042.20
225. PIPER, Elizabeth. Adm. Daniel 4/3/19; John, Elizabeth Kephart, heirs of Catherine Hammond, Margaret Hammond, Jacob, Mary Stone, Barbara Johnson, Rosanna Brown, Daniel.... (end of text in original)
226. PIPER, Jacob. Adm. Daniel 4/3/19; 9 heirs T $95.05
227. POFFENBERGER, John. Adm. Robert Smith, Henry 5/16/12; Adam. Henry Eakle, Valentine, John, Henry, Christian, Simon, Philip Shame? T309.7.8
228. POSTATOR, Andrew. Adm. Jacob 3/9/20; 7 heirs T $1,597.32
229. POWLES, Elizabeth. Adm. Jacob 2/15/21; 5 children T $66.35
230. PROTZMAN, John. Adm. David Harry, Peter Heffley 3/13/12; Michael McKeernan, Catherine, John, Henry T235.0.9   5/24/25 (Catherine now Bateman) T $124.18
231. RAGAN, Amelia. Adm. John Harry 3/24/24; 3 heirs T $2,107.39
232. REEDER, Jessee. Adm. Philip 12/17/22; widow, 8 heirs T $67.84   4/13/23 T $87.80   5/3/25   T $177.26   4/4/26   T $87.88

DISTRIBUTION OF ESTATE ACCOUNTS

233. RENCH, Jacob. Adm. Daniel Schnebly, Isaac S. White 10/14/20; widow, Peter, Samuel H., Joseph, John A., Catherine, Mary, Elizabeth, Margaret, Theresa T $53,629.52 n.d. T $1,698.75
234. RESH, Joseph. Adm. Daniel 5/23/26; Elizabeth Smith received advance $147.12, entitled to no part of distribution; widow, 12 children T $940.62
235. RIDENOUR, Charles. Adm. Adam 4/10/17; widow, Daniel, Anna, Mary T $275.88 4/22/18 T $267.44   4/3/19; each child $89.15 T $267.44   3/3/19; each child $75.77 T $227.33
236. RIDENOUR, David. Adm. Samuel 12/11/11; Samuel, Susanna Markle, Catherine Miller, Jacob, Conrad, Sarah Foster, Milly Kealhoofer, Mary T1613.15.9
237. RIDENOUR, Eve. Adm. Gerard Stonebraker 11/30/24; Amelia, Nancy T $97.80
238. RIDENOUR, George. Adm. Conrad Flora 6/20/17; Margaret Flora, heirs of George, Sarah Small, heirs of Henry, Magdalena Singer's heirs, Eve T89.5.4   5/9/18; T $238.04   8/5/18 T $238.04   4/28/12 T89.5.4
239. RIDENOUR, Henry. Adm. Andrew Kline, William Kreib, Philip Kreib 4/4/26; widow, 6 heirs T $9.29
240. RIDENOUR, Jacob. Adm. George Seibert 5/11/27; mother of deceased, George Seibert and wife, Mary Clapsaddle's heirs, George Kline and wife, Elizabeth, Daniel, Rebecca, John, Margaret, Archibald, Nancy, Upton, Lydia A. each $60.87 T $791.30
241. RIDENOUR, Sarah. Adm. Samuel 8/14/25; Samuel, Susanna Markley, Jacob, Catherine Miller, Conrad, Sarah Hoffman, Amelia Anderson, Mary Hobletzell T $1,199.10
242. RICHART, Jacob. Adm. Jacob, Daniel 4/20/12; specific legacy to Maria Buck's heirs, Eliza Holsinger, Catherine Long, Barbara, Christian, Jacob, Daniel each 100.0.0; Eve 500.0.0; 2d paid to Buck heirs, Holsinger, Isaac Long, Barbara each 100.0.0 T1641.15.6
243. RINGGOLD, Samuel 10/11/11; received $353.94 as guardian of child; signed Samuel Ringgold
244. RITCHIE, John. 9/6/11; distribution of personal estate of deceased by Jonas McPherson who was attorney in fact for Esther Ritchie who's also since deceased; 1/3 to the devisee of Esther Ritchie deceased 430.5.6¼; Archibald, son and heir of deceased 860.11.1½ T1290.16½.0
245. RITZ, Solomon. Adm. Henry Locher n.d.; Elizabeth, Daniel, Sarah T $262.25
246. ROBB, Michael. T191.10.5 (entry crossed out). Second entry: Adm. Christian Lantz. 3/3/12; Peter, Elizabeth Tailor, Rosanna Gainer, Christian, John, Eve Dick T114.3.4
247. RODICK, Jacob. Adm. Joshua 3/31/18; widow $67.47; 6 children each $24.15
248. ROHRER, Jonathan. Adm. Samuel 5/4/19; widow, 3 children T$659.90
249. ROOT, Elizabeth. Adm. Jacob 8/23/24; Elizabeth Ott, Catherine Reneberger T $2,844.80
250. ROOT, Jacob. Adm. Jacob 3/11/12; widow, 8 children T41.10.6
251. ROTENBELLER, Rachel. Adm. Jacob Powles, William McCardle 6/11/23; each received 2 sums: (1) a legacy and (2) a distribution share; Daniel Ritz, Daniel Thomson, Jacob Conrad, Mary Thomson each (1) $266.67 (2) $171.96; Elizabeth Ritz, Sarah Ritz, Valentine Ritz each (1) $133.33 (2) $85.98; Jacob Wise, Susanna Wise, Sophia Wise, Rosanna Wise, Margaret Wettle, Valentine Thomson each (1) $106.67 (2) $68.80 T $1,272.59
252. ROUGH, Barney. Adm. Jeremiah Mason 6/3/23; latent claim $66.01; widow, 8 children T $802.90   5/21/26; Adm. Jeremiah Mason, Margaret; widow, 8 children T $143.52
253. ROUGH, William. Adm. John Jones, Philip 7/4/17; widow, Barnhart, Henry, John, William, Philip, Margaret Houtzer, Catherine Teatherhoof, Barbara Jones T $373.88 6/3/19; John Leiter grandson of deceased $169.33; Barbara, Henry, John, William, Philip, Margaret Houtzer, Cather Teatherhoof, Barbara Jones, each $17.12; John Leiter $8.56 T $145.52   5/29/26; Barnhart, Henry, John, William, Philip, Margaret Houtzer, Catherine Teatherhoof, Barbara Jones each $155.41; John Leider $77.68 T $1,320.96

1817 - 1828

254. ROULETT, William. Adm. John Sisler 2/7/26; widow, Daniel, Mary Sisler, John, Sarah Ann T $573.97
255. RUSSELL, John. Adm. Susanna, William Gabby, Jacob Lambert 12/19/18; widow, Catherine, Christian, Mary, Rebecca, Susanna, John T1158.3.2
256. SANDMAN, Jacob Adm. John Beard 4/16/23; specific legacy to William's heirs $400; William's heirs each $395.22; George Kretzer's 8 heirs each $123.52 T $3,364.16
257. SCHENK, John. Adm. Christine and Daniel 8/24/22; each heir $69.87 T $628.89
258. SCHENK, Magdalena. Adm. Christian 8/24/22; 9 heirs T $795.72
259. SCHNEBLY, John. Adm. John Showery 12/3/23; widow, 2 children T $629.73
260. SCHNEBLY, Susanna. Adm. Daniel Miller 1/19/17; Abraham Woodring, heirs of Leonard, Christian Roudebush, Elizabeth Miller T $1,865.42
261. SCHRODER, Henry. Adm. Peter Martz 4/15/24; widow equal share, 8 heirs T $664.53 Deduct latent claim $3.00
262. SCOTT, George. Adm. George French 3/31/18; Elenor Kennedy, Alexander Mitchell, each 803.2.7 3/4; deduct for commission interest 31.9.3½ T1606.5.3½
263. SEIBERT, Mary. Adm. Michael 1/18/23; 6 children T $909.74
264. SEIBERT, Nicholas. Adm. John Beard 4/16/23; widow $688.69; deduct specific legacy $300; 4 heirs each $249.35 T $2,066.09
265. SEIBERT, Peter. Adm. Henry n.d.; Catherine Cushwa, Jacob, Henry, Elizabeth, Michael T $1,095.05   4/19/26 T $2,163.27   6/5/26 T $9.11
266. SHAFER, George. Adm. Christian Ankeny 4/2/12; specific legacy Henry 200.0.0; Christian, Jacob Lauer?, Simon Hager, Henry, heirs of Peter, each 993.6.8 T4966.13.0
267. SHAFER, Solomon. Adm. Theobold Eckelbarger 8/14/16; widow, Charles W. T $391.50 1/17/23; 1/7 to widow $60.36, Charles W. $363.36 T $423.91
268. SHANE, Daniel. Adm. Theobald Eichelberger 10/26/25; 11 heirs T $33.13
269. SHANE, Henry. Adm. Theobald Eckleberger 4/15/17; deducted for lottery tickets $50; widow, John, Henry, Adam, Peter, George, Daniel, Elizabeth, Catherine, Susanna, Mary, Lucretia Glossbrenner T $473.20   11/18/24; 1/3 of whole and ½ of Daniel's proprotion of the 2/3 to the widow $21.13½; John, Henry, Adam, Peter, George, Elizabeth, Catherine, Susanna, Mary, Lucretia Glossbrenner each $4.12¼ T $62.36
270. SHARER, Henry. Adm. Jacob Towson 4/30/24; John Towson, John I. Porterfield T $311.53
271. SHEARER, Elizabeth. Adm. Abraham Schmutz 8/12/24; Abraham Leib, Jacob Leib, William Leib, Gabriel Leib, Mary Leib, Susanna Leib, Daniel Hogmire, Henry Beckley Jr., Elizabeth Heitt, Catherine Hogmire, Andrew Hogmire T $1,215.45; John Leib discovered later received $101.28; specific legacy to children of Catherine Heitt $141.33
272. SHECTOR, Daniel. Adm. Jacob, Joseph Emmert 11/5/25; widow, Lydia T $1,256.53
273. SHEITZ (SHOOTZ, SHEETZ), Peter. Adm. Daniel and wife Elizabeth 1/29/21; widow $199.71; 7 years interest on $600 for the support of Maryann $252.00; Mary Ann balance $147.42 T $599.13
274. SHENK, Daniel. Adm. Christian 11/14/18; Christian Newcomer, John, Andrew, Christian, Henry, Jacob, Peter Witmer, Abraham, Daniel each $11.37
275. SHEPHERD, Christian. Adm. John, David 11/20/27; specific legacy to John $300; John, Peter, Jacob, George, David, Michael, William, Elizabeth, Samuel each $49.90 T $749.08½
276. SHEPHERD, Thomas. Adm. Adam Myers, John Blackford 11/18/18; specific legacy John $400; 1/5 to widow $1,007.78; John, Sarah, Joseph, Davis each $1,007.78 T$5,038.92
277. SHERLEY, Joseph. Adm. Levin Mills 2/24/24; widow, 5 heirs T $1,693.83
278. SHIFFLER, Nicholas. Adm. Nicholas, John 3/6/20; specific legacy John, Nicholas, Elizabeth Mourer's children, Mary, Margaret Nekark children, each $900.00; specific legacy to Margaret Nikark and Elizabeth Mourer each $1.00; John, Nicholas, Elizabeth Mourer, Mary, Margaret Nikark, each $149.75

DISTRIBUTION OF ESTATE ACCOUNTS

279. SHOWMAN, George. Adm. George, Adam Myers n.d.; deduct claim of T. Myers $525.03; Brien McPherson $33.91; widow $538.26; George, Jacob, David, Elizabeth Benner, John, Peter, Catherine each $440.44 4/6 T $3,621.52
280. SHOWMAN, Mary M. Adm. David, Peter 5/9/25; George, Jacob, David, Elizabeth Benner, John, Peter, Catherine Cline, each ($600) is $576 (received 96¢ on the dollar) T $5,774.47
281. SHRADER, Henry. Adm. Gerard Stonebraker, Leonard Shafer 12/7/25; widow relinquished under will; widow $3,696.49; Bank stock to Gerard Stonebraker $440; one morety? household furniture to Sarah $206; distribution of balance 73 1/3 cents on the dollar; children of Frederick ($700) $513.33; children of Elizabeth Hammond ($1500) $1,100; children of John ($1000) $733.33. The interest on these 2 sums to be paid to Elizabeth Hammond during her life; Sarah ($3000) $2200; Henry, Catherine Stonebraker, Mary Shafer, children of Frederick each ($750) $550 T $11,089.49 12/19/26; sums to be deducted from distribution, consequence of a deficiency in the lands sold to Upton Hammond; widow $107.47; children of Frederick $16.33 and $17.52; children of Elizabeth Hammond $35.02; children of John $23.35; Sarah $70.16; Henry, Catherine Stonebraker, Mary Shafer each $17.52 Total deducted $322.42
282. SHUMAN, Samuel. Adm. Christine, William Moffett 6/22/25; widow, Sarah E. T $1,917.20 Note: error in adding last account $2 deducted from above. 11/21/27; widow, Sarah E. T $ 344.44
283. SHUPE, Adam. Adm. John Hammon 10/3/23; specific legacy Elizabeth $2,500; specific legacy children of Susanna $2,400; Catherine Evey, Polly each $300; 4 heirs each $195.77 T $6,283.07   n.d.;John Hammond and wife each $67.16; Elizabeth, John's heirs, Susanna Newcomer's heirs each $67.16 T $268.65
284. SIBERT, Jacob. Adm. John Cushwa, Henry 10/1/11; distribution of sum received for a bond due estate of Harry Anky 220.0.0; 1/3 to widow 340.2.6; Catherine Cushwa, Jacob, Peter, Henry, Elizabeth, Michael T1240.7.6
285. SMITH, Hezekiah. Adm. John Duffy and Mary his wife 6/22/24; mother $62.89; 4 heirs each $62.89 T $314.48
286. SMITH, Joseph. Adm. Michael 12/18/23; Peter, Susanna, Joseph, Elizabeth, John, Jacob's heirs, Margaret, Michael T $5,265.28   7/20/25 T $113.03   7/20/25 T $1,286.32   5/30/26 T $293.18   4/26/27; Peter, Susanna Barkman, Joseph, Elizabeth Stewdard, John (use of Jacob's heirs), Jacob's heirs, Margaret Adams, Michael T $201.32
287. SMITH, Joseph. Adm. Frederick Woolf n.d.; Sophia Stives specific legacy $40; Alexander, Henry, Joseph, Elizabeth, Margaret, Christian's heirs, Ann Eliza, Magdalena, Sophia each $38.78 T $349.04 Note attached: "John Keplinger and wife, see list of debts"
288. SMITH, Maria. Adm. John Duffy 6/22/24; mother $7.16, 3 heirs each $21.50 T $28.66
289. SMITH, Martin. Adm. Martin Myers 6/23/24; widow, 4 heirs T $493.69
290. SMITH, Nicholas. Adm. George Keller, Benjamin Swingley 6/14/17; Benjamin Swingley, Jacob Wagoner, Frederick Raimer, George Keller, Catherine T $479.60 4/22/24; Nicholas, Mathias, George, Benjamin Swingley, Jacob Wagoner, Frederick Raimer, George Keller, Catherine T $6,017.40
291. SMITH, Zebina. Adm. Sarah, William Towson 8/27/27; widow, John, William, Zebina T $1,137.39
292. SNYDER, David. Adm. Jacob Woolf 1/28/24; John, Mary, Henry, Catherine T $53.64
293. SNYDER, George. Adm. Martin 12/19/26; Michael, Jacob, John, Polly Umbarger, Catherine, Martin, Elizabeth Potts, Adam, Magdalena Baker's heirs T $69.44
294. SNYDER, Margaret. Adm. Jacob Howell, Daniel Howell 2/18/14; 10 heirs T73.11.1
295. SNYDER, Margaret. Adm. John Dovenberger 12/19/27; John Dovenberger ($300) $257.63½; Magdalena Camus?, Jacob Long, Henry Long, Catherine Getz, Maria Ash, Christine Coback, Margaret Shanberger's heirs ($100) $85.87 3/4; Margaret Hall ($56) $48.09 3/4 T $906.88 Note the difference between the two figures - there was no mention of a reason for the deduction.

1817 - 1828

296. SNYDER, Michael. Adm. Henry Shafer 8/16/16; John's heirs, Michael's heirs, Martin T $1,340.36
297. SNYDER, Michael (alias Taylor). Adm. Henry Shafer 2/23/26; Martin $532; Peter, Elizabeth Fausnaught, Mary Yontz, John, Catherine Byers, Barbara Nighswander, David, each $76 T $1,064.00
298. SPEACE, Daniel. Adm. Joseph Woolf 4/27/20; specific legacy $533.33; to Joseph Woolf's child provided she attained her full age, but dying in her minority, ½ to the father Joseph, $800; Daniel Woolf, Elizabeth Fausnaught, John Woolf, Susanna Shector, Hannah Woolf, each $160; Daniel Woolf, Joseph Woolf, John Woolf, Elizabeth Woolf, Susanna Shector, Hanna Woolf, each $241.29 4/2/23; 6 heirs T $1,800   4/2/24; 6 heirs T $1,795
299. SPEACE, Margaret. Adm. Joseph Woolf 3/31/21; D. Woolf, John Woolf, Joseph Woolf, Elizabeth Woolf's heirs, Susanna Shector, Hannah Woolf T $2,311.68
300. SPICKLER, Nicholas. Adm. John, Samuel 3/24/23; 1/3 to widow $384.79; specific legacy Samuel $190; specific legacy John $20; 4 heirs each $139.89 T $1,154.37
301. STARTZMAN, Henry. Adm. Martin, David 12/31/28; Martin, Henry, Rebecca, Julianna Householder, Susanna Fiery, David, Eve Kershner T $1,046.59
302. STEPHENS, David. Adm. Harriet 10/17/27; widow, Samuel M., Elmira, Amanda, Nancy, James H.B., Upton T $2,784.42
303. STONEBRAKER, Michael. Adm. George 9/17/27; Catherine Bentz, Gerard, Jacob Seibert and wife, George, John T $18,985.45
304. STOUFFER, Jacob. Adm. Christian 3/1/23; sum reserved for latent claims $3; specific legacy Samuel $20; 12 heirs each $278.21 T $3,639.71
305. STOVER, Jacob. Adm. Christian, Margaret 9/11/11; widow excluding advance 43.2.4; Ann Troup, Jacob, Christian, Elizabeth Rowland, Barbara Hoover, Mary Ridenour, John, David each 20.6.6½ T205.14.8
306. STULTZ, Henry. Adm. Andrew Cline, Philip Kreich 5/4/18; specific legacy to the mother $200, to John $100; Peter, David, John, Susanna Knable each $134.39 T $837.57
307. SUMMERS, Jacob. Adm. George Fague 1/6/26; widow, Alfred, William T $191.95
308. SWEARINGIN, Charles. Adm. John V. 5/19/20; specific legacy to the boy $1,200; to Martha ___ackling $133.33, 11 children each $792.49 T $8,717.45
309. SWINGLEY, John. Adm. Nicholas n.d.; widow, Nathaniel, John, Elizabeth T $4,600.28
310. SWOOPE, Peter. Adm. Catherine, Daniel Griffith n.d.; Catherine (the widow) $843.43; Catherine Seibert, Christian Davis, Susanna Yontz, Sarah Griffith, Rosanna Crouse, Elizabeth, Jacob S.W., Magdalena each $210.86 T $2,530.31
311. TEISHER, John. Adm. John Seibert 7/9/25; widow, John and wife, Jacob and wife, Jacob Hart and wife, David Stoner and wife, Mary, John, Jacob T $2,497.13 n.d.; widow, 6 heirs T $28.92
312. TEISHER, Mary. Adm. John Seibert 7/9/25; 6 heirs (see heirs of John Teisher) T $956.19
313. THOMAS, Jacob. Adm. Jacob, Christian Core 8/13/12; specific legacy Henry 700.0.0; George, Michael each 500.0.0; George, Michael, Sodwick, Abraham each 65.17.6; Jacob, Henry, Sodwick, Abraham, George, Michael, Christine, Eliza Core, Magdalena Core, Catherine Doup, Lavinia Fry, each 146.7.7 T3569.7.6½
314. THOMAS, Susanna. Adm. Jacob 11/7/26; Jacob, Henry, Abraham, Lewis, George, Michael, Christine Shutt, Elizabeth Core, Catherine Doup, Susanna Fry T $897.10
315. TOMS, Maria. Adm. John Shearer 11/13/27; Elizabeth, Ezra, Catherine each $406.99
316. TROUP, David. Adm. John 3/13/19; John, Elizabeth Weiland, Jacob, Peggy, David, Christine, Nancy T $959.54   4/13/20 T $538.30; 7 cents to be deducted from each share
317. TROVINGER, Christian. Adm. John, Joseph 4/29/24; Jacob's heirs, Samuel, John, William, Daniel, Joseph, Mary Keeler, Rebecca Landis, Sarah Hatter, Catherine Smith each $647.93; each received additional $281.55 T $9,294.95 n.d. T $5,556.10   8/2/25 T $987.16   7/28/27 T $3,141.42

37

DISTRIBUTION OF ESTATE ACCOUNTS

318. TYSHER, Peter. Adm. John 5/22/12; Peter, Joseph Ridenour, Susanna Pottorf, Dorathy T243.7.5
319. VERVIL, John. Adm. John, John L. Hoovermail 1/4/12; 5 children T170.2.9½
320. VERVIL, Peter. Adm. Joseph Mumma n.d.; widow, 8 heirs $53.40
321. WADE, John. Adm. Henry, Elias 4/25/26; sum placed in hands of some suitable person, interest to go to the use of Priscilla $1,000; Roan Buroll, William, John, Elias, Henry T $1,723.90   3/31/27 T $1,508.96   6/1/27 T $501.38
322. WACHTEL, John. Adm. Elizabeth, Jacob Kershner 3/16/12; widow, 11 children T66.5.10
323. WATSON, Richard. Adm. Jacob Miller 4/1/23; widow, 7 heirs T $242.15
324. WATT, John. Adm. John, William 1/15/19; specific legacy to Archibald $500; money for future claims $460; to John, William, Mary Parrott, Eliza T $1,482.24
325. WAUGH, Archibald M. Adm. Catherine 11/25/25; widow, Mary Ann, Thomas Moors, Henrietta M.A., James, Archibald T $3,816.31   6/21/27 T $1,094.50
326. WEBB, John. Adm. William (nephew) 2/28/18; widow, 5 children T $106.42   8/26/19; widow, 2 children 73.8.10
327. WEBB, William. Adm. William 2/28/18; widow, William, Margaret Baker, Ann Rusell, Mary Baker, Peter, John's children T $1,019.47
328. WELLER, Adam. Adm. Jacob, Adam 12/31/24; 7 children T $1,503.52   4/5/27 T $300.78
329. WELTY, Frederick. Adm. John, Christian Snyder 4/7/17; widow, 8 children T $147.44
330. WELTY, Henry. Adm. Jacob Hestand, Henry 2/17/18; Jacob, 2 ___ each $25.00; Jacob Garber, Benjamin Hestand, Jacob Moyer, Henry Stoufer each $476.10   T $6,904.41   4/7/19; one acre land left the mother, each of the above $318.61   T $1,374.44   6/7/20 (excluding mother) T $694.19   Adm. John Hestand n.d.; T $96.46   Adm. Jacob Housland, Henry 2/17/23; deduct $1 from each T $697.19   Adm. Daniel n.d.; widow, 5 heirs T $1,675.40
331. WESTENBARGER, David. Adm. Henry Schleigh 12/20/26; widow, Nancy Kershner, Catherine, Elizabeth, Samuel T $1,485.37   interest from 11/21/22
332. WILSON, Isaac. Adm. Phebe 6/3/25; widow, Lidia, George, Elias P., Isaac, Mary T $316.30
333. WINEBRENNER, Christian. Adm. William Kreps 9/9/18; Bastian, Jacob, Philip, Christian, Peter, Christian?, Catherine Schrader T $222.28
334. WITMER, Christian. Adm. Daniel Schnebly 5/9/18; widow, 1 child T $232.42
335. WOLFINGER, Michael. Adm. Joseph Gabby 3/18/23; widow, 6 heirs T $3,642.85   Adm. William Gabby 3/18/23; 1/6 to mother, 5 heirs T $390.60
336. WOLFKILL, Jacob. Adm. Jacob, Michael Seyster 12/6/25; Jacob, John, Michael Seyster T $660.55
337. WOLFORD, Michael. Adm. John Carr 8/26/25; widow, 9 children T $152.80
338. WOOLFKILL, John. Adm. Elizabeth 11/18/16; widow, 1 child T443.19.4
339. YOUNG, Jacob. Adm. Jacob, Jacob Hershey 11/24/17; Jacob, Lodwick, Mary Kinsoe, Catherine, Matilda, Sarah, Margaret Hershey, Elizabeth Bentz T $36.61
340. ZEIGLER, ___. Adm. William Gabby, Frederick 1/2/19; widow, George, Jacob, Catherine Poe, David, Elizabeth, Nancy, Barbara, Samuel T $2,470.69
341. ZEIGLER, William. Adm. George Smith, Elias Baker 5/23/26; Elias Baker, Cornelius Stiffler T $4,425.84

DISTRIBUTION OF ESTATE ACCOUNTS
Washington County, Maryland   1828 - 1835

1. ADAMS, Henry. Adm. David Newcomer 10/18/31; widow, Rebecca, Sarah Ann, Catherine, William H., Samuel H. T$644.42½
2. ALBERT, William. Adm. John 2/26/29; widow, Ann Weaver, Mary, Catherine, Eleanor T$1892.00
3. ALTER, George. Adm. Catherine, Gerard Stonebraker 10/27/30; widow, Elias O'Neal and wife, Samuel, Susan, David, Mary, Amelia, Jacob, Rebecca, Catherine T$141.65
4. ALTER, Susan. Adm. Jacob Ott 1/5/33; Catherine Kealhofer specific legacy $100; Joseph Good and wife, William Moreland and wife, Samuel Boyd and wife, Stewart Hammaker and wife, Elizabeth Kerflick, each $428.27 3/4 T$2241.38
5. AMEN, John. Adm. John Highbarger 9/15/35; John Highbarger and wife, Margaret Smith, Catherine Harman T$72.94
6. ANGLE, David. Adm. Jacob Sr., Jacob Sr. n.d.; (a) Jacob, Jacob Brewer, Martin Myers, each $116.56 5/7 (b) John Stah's heirs (Susanna, Catherine, Elizabeth, Jacob) each $29.14 (c) John's heirs (Henry, Samuel, William, David, Elizabeth Brumbaugh) each $23.13 1/5 (d) Henry's heirs (Elizabeth Stone, Catherine Smith, Polly Waltmire, Sophia Cushwa, Sally Teach) each $23.31 1/5 (e) Frederick $116.56 T$816.07   11/3/25; each group A-D received $9.93 1/7; Frederick not named; David added
7. ANGLE, Elizabeth. Adm. Jacob 6/30/35; John legacy $99.60; Henry's heirs (Elizabeth, Catherine, Polly, Lovena, Sally) each $10; Susanna $30; David $250 T$429.60; Mary Brewer, Catherine Myers, each $436.01 T$1301.62
8. ANGLE, Henry. Adm. Jacob 6/23/35; John, Jacob, Henry, David, Daniel, Mary Brewer, Catherine Myers T$1597.85
9. AVEY, Jacob. Adm. Susanna 4/10/33; widow, Margaret Emmert, Joseph, Rachel, John, Susanna, Jacob, Henry, Ezra, Elizabeth, Therasa T$452.11
10. AVEY, Peter. Adm. Isaac Long 2/12/28; (a) Catherine (dead, share to John Coffman) $110.95 (b) Mary (m. John Wolgamot) share to children: Barbara m. Henry Coffman, Elizabeth m. Andrew Hershey, Susannah m. John Bovey, Mary m. John Coffman each $27.73 3/4 (c) Barbara (m. George Strome) share to children: Henry, George and David each $36.98 1/3 (d) Henry (dead) share to children: Jacob, Henry, John, Mary m. George Gingrick each $27.73 3/4 (e) George (dead) share to children: John, Henry, Peter, Barbara m. John Gossard, Nancy m. Samuel Feas each $22.19 T$554.75   Note: brothers and sisters of Peter Avey (A,B,C,D, and E) all died intestate
11. BACHTEL, Isaac Sr. Adm. Joseph Snively 4/28/30; Marian Schriver, Elizabeth Rowland, Isaac Jr., Susanna Barr, Nancy Snively, Christine Hull T$38310.38   4/27/31 T$1733.82   5/14/32 T$457.35   4/23/35 T$195.27   4/15/53 T$496.15 (Christine Hull now Christine Barr)
12. BACHTELL, Isaac. Adm. Joseph Snively 4/23/35; Hamet? the widow, Samuel, Joseph T$15.71
13. BACHTELL, Jacob. Adm. Martin 5/22/33; Samuel, Isaac, Henry, Andrew, Samuel Reichard and wife, Philip Beard and wife T$234.55
14. BACHTEL, Samuel. Adm. Martin 1/29/33; Isaac, Magdalena Funk, Esther Bowman, Susanna Moyer, Ann Kessler, Martin, Elizabeth Wingert, Barbara Wingert, Jacob T$2281.69
15. BAKER, David. Adm. Fredericka 4/23/29; widow, Ann, Sarah, Susanna, David T$214.26
16. BAKER, Lucas. Adm. John 7/29/30; the mother, Peter, John, Jacob, Samuel, Nicholas T$652.16
17. BAKER, Samuel. Adm. Jacob 1/21/30; Elizabeth Downer, Mary Long, Magdalena Cost, Rosanna Betebrenner, Rebecca, Frederick, David's heirs, Christine Core T$197.99
18. BARE, Isaac. Adm. Isaac, John, Martin 6/6/35; Isaac, Martin, John, Nancy Wolgomat, Barbara Rowland, Mary Lysickler T$8312.10
19. BARKMAN, Eve. Adm. Jacob 8/6/28; Joseph Smith and wife, Eve, Daniel Heller and wife, Lewis Meyers and wife T$496.02

DISTRIBUTION OF ESTATE ACCOUNTS

20. BARKMAN, Michael. Adm. Jacob 8/6/28; Michael, Jacob, Joseph Smith and wife, Eve, Daniel Heller and wife, Lewis Meyer and wife T$1650.24   4/14/32 T$1146.40
21. BARKS, John. Adm. John 11/15/31; John Myers, Margaret Myers, Elizabeth Crise, Rosanna Myers T$766.47
22. BARKSTREFER, Adam. Adm. Daniel Bovey, Henry Bovey 5/5/35; widow T$822.64
23. BARR, George. Adm. Lewis Fletcher 9/17/34; Nitericia? T$39.91   6/24/35; Nitericia T$45.72
24. BEAN, Charles. Adm. Barton n.d.; 1/3 to widow, 1/3 each to William, George W. $173.08 1/3 T$519.25
25. BEATTY, William. Adm. John T. Miller for Peter Miller, deceased 5/22/32; Ann E., only heir T$498.20
26. BELL, David. Adm. Jacob   3/11/35; Daniel, Jacob, John's heirs, Catherine Lyday each $147.77 2/5; Jacob Mentzer, John Mentzer, David Mentzer, Conrad Mentzer, Polly Mentzer, Catherine Mentzer each $24.63 T$738.87
27. BELL, John. Adm. Jacob, Peter 4/22/34; Catherine, Rosanna, Mary, George, Sophia, Frederick T$245.50
28. BELL, Leonard. Adm. Henry Schleigh 10/16/28; Catherine Kritzer, Betsey Coleman, Rachel Sheetz's heirs, each $257 legacy plus $8.75; Peggy, Daniel, John, each $300 legacy plus $10.23 T$56.96
29. BENTZ, Jacob. Adm. William Eakle, Jacob 5/7/29; widow, Elizabeth Knight, Susanna Barr, Mary Short, John Moninger and wife, Jacob, Catherine Neikirk's heirs T$59.62
30. BINKLEY, George. Adm. Jonathan 4/12/31; the mother, Catherine, Elizabeth, Jacob, Jonathan, Sally Burgan T$454.63
31. BISH, David. Adm. George Brumbaugh 3/3/30; widow, Henrietta H., Amanda C. T$103.07 10/31/31 T$73.49   11/2/31 T$62.56
32. BLACKMORE, William. Adm. Lancelot Jacques 2/12/28; William Arnold, Mary Arnold, Elizabeth Digon (Dixon?), Caleb's eldest son (not named), Hester Lynn, Elijah Lynn, Kitty,Catherine T$1441.19   4/7/31 T$93.98   5/22/32 T$7.68½
33. BLAKE, Thomas. Adm. Burdine 11/2/30; widow, Elizabeth, John, Sarah, Mary Jane, Charlotte, Jeffrey, Ann T$266.18
34. BLECHER, John. Adm. John with will of Henry Poffenberger, settled by Jacob 6/9/35; Samuel Poffenberger, Mary Monager, Susan Poffenberger, Jacob Poffenberger, Margaret Poffenberger, Mahala Poffenberger, John Poffenberger, Henry Poffenberger T$102.74
35. BLECKER, John. Adm. Jacob 11/18/35; widow, Leah Huffer, Catherine Mulendore, Jacob, Samuel, Maria A., Susanna, William, Elizabeth, Barbara, Margaret T$2592.00
36. BLOOD, Parker. Adm. William M. Marshall 2/2/35; widow, Elizabeth T$432.32 6/24/35 T$191.22
37. BODMAN, Lewis G. Adm. Ferdinand 6/2/29; Ferdinand, William, Philip T$25486.97
38. BOTELER, Thomas C. Adm. Washington, Thomas 8/9/33; widow, Washington, Thomas, Bartholemew, Hannah Garret, Sarah T$5991.39; Mary A. Moore previously received large advance from her father
39. BOWERS, Elizabeth. Adm. Ludwick Protzman 3/13/29; to mother B. Bowers, Jacob, George, Mary D., Barbara, Sarah Ann T$82.98
40. BOWART(D), Margaret. Adm. George Brumbaugh 4/14/30; Mary McDaniel, George, Margaret Figaley, Christine Kifer, Michael, Jacob, Andrew, Sarah Creager T$111.07
41. BOWMAN, Jacob. Adm. George Confer 5/14/31; George Confer (wife Elizabeth), Pointon Webb (wife Margaret), James Flemming (wife Mary), Henry Gordon (wife Matilda), George Lawrence (wife Catherine), John Koontz (wife Susan), Sally T$28.12½
42. BOWMAN, Susanna. Adm. George Confer 2/13/30; same as Jacob #41 (except Koontz spelled Coon) T$65.11
43. BOYER, Jacob. Adm. John 4/17/29; widow, 7 heirs T$725.13   5/6/30; widow, Jacob, John, Peter, Joseph Byers, Elizabeth Kendle, Margaret Bowser, Catherine Beard T$609.85

1828 - 1835

44. BOYER, Jacob. Adm. Catherine, Jacob 6/27/31; widow, Jacob, Susan Newson, Thomas, Catherine, Obedia, Upton, Rachel, Sarah, Eliza McClannahan, Mary T$721.05
45. BRADY, John. Adm. Robert Mason 8/19/29; widow, Robert, Mary, John A. T$3755.66 8/23/31 T$2013.54 4/4/33 T$1178.24 9/11/34 T$546.48
46. BRADY, John A. Adm. Susan 8/26/31; the mother, Robert W., each $804.94 T$1609.88 4/4/33 T$324.74 8/4/35 T$154.08
47. BRADY, Mary. Adm. Susan 8/26/31; the mother, Robert W., John A. T$1238.37 4/4/33 T$246.49 8/4/35 T$117.22
48. BRANSTETTER, Magdalena. Adm. Benjamin Camer 5/14/32; legacy Daniel $200; legacy Mary Fishack $50; Susanna Bargdoll $986.77 T$1236.77
49. BRANTNER, Eliza. Adm. Lewis Fletcher 5/18/32; widow ½; Samuel, Michael, Ann, George, Mary each $4.95; Jacob's heirs (to wit: Jonas, Levi, Samuel, Susan) each $1.23 3/4 T$59.39
50. BRANTNER, John. Adm. Henry Nyman, Michael 3/7/28; 7 heirs T$123.27 6/9/28 T$171.06 12/29/28 T$181.58 5/11/29 T$339.32 8/25/30 T$132.93 9/26/31 T$177.45 1/14/33 T$570.43
51. BRENDLE, John. Adm. Hannah 1/17/32; widow, John, Maria Antoinette T$89.59
52. BREWER, Adam. Adm. Jacob, William Beard 9/5/35; John, Mary Beard, Catherine, Matilda, Elizabeth T$619.57
53. BREWER, Martin. Adm. Jacob 9/15/35; Jacob, John, Mary Beard, Catherine, Elizabeth, Samuel Haynes T$266.59
54. BROWN, Benjamin. Adm. William Drury 5/14/32; Barton, Lewis, Hanson, Ignatius, George Willmouth and wife, Samuel Burch and wife, Margaret McClain T$412.15
55. BROWN, George. Adm. Benjamin 2/14/33; widow, William, Edward Leary, Benjamin, Eleanor, Anna, Maria, Haddalla? T$160.76
56. BROWN, Mary A. Adm. Tobias 7/29/28; Abraham Grim and wife, Tobias, John, Daniel, Abraham, Samuel, George's heirs, Abraham Yerty and wife, George Knode and wife, Jacob Gitman and wife, George Jennings and wife T$61.25
57. BRUMBAUGH, Daniel. Adm. George 3/10/28; widow, Susanna, Elizabeth, Daniel, Maria, Louisa, Thomas, Samuel, Isabella, Caroline T$324.17 6/16/30 T$192.72
58. CARDLE, Mary. Adm. George Brumbaugh 5/10/34; David, William, Sarah T$38.11
59. CARLES, Moses. Adm. John Woolf 8/10/30; widow, Daniel, John, David, Moses T$42.30
60. CARTER, Josiah. Adm. Jacob Slagle, Elizabeth his wife 8/3/31; widow, legacy to Elizabeth $2000; Negroes willed to Jane $280; Negroes willed to Rebecca $300; Negroes and other property willed to J. $338.75; balance due executor $292.89 T$3938.79 (Note: distribution crossed out)
61. CAUFFMAN, Jacob. Adm. Jacob 12/10/35; widow, Simon, Samuel T$558.64
62. CELLAR, George. Adm. Thomas Keller 4/13/30; George Keller $414.57; heirs of Margaret Hager (to wit: Matilda, John, Maria A.) each $138.19 T$829.14 4/22/31; George Keller $308.97; Margaret Hager's heirs each $102.99 T$617.94 12/22/35; George Keller $433.37; David Hager's heirs each $144.45 2/3 T$926.00
63. CHANY, Jeremiah. Adm. _____elly 11/14/33; J____ the mother $66.32 4/7; Neoma Funk, Matilda Heister, Mary Knode, Prudence Boetler, each $66,32 4/7; Ann's? heirs (Elanora, John B., Samuel) each $22.11; Robert's heirs (William, Prudence) each $33.16; Luke's heirs (Amanda, ____, Lucretia) each $22.11 T$464.28
64. CHANEY, Jeremiah (of Charles). Adm. Thomas 12/9/29; Thomas, Drusilla, Rebecca, Johnston, Eliza, Robert T$74.38 Second distribution: 12/9/29 T$157.03
65. CHANEY, Luke. Adm. Samuel Newcomer, Robert 4/2/29; widow, 3 heirs T$115.45 Note: the name William J. Chaney appeared in the corner of the page
66. CHANEY, Mary. Adm. Michael Funk 9/30/28; Henry Heck and wife Drusilla, Thomas, Rebecca, Eliza, Johnson, Robert T$93.17
67. CHANEY, Robert. Adm. Jelsy? 4/27/32; Prudence, Matilda widow of Luke and 3 children, Neomy Funk, William B., Mary Knode, Jeremiah, Robert T$4242.36 4/27/32; widow

DISTRIBUTION OF ESTATE ACCOUNTS

68. CHANEY, William B. Adm. Samuel Newcomer 6/6/31; Ellen, John, Samuel T$3556.45 9/7/32 T$99.97 8/6/34 T$534.23
69. CHRISTIAN, Jacob. Adm. Daniel, Jacob Hoffer 12/10/32; ½ toward Daniel the father $740.55 T$1481.11 1/3/34 each $316.86 T$633.72
70. CLAGETT, Zachariah. Adm. Robert, Horatio, Alfred 10/18/28; Robert, Mary Ann Garrett, Sarah Boteler, Eliza, Elizabeth Gray, Matilda, Aleatha Boteler T$1057.40 11/25/29 T$1039.52½ 6/6/31 T$74.64
71. CLAGETT, Rachel. Adm. Robert 1/5/50; $500 to support two old Negros; Robert, Mary Ann Garrett, Sarah Boteler, Eliza, heirs of Elizabeth Gray, Matilda, Aleathea Boteler, Haratio, Alfred each $612.22 T$5509.97 1/19/30 T$498.12 6/6/31 T$32.58
72. CLAPSADDLE, Daniel. Adm. Conrod Worley 12/5/34; Jacob the father T$77.72
73. CLINGAN, William. Adm. David Brookhart 7/28/34; widow T$360.27
74. COLLIFLOWER, George. Adm. George, William Eacle 10/22/33; widow, Peter, John, George, William Eacle and wife T$5317.16
75. COOK, John. Adm. John, David 5/14/33; specific legacy Henry $400; George's heirs $200; Mary Scyafoose $300; John, David, Samuel, Susan Bragonier, Elizabeth, Catherine Fritz (Fitz)?, Charlotte, Henry, Alexander, William each $128.24 T$2182.44 2/10/35 T$38.77
76. COON, John. Adm. John Newcomer 2/20/28; widow, John, Joseph T$478.02
77. CRAMER, Jacob. Adm. John Gibbeny 6/11/28; widow, Jacob, Mary, Daniel, Elizabeth, David T$696.07
78. CRAMPTON, Elias. Adm. John, Elie 5/4/29; widow, John, Elie, Elizabeth Rohrer, Thomas H. T$2067.15 5/2/32 T$120.49
79. CRAMPTON, John. Adm. Henry Wade 8/2/28; widow, Henry Wade and wife Ann, Susanna, John, Harmon, Josiah, Joshua, Oliver, Elizabeth, Sarah E., Thomas W. T$3676.64 8/8/29 T$1601.72 11/21/31 T$124.71
80. DARBY, Henry. Adm. John.D. Breisch 9/29/35; John, Catherine Ogle, Elizabeth Augustine, Mrs. Allison's heirs T$540.73 Second distribution: n.d. T$137.37
81. DICK, Henry. Adm. David Barkman 2/22/30; widow, Jacob, Catherine, Mary, David, Henry, John T$90.12
82. DICK, Eve. Adm. Christian 9/17/33; Christian, Jacob, John, Adam, Catherine Parther, Lancelot Jacques for use of Margaret Gower's heirs T$996.06
83. DICK, Jacob. Adm. Lancelot Jacques 12/7/30; widow, Margaret Gower, Christian, Jacob, Catherine Prather, John, Ann Gelwicks, Adam, Mary T$2659.38 6/5/32 T$435.47 (Mary became Mary Otto) 2/26/33 T$14.04
84. DICKEY, William. Adm. Samuel S. Cunningham 6/3/33; John, Samuel, Ezekiel, Matthew, Archibald T$2152.68 12/16/33 T$134.78 5/6/34 T$67.34
85. DITTO, Abraham. Adm. William 4/3/34; Martha Wilson, Mary Hitchcock, William, Nancy A. _____ owden, James B. T$1997.42
86. DONAVAN, John. Adm. 12/29/29; Jane Wilkinson, Agnes Wilkinson, Elizabeth Wilkinson, Rebecca Wilkinson each $463.39; Robert $741.42; William, James D. each $185.35½
87. DORSEY, Francis. Adm. Philip Crow? 3/25/34; widow, John, Eliza, Edgar, Margaretta, Philip, Edward, Mary I., Benjamin T$487.33
88. DOWNES, William. Adm. George Smith 1/21/28; Lewis ($50) $14.87½; Washington, Adaline, Arey, each ($70), $20.82½ T$77.35
89. DUSING, Philip. Adm. John 4/4/33; John, Elizabeth, Catherine T$28.34
90. EACLE, Fanney. Adm. Daniel Funk 6/14/33; John Funk, Daniel Funk, David Funk, Absolem, Martin each $9.58 1/6; Martin Rohrer, Henry Rohrer, Mary Rohrer each $3.19 1/3 T$57.49
91. EAKLE, Henry. Adm. John 6/15/31; reserved for Christian, purchaser of the land $50.00; Henry, Catherine Perry, Christian, Jacob, John, Mary Dovenberger, Absolom, Martin each $841.61 T$3032.10
92. EMICK, George. Adm. Susannah 10/24/35; widow, George, William, Jacob, John, Amelia, Susannah T$419.33

1828 - 1835

93. EMICK, Susannah. Adm. Susannah 10/24/35; mother 1/6 $4.78; George, William, Jacob, John H., Amelia each $4.78   T$28.68
94. EVANS, Daniel. Adm. Robert Clagett 6/24/34; John   T$381.24
95. FECHTIG, Christian. Adm. George, _____ McComas 5/19/35; Frederick, Margaret Amos?, Christian C., Susan McComas, George, John H., Jacob T$2417.87
96. FELKER(S), Henry. Adm. Abraham 3/5/30; widow, John, Jacob, Ezra T$666.68
97. FESSLER, Elizabeth. Adm. Christopher Flory 8/19/34; Susannah Goody, Mary Thomas, each $200; Jacob $236.58
98. FESSLER, Mary. Adm. John Welty, Elizabeth Welty 10/20/28; 4 heirs T$404.72
99. FIERY, Jacob. Adm. Jacob 6/6/32; deduct for widow $500; Catherine E. Swingley $400; Jacob use? of Samuel Ditto $1700; Jacob, Mary Ann Wolgomot, Catherine E. Swingley, Joseph, William H., Benjamin F., Daniel each $897.08 4/7 T$6279.60 5/21/33 T$497.45   6/6/34 T$497.45   5/19/35; expenses $25.91 T$71.17 5/8; William Swingley added, Catherine E. Swingley omitted in this last entry
100. FIERY, John. Adm. John Troup, Joseph Brewer 4/17/28; widow, Joseph Brewer and wife, John Brewer and wife, Joseph, Solomon T$1449.40   5/20/29 T$792.24 4/17/30 T$805.66   6/3/31 T$140.31 (Mary wife of Joseph Brewer, Elizabeth wife of John Brewer)   6/10/34 T$274.33 (Elizabeth Brewer now Elizabeth Fiery)
101. FIERY, Joseph. Adm. John and Henry 1/22/35; Mary C. Moatz, Mary Eve Zellar each $1918.49 1/3; William Ditto, Joseph F. Miller each ½ share or $959.25½ T$5755.48   8/12/35; same full shares $433.06 2/3; half shares $216.53 1/3 T$1299.20
102. FINK, Jacob. Adm. Mary and George W. 10/15/28; widow $190.87; George W., Mary, Andrew, John, Barbara, Susannah, Christina, Michael, Jacob, Daniel each $38.17½ Interest from 8/25/24
103. FOUTZ, Susanna. Adm. Jacob 7/31/28; Nancy Thumb, Jacob, Henry, Jacob Alter and wife Elizabeth, Frederick, William, David, William Creager and wife Mary, William Brentlinger and wife Charlotte, George T$119.15   9/30/28 T$57.35
104. FRAZIER, Loyd. Adm. Lewis Fletcher 3/25/35; ½ to widow; Finley, Falder, Jeremiah, Otho H., Horatio, Hale, Sophia, Henry T$241.48
105. FOLTZ, George. Adm. Jacob 1/28/30; widow, Catherine T$238.74
106. FUNK, Susannah. Adm. Daniel Reichard 11/26/29; Margaret Gehr, Susannah Mong, Elizabeth Rohrer T$542.44
107. FURGASON, James. Adm. John Kennedy, John McCurdy 3/24/35; Mary Ann Patton, John McCormack, John Moreland, John Boyd, James Warden each $15,148.75; Sarah Clarke, Robert Clarke each $7574.37½; Hugh Moreland, William Moreland, Thomas Williamson each $3787.18 3/4   T$106,041.25
108. FURRY, Frederick. Adm. John Blecher 9/9/35; David T$188.96
109. GABRIEL, John. Adm. Josiah 4/26/30; Margaret Zeller 1/5 or $40.38; Catherine, Josiah each $80.76½   T$201.91
110. GARY, Elizabeth. Adm. Mary Stebler, Abigail Davis 7/22/30; Judith Acle, Sarah Stiffler, Jacob Moats, Mary Stebler, Abigail Davis T$267.54 1/3
111. GARY, George. Adm. Jonas Hogmire, George Smith 9/7/29; Judith Eakle, Sarah Stebler, Susannah Motes, Mary, Eve Davis, Elie Motes T$2531.08
112. GATES, William. Adm. Joseph n.d.; widow, Elizabeth, Sarah, Susan, _____, William B. T$1458.15
113. GEETING, Elizabeth. Adm. Christian Deaner 6/23/35; Jacob Detwiler, Samuel Detwiler, Mrs. Hen___ing heirs, Mrs. Hamish (Harnish?), 1 heir unknown T$132.83
114. GEHR, Catherine. Adm. Isaac 8/27/33; David Welty and wife $105.40; George's heirs (Daniel, William, Denton, Mary) each $26.35; Daniel, Ann, John Price, George Beard and wife, Samuel, Eliza Mumma, Isaac each $105.40 T$948.60
115. GEISER, Elizabeth. Adm. David Weise 2/24/35; Henry Weise $33.57½; John Weise $10.00; Andrew Weise $9.00; David Weise $620.80 T$673.37
116. GEISER, Frederick. Adm. John 12/15/30; David Branteter and wife Catherine, Abraham Snyder and wife Mary, Jonas Leiser and wife Judith, David Bachtel and wife Susanna, Benjamin Oswald and wife Sarah, Thomas B. Murry and wife Mary Ann, Martin, Peter, John T$106.83

DISTRIBUTION OF ESTATE ACCOUNTS

117. GRIM, David. Adm. Samuel Clagett 4/4/23; widow, Elizabeth, Cassandra, Amelia, Nathaniel, Mary Ann T$71.60
118. GROUND, Philip. Adm. George Sr. 9/26/28; George, John's heirs, Elizabeth Russell T$3126.50
119. HAGER, Christian Sr. Adm. Jonathan J.? 12/12/33; Christian, the father $1405.09
120. HAGER, Elizabeth R. Adm. Jonathan 12/12/33; to Christian, the father $1405.09
121. HAMILTON, Henry. Adm. George Brumbaugh, George Hess 1/21/33; William I., Ann Mary, James H., Julian T$926.10
122. HAMM, Peter. Adm. Margaret, George Hedrick 6/1/30; Peter, George's heirs, Catherine, Elizabeth Sheets, Sarah Runner (distribution voided) 8/17/30; widow, $1299.37; Peter, Sarah, Catherine, Elizabeth Sheets, Sarah Runner each $779.62 T$5197.47 9/27/31; Adm. Margaret; widow $172.93; Peter, Sarah Runner, Catherine, Elizabeth Sheets, Sarah Sharrick each $103.76 T$691.72
123. HAMMOND, Joseph H. Adm. Benjamin Youtz 11/29/31; Philip, Mary Ann Avery, Elizabeth Ninenheller, Luciann, Elias, Faney Welty, Levina, David T$323.47 3/30/32 T$7.00 (held by Joseph Rench)
124. HAMPTON, William. Adm. Elias Baker 8/10/30; Susannah Toulson, John, Thomas T$1146.00
125. HANER, Anthony. Adm. George, Daniel 7/20/30; George, Polly Tice, Daniel, Jonathan, Martin, Rosannah, Henrietta R. Knepper T$696.22
126. HARLAND, Esther. Adm. George R. Beall 2/28/32; John, James, Samuel, Daniel, Solomon, Braden? and wife, Joseph Boultz and wife Elizabeth T$175.64 3/23/33 T$9.20
127. HAWKEN, Juliana. Adm. William 6/8/30; Jacob, Samuel, William, specific legacy each $300; Nancy, Lewis and George each $223.93½ T$1347.87
128. HAYS, John. Adm. John D. Eacle 11/20/34 1/3 to widow $196.54; Christina M., Daniel each $196.54 T$589.63
129. HECKMAN, Benjamin L. Adm. Samuel M. Hitt 5/5/35; Samuel P.C. $1150.27
130. HEFFLICH (HEFLEIGH), Peter. Adm. John H. Smith, Daniel Carver 8/28/28; heirs of Peter $207.10; David Nead Jr., Peter Nead, John Nead, heirs of Daniel Nead each $124.28 2/3 T$579.96 (Note added: By will of deceased executors are to pay heirs $221.95 plus interest from 1/1/14 in addition to $207.10)   5/11/30; Peter's heirs, for use of John's heirs $125.62; Nead heirs each $52.34½ T$282.65 4/7/31; Peter's heirs $1252.00, for use by John's heirs $332.72; balance due by will of deceased $111.15; Peter's heirs balance $806.13; Nead heirs under two former distributions $529.89; to each Nead heir $573.37 T$2514.94 10/23/32; Catherine Smith $97.32; Nead heirs each $32.44; Peter's heirs $97.32, John's heirs, Amelia Carver, Ann M., Elizabeth, Otila R. Weast each $24.33 T$389.28
131. HEISTER, Rosannah. Adm. Christian Hager, Philip Wingert 12/12/33; specific legacy Philip Wingert $3851.24; Rosannah H. Kershner, Rosannah H. Hower, Mary R. Barr, Alexander Swann each $26.27; Magdalena Hager, Christian Hager, Elizabeth R. Hager each $625.20; interest from 1/17/11 T$5833.82
132. HERSH, Frederick. Adm. Christian Shank 4/11/31; Elizabeth Hersh for Jacob Poarch Trustee $332.05¼; Catherine Poarch $332.05¼; Sophia Shank's heirs (Henry, Jonas, Christian, John, Jacob, Frederick, Noah, Sophia) each $41.50½; Mary Carbaugh's heirs (Susanna, Jacob, Mary) each $110.68¼ T$1328.31   1/17/32: Poarch heirs and Sophia Shank each $348.35; Shank heirs each $43.54 3/4; Carbaugh heirs each $116.11 2/3 T$1393.40 3/29/32; same as above with $173.33 1/3, $21.66 5/8, $57.77 2/3 respectively T$693.33 4/1/33; same as above with $173.41 3/4, $21.67 3/4, $57.80 1/3 respectively T$693.67
133. HERSHEY, Christian. Adm. Samuel M. Hitte, Jacob Fiery 5/28/31; legacy to Mary, Susan, Catherine, Nancy each $3.00; Joseph Emmert and wife, Jacob Fiery and wife, Mary, Susan, Catherine, Nancy each $1368.93 1/3 T$8213.60

1828 - 1835

134. HETZER, John. Adm. John Nitzell 4/18/31; widow, John, Mary, Eliza, Catherine, Jane, George, Charles T$247.64
135. HEWIT, Ludwick. Adm. Jacob, Daniel 11/12/33; John, Jacob, Daniel, Margaret Hogmire, Mary Knode each $2634.55 1/3; Faith heirs (Jacob, Lewis, Margaret, Elizabeth, Susannah) each $526.91 T$15,807.32
136. HIGGINS, Jamima. Adm. Charles A. Warfield 3/19/33; the mother T$162.02
137. HIGGINS, Upton. Adm. Charles A. Warfield 11/24/32; widow, Irmma T$250.53
138. HILL, Valentine. Adm. John Clopper 10/18/28; 8 children T$117.98 Second, third and fourth distribution: 11/16/29; 5/15/30; 6/11/30; same amount as first 8/27/32; Jacob, Daniel, Jonathan, Jacob Barks, Elizabeth Rohrback heirs, Barbara, Peter T$374.05
139. HIVENER, Jacob. Adm. George Smith 2/4/28; Joseph, Catherine, Polly Schnebly, Sarah Knestrick, Elizabeth Dillon, George Keifer Sr. T$1282.09 6/12/28; T$2012.35 6/17/28; T$1192.61 4/8/31; T$205.43 10/31; T$58.88
140. HOFFMAN, Barbara. Adm. John 11/13/32; legacy to Joseph Foreman $200; legacy to Ann Roberts $1000; John $416.16½; Nathaniel Swingley $208.08¼; Elizabeth Ankeney $208.08¼ T$832.33 10/30/34; legacy to Nathaniel and John Swingley $200; John $133.75; Nathaniel Swingley $66.87½; Elizabeth Swingley $66.87½ T$467.50
141. HOLLIDAY, James. Adm. William 8/6/35; Susan, Henry, George S., William, Richard T$157.92
142. HOSE, Peter. Adm. Peter, Philip 7/24/30; Magdalena Baker's child, Mary Carl, Catherine Price, Elizabeth Needy each $44.35½; Philip $88.71 T$266.39 12/26/31 (Elizabeth Needy excluded); each $31.30, Philip $62.60 T$187.81
143. HOWELL, Elizabeth. Adm. George Brumbaugh 5/10/34; James T$67.84
144. HOWER, Jacob. Adm. John Witmer 12/4/32; John, Susanna Ridenour, Mary Smith, George's heirs (Elizabeth, Maria, David, ____) each $6.19 T$344.76
145. HUGHES, Ann. Adm. Joseph Martin 5/1/29; Joseph and wife, Jessee D. Elliott, Daniel Duncan T$1079.92½ 8/15/31; Rebecca Martin, Jessee D. Elliott; Hamet A.L. Duncan T$196.33
146. HUTZELL, Matthias. Adm. Jonathan 1/19/35; Susannah, Sarah, Elizabeth, John, Nancy, Adam, Jacob, Samuel T$1576.74
147. HYLAND, John R. Adm. Charlotte, Andrew Kershner 5/2/28; widow, Mary Ann, Hugh, Ann, Thomas T$29.23
148. IRWIN, John. Adm. Jacob T. Towson 12/19/32; ½ to widow; Rachel Sterrett, Nancy Sterrett, John Hogg, Sarah, William T$426.63
149. JAMES, Abraham. Adm. Bennett 6/4/33; widow, Amos, William, Hiram T$770.03
150. JOHNSTON, John. Adm. George H. Lambert, n.d.; George H. and Jane his wife, Margaret, Sarah Simpson, Adam Brewer and Mary his wife, each $188.50 The above plus Susan Dowin each $55.60 1/5 T$1032.01
151. JONES, Jonathan. Adm. Jacob 5/17/31; Elizabeth, John, Jacob, Henry's heirs, Mary, Margaret, Jonathan, Catherine T$137.36 4/10/32 T$26.56 4/12/33 T$36.57 4/24/34 T$158.20 4/12/35 T$60.22 Note: Elizabeth now Elizabeth Long
152. JULIUS, John. Adm. Joseph Graff 5/4/33; widow, Samuel, H. H____worth and wife, Elizabeth, Catherine, John, Ann, George T$232.00
153. KAILOR, Frederick. Adm. Jacob 7/21/30; Jacob, Catherine T$26.02
154. KELLER, Elizabeth. Adm. Elie Crampton 5/4/29; Ann Marie, Alford T$1673.80 5/2/32 T$664.37
155. KELLER, Joseph C. Adm. Isaac J. White 3/15/28; widow, Ann Marie, Alfred each $90.93 1/3
156. KELLY, Susan. Adm. Leonard Smeltzer 12/19/35; Marie Kelly's heirs, Elizabeth Gower's heirs, Martha Kelly's heirs T$6.59
157. KENSEY, Samuel. Adm. Adam 5/20/35; Ann $42.63, James W. $85.26

DISTRIBUTION OF ESTATE ACCOUNTS

158. KEPLER, Ann. Adm. Martin Bachtel 1/11/31; (Note: distribution has been divided into groups) Group A: Ester Bowman, Martin Funk and wife, Martin Bachtell, Maria Woolf, Barbara Wingert, Elizabeth Wingert each $799.79 2/3 Group B: David Shiver and wife, Jacob Rowland and wife, Joseph Snively and wife, Christian Barr and wife, Henry Hall and wife each $159.96 Group C: Jacob Moyer, Samuel Moyer, Patrick Mooney and wife, Peter Hose and wife, Barbara Moyer, Henry Moyer, John Moyer, Isaac Moyer, Christian Moyer, Jacob Ridenour and wife, Peter Wetzel and wife each $72.71 Group D: Samuel Bachtel, Isaac Bachtel, Samuel Rich and wife, Henry Bachtel, Andrew Bachtel each $133.30 T$7198.17 1/29/33; Group A: $250.30 2/3 (Martin Funk's wife Magdalena) Group B: $50.06 Group C: $22.75 Group D: $41.71 2/3 T$2252.76 n.d.; Group A: $94.47 2/9 Group B: $18.89 2/5 Group C: $8.59 Group D: $15.74, Philip Beard and wife added to Group D. T$850.25
159. KERSHNER, Christiana. Adm. Isaac 4/4/28; specific legacy Polly, Elizabeth Heller each $10.00, Jacob $1.00; Peter, Isaac, Philip, John, Jonathan, Martin, Daniel, Polly, Elizabeth Heller each $39.30; Solomon, John Sterret, Philip Sterret, Polly Sterret, Natha Sterret each $7.86 T$393.00 ($30.00 charge in will deducted from Sterrets $7.50 from each)
160. KERSHNER, John. Adm. Jacob 4/5/31; David, John, Solomon, Jacob, George, Samuel, Elizabeth Belch T$4944.72 (legacy to Mary Tice $100.00) (Note: each distribution hereafter included Mary Tice) 4/3/32 T$877.99 4/2/33 T$877.99 4/2/34 T$892.89
161. KERSHNER, Martin. Adm. Andrew Sr. 11/21/29; Catherine Bachtel, heirs of Barbara, heirs of Elizabeth Rockerfield, Solomon, John Dunn, heirs of Ann Ankeney, Susannah Schnebly, Jacob Dunn T$5237.17 12/13/32; each $393.80½ (John and Jacob Dunn were both married)
162. KING, John. Adm. Martin, Daniel, George Fectig 8/2/34; Daniel, Martin, Sophia Hershey, Eliza Moore, Rebecca Graff, Abraham, Otho, Levi, William T$1297.87
163. KLINE, Samuel. Adm. Christian C. 3/8/34; George, Daniel, John, Charles, Christian C. T$707.12
164. KLINK, George A. Adm. John Hershey 7/5/28; John Zimmer, Margaret Zimmer, George F., Mary B. T$1656.67 9/4/32 T$41.27
165. KNODE, Jacob. Adm. John, Peter Seibert 4/6/29; Mary, Margaret Seibert, Catherine Bussard, John, Henry, Jacob, heirs of Amelia Harry (3 children) each $1090.67½ (each had received advancement, plus the balance totaled the $1090.67) T$7634.73 8/13/30 T$1153.59(Amelia Harry's children were Jacob, Margaret, Amelia) 2/5/31 T$1123.93
166. KOONTZ, Catherine. Adm. Nancy Pfoutz 5/22/33; William, Elizabeth, Thomas, John T$44.11
167. KREAGER, Henry. Adm. Jacob Renner 12/17/34; Jacob Benner and wife, John's heirs, Daniel, William, George, Jacob Suter and wife, Henry, Henry Christ and wife T$333.64
168. KREIGH, Elizabeth. Adm. William 6/4/33; Catherine $108.09 1/5; William, Phillip, Elie, George, Mary, Daniel, Benjamin, John each $13.51; Nicholas, Barbara Fessler, George Sponslor? and wife each $108.09 1/5 T$540.46
169. KRETZER, John. Adm. Daniel Grim 5/4/29; widow, Jacob, Margaret, John, Aaron, Sarah, Noah T$241.02
170. LAMBERT, Eve. Adm. George H. 5/18/29; Margaret Hahn, Thomas Noland and wife, Jacob, heirs of Eve Gearhart, George H., John, Michael Graybill and wife, Barbara Ann Zeigler, Jonas, William Garver and wife, Shem T$159.55½ 6/7/30 T$101.72 5/2/31 T$69.40 4/26/32 T$69.40 4/26/33 T$48.16 4/4/33 T$69.50 (Jonas's heirs replaced Jonas)
171. LAMBERT, George M. Adm. George H. 4/26/33; same heirs as Eve above T$48.16 4/4/34 T$5681.28 (statement mentions Susannah Nowland, probably wife of Thomas Nowland)

1828 - 1835

172. LANDIS, Abraham. Adm. Henry 12/11/32; Mary the mother, Nancy Stonebraker, Elizabeth Contz, Sarah Winters, Henry, Salina, Susan, Amelia, Henry McCauley T$948.25
173. LEAR, Jacob. Adm. Samuel Blair 6/2/31; widow, Philip, Charles?, Jacob, Delila, Mehala T$303.18
174. LECKRONE, Catherine. Adm. John Wolfelsburger 11/14/35; the mother, Elizabeth, Rebecca, Mary, John T$155.44
175. LECKRONE, Jacob. Adm. Samuel Bachtel, Jonas 10/30/35; Jonas, Henry Mitter and wife, James Dillahunt and wife, John Hartle, Lewis Keller and wife, John Miller and wife, Daniel Davis and wife, Abraham Shanafeltz and wife, Esther, Jacob (son of Jacob Sr.) T$3376.42 Note: Peter Spessart heirs (Margaret, Peter, Susannah, John, Mariah, Elizabeth) each $43.28 2/3; Henry Miller heirs (Jacob, Christina, John, Daniel, David, Samuel) each $43.28 2/3; Jonas heirs (Elizabeth, Rebecca, Catherine, Maria, John) each $51.94 2/5
176. LECKRONE, Maria. Adm. Samuel 12/16/34; Jonathan, Nancy Clopper, Polly Hammaker, Rebecca Row, Sarah Mitchell, Susan, Samuel, Daniel, Catherine, Elizabeth Bachtell T$944.15
177. LECKROON, Simon. Adm. Jacob, John 4/3/29; Jacob, John, Lemuel, Daniel each $264.04½; Ann, Mary, Elizabeth, Sarah, Margaret, Catherine, Susannah, Maria each $176.03 T$2464.42 3/16/30; the males $120.54, the females $80.36 T$1125.04
178. LEITER, Jacob. Adm. David 10/15/28; widow, David, John, Jacob, George, Ann Maria, Samuel, Felix, Henry, Abraham, Ann Catherine T$550.50
179. LESSLEY, John. Adm. Elizabeth I. 6/30/33; widow, Sarah, Joseph, John, Alexander, Delila T$1026.97
180. LEYDY, Henry. Adm. Samuel Lantz 6/4/33; widow, John, Elizabeth, Barbara, Mary, David T$377.11
181. LEVERNEICKT (-NEIGHT), Christopher. Adm. Christian Bair 11/1/32; widow, Peter Hull, Adam Beard, Robert Shives T$414.28 12/2/34; widow $4.95, others each $3.30 T$14.85
182. LIND, John. Adm. Dr. John Reynolds 5/16/31; widow, 6 children T$28.99
183. LITTLE, Jacob. Adm. Frederick Miller 7/24/30; Catherine Miller wife of Adm., Susannah T$1304.44
184. LOCHER, George. Adm. Henry I. Shafer 3/20/32; widow, Ann B., Charles H., Henry, Mary, George H., Elizabeth T$3032.05 9/1/35; Ann R., Henry L., Ann M., George H., Ann E., Charles H. T$493.00
185. LOCKER, Henry. Adm. Leonard Stonebraker 10/6/35; Elizabeth, John, Henry's heirs, Mary Ann, William, Isaac, Barbara T$239.99
186. LOCKRIDGE, George. Adm. William Eakle 1/19/30; George, John, William T$60.53
187. LOWMAN, Jacob. Adm. John 9/16/30; widow, John, Jacob, Henry, David, Susanna, George, Mary T$686.42
188. LYNCH, John B. Adm. Alexander Neill 12/4/29; widow, Susan, Blackison T$1814.21 4/13/31 T$200.27 4/17/32 T$183.12
189. McCLAIN, John. Adm. Elizabeth, Josiah 3/22/32; widow, Maria Tice, Josiah, Otho, Richard Reuben, Owen, Andrew, Elizabeth, Lucretia T$1755.15 3/20/34 T$698.90
190. McCLAIN, John Jr. Adm. Mary, Michael P. Smith 5/7/33; widow, Maria, Elie, Leonides, Ann C. T$2104.19 8/21/33 T$757.24
191. McCLUNG, William. Adm. Daniel Hauer 3/7/31; Maria, Elizabeth, William, Eve, Silas T$532.21
192. McCOY, Mary. Adm. Daniel Welty 1/29/23; Emanuel, Vincent, Mary T$909.95
193. McFERRAN, Alexander. Adm. Precila 4/16/28; widow, Daniel Johnson, James B., Alexander T$478.90
194. McGLOUGHLIN, John. Adm. William 10/22/33; the father John T$189.00
195. McKESSIC, James. Adm. Thomas Roulet 1/27/34; widow, Thomas Roulet and wife, Mary Nuse, James, Nancy Flory, John, Robert, Jane, Henry T$305.48
196. MALOTT, Theodore. Adm. Benjamin, Daniel 3/5/33; ½ to widow, Benjamin, Elias, John's heirs (Mary Ann, Rebecca Snell), heirs of Catherine Gale (Jim, Benjamin, Mary Gordon) T$2753.96 5/16/34 T$12858.70

47

DISTRIBUTION OF ESTATE ACCOUNTS

197. MALOTT, Benjamin. Adm. Benjamin 3/19/33; Theodore, Elias, Rebecca Snell, Catherine Gole, Mary Ann T$1879.66
198. MALONE, Benjamin. Adm. James Powell 11/15/31; Nancy Powell $150.00/$6.00; Sidney Powell, Mary Ann Powell, Eliza Ann Powell, George Powell, Elias, James, Mary Ann, Maria, John Dean, Rebecca Dean, Hezekeah Dean, Eliza Ann Asherman, Mary Asherman, Maria Asherman, Elizabeth Asherman, Elizabeth Burrie (Burrel), Mary, Amey, Sallie each $100/$4.00; Benjamin Powell $400/$16.00; Maria $50/$2.00 T$2600.00/$101.70 (Note: no explanation for two amounts)
199. MARTIN, David. Adm. Joshua Newcomer 4/13/30; widow, Nicholas T$699.98 4/9/31; widow, Nicholas T$710.70
200. MARTIN, Nicholas. Adm. Jacob Angle 3/17/35; widow, Rosanna, David T$2258.86
201. MARTIN, Samuel. Adm. Thomas 3/19/28; widow, Thomas T$925.80
202. MIDDLEKAUFF, Christian. Adm. Jacob, John J. Keedy, Daniel Finefrock 8/7/32; Elizabeth Stoups, Rebecca Smith, *Mary Ann, Nancy, Susannah T$3674.18 8/7/32 T$1778.98 (*Margaret replaced Mary Ann in second entry)
203. MIDDLEKAUFF, Jacob. Adm. Jacob, Daniel, John, David Woolf 3/16/35; Elizabeth Woolf's heirs (John Welty and wife, Daniel, Jacob, Elizabeth, Susannah, John) T$2569.40 6/29/35 T$5360.32
204. MIDDLEKAUFF, Peter. Adm. Samuel, Daniel 1/8/29; widow, Samuel, Daniel, Elizabeth, Susannah, Sarah Ann, Mary Ann T$3378.52
205. MILLER, Daniel. Adm. Lancelot Jacques 3/31/30; widow, Louisa T$809.75 5/10/31 T$100.94
206. MILLER, Elizabeth. Adm. John Hall 2/26/30; Nancy Filengame, Levin Mills, William H., John, Sophia Haslett, Samuel Mills, William Mills, Eliza I. Hall, Emily H. Hall, Hannah M. Hall T$425.38
207. MILLER, Jacob. Adm. Jacob 5/7/30; widow, Mary Barr, Jacob, Susan Funk, Tobias T$112.86
208. MILLER, Jacob F. Adm. Frederick 3/12/29; widow, 10 heirs T$118.26
209. MILLER, John. Adm. Ann, Henry Fiery 11/3/35; widow, Alexander T$2111.07
210. MILLER, John. Adm. John, Andrew Beck 3/15/30; widow, John, Susannah Beck, heirs of Elizabeth Binkley (William, Thomas, Louisa, George, Ferdinand, Jacob) T$274.06
211. MILLER, Michael. Adm. Jacob, George Smith 2/14/33; William Oldham and Mary Oldham (Olden), Catherine Keedy, Susannah Sheelman, John Geeting and wife, Barbara, Frederick F. and wife, John, Magdalena, Elizabeth, Jacob, George Smith and wife T$999.60 6/3/33 T$2601.75
212. MILLS, Michael. Adm. James P. n.d.; Thomas, James, Elizabeth, Robert Thedrick and wife, Jacob, Rach? Ward, Ellen Ward T$88.70
213. MITTAG, John G. Adm. George Brumbaugh 6/1/30; widow, Catherine, John F.G., Eliza Howell, Alexander McCammel and wife Susannah, Maria, Sophia, Thomas E. Helm (no amount)
214. MORRISON, Alexander. Adm. Burdine Blake 11/2/30; widow, Jane, John, Alexander T$351.74
215. MOYER, John. Adm. Christian, John 4/11/29; Jacob, Elizabeth Dusing, Samuel, Barbara, Mary Abrecht, Susannah Hose, Henry, Christian, Isaac, Esther Ridenour, Nancy T$267.00 5/1/32 T$112.75 9/1/32 T$871.13 11/10/32 T$171.01 3/3/35 T$1104.87 3/7/35 T$930.19
216. MOYER, Susannah. Adm. Christian 1/29/33; Jacob, Elizabeth Dusing, Samuel, Barbara, Mary Abrect, Julianna Hose, Henry, Christian, Isaac, John, Esther Ridenour, Nancy T$226.98
217. MURRY, John. Adm. Charles 2/18/35; given the father T$367.31
218. MYERS, Jacob. Adm. Jacob Miller 6/4/32; Elizabeth, widow T$41.49
219. MYERS, John. Adm. John 12/21/31; John, Mary, Elizabeth Grice, Rosanna T$395.78
220. MYERS, Margaret. Adm. John 9/7/32; John, John (of Jacob), Jacob Grier, Rosanna T$397.15

1828 - 1835

221. MYERS, Mary. Adm. Jacob H. Grove 1/25/31; Frederick Hoskins, Jacob Hoskins, George Hoskins and wife, John's (Jacob, Joseph, Elizabeth, Polly, Mary A., Benjamin), John Hoffman, Samuel Hoffman, Mary Hoffman, Jacob Hoffman, James Hoffman T$5293.97   11/27/32   T$77.96
222. MYERS, Sarah. Adm. Jacob Miller 6/4/32; Henry, Peter, Frederick, Elizabeth, Daniel Clayton, Polly Kingerey heirs (Samuel, Rosanna, Jacob, Thomas), John's heirs (John, Polly, Jacob Grier, Rosanna) T$2664.42
223. NEFF, John. Adm. John 5/7/30; Henry's children, Jacob's children, Magdalena Shideler, Francis, Adam's 9 children, Catherine Bucher's 8 children, Esther Swinehart's 9 children T$410.15
224. NOWELL, James. Adm. Gilbert 5/21/28; Betsey, Rebecca Pool, John, Gilbert, James, Joseph, Sarah Herbert, William T$485.03
225. NEWCOMER, Christian. Adm. John, Daniel 6/2/35; Martin, Joseph, David, Christopher, Bran?, Ann Hammond, Maria, Elizabeth, Sarah T$278.30 5/8
226. NEWCOMER, Daniel. Adm. John G. Miller 5/19/31; Sarah Chaney, John G. Miller and wife, Elizabeth, Susannah, Michael, Henry, Nancy T$777.49
227. NEWCOMER, John. Adm. Christian, Peter 3/31/28; Christian, Margaret Welty, Elizabeth Stoufer, Fanny Stover, Nancy Hoffman, John, Andrew, Jacob T$187.76 Peter received $779.21¼ beforehand   5/2/29   T$187.76
228. NEWCOMER, Jonathan. 2/24/30; Entry voided, listed Jonathan, Emanuel, Elizabeth, Ann Funk, Barbara Negley, Isaac, Daniel, Joshua, Mary Wingert, Catherine, Peter
229. NEWCOMER, Peter. Adm. Jonathan 2/24/30; Jonathan, Emanuel, Elizabeth Nighwander, Ann Funk, Barbara Negley, Henry (son of Isaac), Daniel, Joshua, Mary Wingert, Catherine Martin, Peter T$8212.92   11/24/30   T$270.81
230. NIGHWANDER, Samuel. Adm. Henry Keedy, Samuel Avey 4/26/25; Elizabeth Houser, Henry Keedy and wife Nancy, Abraham, Joseph, John, David, Jacob, Martin Barnhart and wife Martha, George Willhouser and wife Elizabeth, Samuel Avey and wife Sophia, Emmanuel, Daniel son of David T$663.84
231. NIGHWANDER, Susannah (same as Samuel above) T$644.10
232. O'BRIEN, Henry. Adm. Joseph Moatz 2/12/33; James T$345.22   11/12/33 T$690.93
233. ONWILER, William. Adm. _____ Maines 11/20/29; Nicholas, Catherine Blair, Joseph T$107.73
234. ORMSTON, Ralph. Adm. John 4/24/32; widow, Andrew, John, Andrew Whiteman, Ralph Stockwell of J., Ann, James Tenant Jr. T$4062.50
235. OSWALT, Eve. Adm. Benjamin Jr. 4/5/31; Daniel Zimmerman, Benjamin, John, Samuel, Solomon, Lydia Kempffer, Henry Keagy, Eve (legacy under will of Phillip) T$108.28
236. OSWALT, Peter. Adm. Christian Flory, Benjamin 7/19/31; Benjamin, John, Jonathan, Samuel, Solomon, Lydia, Adam, Elizabeth, Catherine T$43.60
237. PALMER, Joseph. Adm. John Moats 1/18/34; widow, Elizabeth, David, Samuel, Jesse T$244.88
238. PFOUTZ, Henry. Adm. Nancy 5/22/33; widow, Nancy, Catherine Koontz, Nancy, Henry, Michael, Samuel, Joseph, Eliza, John, Jacob T$716.34
239. PRATHER, Louisa. Adm. Tobias Johnston 4/7/35; Delila Townsend, Catherine Townsend, Charlotte Johns, Ellen _____, Pricilla Jamison, Mary Johnston, Mariah Boon, Harriet Philpot, Sarah Boon, Nancy Morrison heirs T$216.90
240. POOROMAN, John. Adm. Jacob 12/10/29; Harry, Elizabeth, Catherine Long, Jacob, Nancy Brown's children (John, William, others not named), Abraham, Nelly Ross T$704.32
241. POTTER, Barbara. Adm. Christian Strite 11/3/35; Magdalena Nichodemus, Barbara Ledy, Mary Basore, Daniel's heirs (John, Barbara, Lewis, Maria), Abraham Baker's children (John, Elizabeth, Daniel, Abraham, Catherine, Barbara, Justiana) T$337.90
242. POTTORF, Andrew. Adm. Henry Seibert 2/12/28; Simon, George, Henry's heirs, Martin's heirs, Elizabeth Seibert's heirs T$981.54
243. PRICE, John. Adm. Keziah 6/7/30; widow, William H., Mary Ann T$726.79

DISTRIBUTION OF ESTATE ACCOUNTS

244. RAGAN, John. Adm. John Henry 4/2/29; Susannah, Amelia T$2636.62
245. REEDER, Frederick. Adm. John Moffet 10/20/29; Ann Elizabeth, Alexander T$467.40
246. REEDER, Jesse. Adm. Philip 2/14/29; widow, 8 heirs T$177.88   7/20/30 T$184.54   5/31/31 T$87.78   6/11/32 T$89.10   5/19/34; names 7 heirs, Elizabeth Miller, Mary Norris, Nelly Brantner, Philip, Joseph, Francis, Hiram T$44.70
247. REEL, Joseph. Adm. John, Joseph Ground 4/5/32; Mary Martin, Henry, Rezin, John, Elizabeth Morgan, Michael, Nancy Smith, Samuel, Daniel, Barbara T$4899.00
248. RENTCH, Peter. Adm. Samuel H. 2/2/35; Margaret Y., S.S. White and wife, Daniel Schnebly and wife, Samuel H., Samuel Nigh and wife, Joseph, John A., David Zellers and wife, Catherine Schnebly heirs (George B. Beall and wife, David H., Elizabeth, Margaret, Calvin, Catherine) T$472.50
249. RENTCH, Daniel. Adm. Ann 2/1/33; Andrew, Catherine, Catherine Miller, Ann Maria Schnebly, John's heirs (Angelica, Lawrence, Ealenora, Daniel S.) T$1092.93
250. REPLEY, George. Adm. John, David Cushwa 10/25/31; widow, Catherine Cushwa, Rosana Garbron, John, George, Jacob, Henry, Lidia, Sarah McComky, Joseph T$118.45¼   5/2/34 T$557.69
251. RIPLEY, Daniel. Adm. Nathaniel Summers 4/2/33; 7 heirs not named T$388.31
252. RICE, Barbara. Adm. Jacob 8/27/30; Jacob, Henry, Joseph Wagner, Catherine Wagner, Anna Boyer, Elizabeth Garvin T$91.95   4/19/31 T$91.85
253. RIDENOUR, Archibald. Adm. Daniel 3/11/35; George Seibert, George Cline, Thomas Beard, Daniel, John, Conrod Worley, Margaret, Nancy, Upton, Lydia T$63.59
254. RIDENOUR, Elizabeth. Adm. George Seibert 3/24/29; George Seibert and wife, heirs of Mary Clapsaddle, George Kluir and wife, Elizabeth, Daniel, Rebecca, John, Margaret, Archibald, Nancy, Upton, Lydia A. T$335.55½
255. RIDENOUR, John. Adm. Alexander Neill, Daniel Schnebly 1/4/31; Dorothy, Susanna Pottorf, D., Peter, Joseph, Mary, Isaac, Catherine Beiry, Jacob, Isaac Kershner, Jacob Kershner, William Kershner, Elizabeth Kershner T$742.43
256. RIDENOUR, Mary. Adm. Lodwick Protzman 3/3/30; John D., Ann, Mary T$1049.30
257. RITCHIE, Esther. Adm. George Ross Bell 2/5/33; Archibald, Jonas McPherson, Thomas James T$1103.94
258. ROHRER, John. Adm. David, John 3/11/29; widow, Samuel, Jacob, Eve Hoseltine, Magdalena, Catherine Huntsberry, Nancy Poffenburger, heirs of E. Geltmaker, Margaret Hine, Susanna Grim   4/6/30 T$1273.32   7/6/35 entry void 9/1/35; entry names E. Geltmaker's heirs as John, Elizabeth, Margaret, Margaret Hine   Second distribution started, crossed out with entry: widow and Eve Hosselton listed
259. ROHRER, Samuel. Adm. Elizabeth 10/8/30; widow, Mahala, Amanda, Elias, Silas, Marietta T$2280.72
260. ROHRBACK, John. Adm. Henry 10/27/34; widow, Mary H., David T$740.63   12/31/35 T$15.83
261. ROSS, Samuel. Adm. David 11/9/33; David C., James Bowls, Robert Bowls, Catherine T$349.28
262. ROWLAND, Henry. Adm. John 4/2/33; Henry, Catherine Wingert, Nancy Long, Hannah Bosteter, Susannah Martin, John, Elizabeth Gruber's heirs (Mary Steinmetz, Jacob, Nancy Soudenberger, Samuel, David, Sarah, Isaac), Mary Foreman's heirs (Hannah, Nancy, Mary), David's heirs (Elie, Benjamin, David) T$2277.37
263. ROWLAND, John. Adm. John, Isaac 8/10/35; Jacob, John, Isaac, Nancy Gruber, Elizabeth Emmert, Sarah Emmert, Mary Rice, Barbara, Lidia T$15345.86
264. RUNNER, Rebecca. Adm. Henry Feiry 5/11/30; Isaac, Priscilla, William T$3260.13
265. SCHLEIGH, Henry. Adm. Leonard Huber, Jacob Swoope 4/14/35; Henry, William Aman, Jacob's heirs (Mary, Isaac, Jacob, John, Gideon, Eza, Hannah Heddeman) T$2309.69   9/18/35 T$4597.45
266. SEIBERT, Henry. Adm. Michael Henny, Catherine 11/3/35; widow, Michael, Elizabeth Ditto, Mary Ann, Henry, John, Susan, Louisa, George P. T$6074.84
267. SEYSTER, Daniel. Adm. Sarah 7/17/30; widow, Elizabeth K., Lewis C., Andrew H. T$3334.19

1828 - 1835

268. SHAFER, Elizabeth. Adm. Daniel Hower 3/17/35; David, Fanny, George T$27.99
269. SHAFER, Leonard. Adm. Mary Shafer 5/10/33; widow, Lewis A., Caroline B., Harriet E., John S., Ann M., Sophia P., Gustavus W., Samuel B., Thomas H., William A. T$1193.40
270. SHANEFELT, Andrew. Adm. Henry, Peter Snyder 5/17/31; Jacob Bowman, Henry, Peter Snyder and wife, Andrew, Daniel, Susannah, Jacob, David, William, John T$424.95
271. SHANEFELT, William. Adm. Jacob Leckroon 3/1/28; Margaret Leckroon, Susannah Bowman, Catherine Artz, Jacob, John, Henry, William, Andrew T$738.52
272. SHANK, George. Adm. Nicholas Shultz 4/10/32; Margaret, George Deihl, Mary Ann Reed, Henrietta, Samuel, heirs of George, Eliza Shultz, Margaret, Samuel T$1794.05 6/18/33 T$157.22 3/28/35 T$304.87
273. SHANK, Henry. Adm. Jacob, Henry 1/22/28; Michael, Jacob, Christian, Henry, David, Barbara T$13603.90
274. SHARER, Catherine. Adm. John Light 6/13/31; Samuel Williams, Henry Williams T$572.29
275. SHELLING, Philip. Adm. David 4/30/33; Philip, Susannah, David, Jonas, Jacob, Elizabeth, William, Lewis T$307.00
276. SHELLMAN, John. Adm. Susannah 4/24/32; widow, Jacob, Mary Ann, Elizabeth, John, Susannah, Catherine, Magdalena T$203.03½
277. SHEPHERD, Thomas. Adm. Adam Myers, John Blackford 4/10/28; John, Sarah Spong, Joseph, David T$2251.79 2/3/29 T$1282.66 2/9/30 T$1112.67
278. SHEPHERD, John. Adm. John Blackford 3/5/29; widow, Alexander, Jane, Sally, Ruhemiah T$643.49 2/9/30 T$262.51
279. STEPHEY, Elizabeth. Adm. John P. 9/10/33; John P., Daniel, Andrew, Jacob, Samuel, Isaac T$350.06
280. SHEPPERD, Thomas. Adm. Thomas 3/4/34; widow, Thomas, Henry, Amanda, Mary, Sarah, James, Joseph T$696.73 4/1-7/35 T$1431.38
281. SHELLEBERGER, David. Adm. David C. Newcomer 2/15/28 T$915.62 1/24/29 T$460.09 5/17/30 T$540.37 4/29/31 T$752.91 2/8/32 T$999.33
282. SHIVELY, Adam. Adm. George Umbaugh n.d.; widow T$407.19
283. SHONG, Matthias. Adm. William F. Hebb 5/18/30; widow, Irvem, Shepherd, Mary E., Matthias, Ellen, Joseph T$548.18 (entry voided)
284. SHOWMAN, George Sr. Adm. David 5/4/33; George Jr., Jacob, David, Elizabeth Benner, John, Peter, Catherine T$276.25 5/4/33 T$13.24
285. SHUPE, Adam. Adm. John Hammond 5/2/28; John Hammond and wife, Elizabeth, heirs of John, heirs of Susannah Newcomer T$228.76 11/24/28 T$195.17 3/23/32 T$112.30 8/29/35 T$2050.56
286. SIMPKINS, William. Adm. Derius 4/2/32; John W., Sarah, Susan, Ruth Ann, Mary, Elizabeth, Macey, Rebecca, Derrius, Nancy Ann T$3518.27 3/30/33 T$1403.31 3/31/34 T$1466.09
287. SLIFER, Ezra. Adm. Henry Nyman 7/6/35; widow, Oliver, Elmira, Catherine, Ezra, Rebecca, Olinda, Randolph T$910.33
288. SMITH, Joseph. Adm. Michael 4/14/28; Peter, Susamiah Barkman, Joseph, Elizabeth Stewetard, John, Jacob's heirs, Margaret Adams, Michael T$245.11 4/28/29 T$169.79
289. SMITH, Joseph. Adm. Michael P. 4/10/30; John McClain and wife Mary, Upton Powell and wife Ann, Michael P. T$2522.52 4/2/31 T$1574.97
290. SMITH, Joseph. Adm. Frederick Woolf 4/22/28; Alexander, Henry, Joseph, Elizabeth, Margaret Spielman, Ann Elizabeth Cromrine, heirs of Christina, Magdalena Woolf, Sophia Stine T$225.50 4/7/29 T$241.00
291. SMITH, Nicholas. Adm. Benjamin Swingle Sr. 10/20/30; Nicholas, Matthias, George, Benjamin Swingle, Jacob Wagoner, Frederick Ramer, George Keller (Kebler), Catherine T$1231.24 4/6/31 T$3456.84
292. SMITH, William G. Adm. William Towson 3/5/33; Sarah Coakley, the mother, Zebina, John A. T$936.14 4/27/33 T$318.57

DISTRIBUTION OF ESTATE ACCOUNTS

293. SMITH, Zebina. Adm. Sarah Coakley, William Towson 2/7/28; widow, John, William S., Zebina T$609.41¼; Philip H. Coakley and wife Sarah 12/13/28 T$558.51 2/25/31 T$1681.22
294. SMITH, Zebina Jr. Adm. William Towson 3/5/33; Sarah Coakley the mother, John A. T$616.29 4/27/33 T$424.86
295. SNEARY, John. Adm. Frederick Humrickhouse 3/11/29; Margaret McElves, Catherine Shell, Nancy, James, Polly Leighter's heirs (Elizabeth Fuss, Polly Miller, Nancy Carbaugh) T$616.70
296. SNYDER, George. Adm. James Beatty, Joseph 6/9/35; John, George, Mary, Jackson T$349.28
297. SNYDER, Jacob. Adm. Abraham 5/28/30; John, Barbara, Henry, George Harbaugh and wife, Jacob Miller and wife, Abraham, Christian, Martin, Joseph Keplinger and wife T$794.04
298. SNYDER, Leonard. Adm. James I. Beatty 1/17/34; widow, Otho, Mary, Louisa, Peter, William B., John T., Sarah A. T$740.68
299. SPEALMAN, David. Adm. Daniel M. Middlekauff 7/15/35; widow, Hiram W., David, Catherine T$408.16
300. SPIELMAN, John. Adm. Jacob Jr. 10/9/28; Samuel Cramer and wife Mary, Jeremiah, John, Sarah, Catherine, Elizabeth T$725.09
301. STAHL, Jacob. Adm. Jacob Woolf, Martin Barr 4/24/33; John, John Brocius, widow, Archibald Fleming and wife, Jacob Woolf and wife, Martin Barr and wife, Daniel Startzman, Christina, Catherine, Sarah, Lydia T$193.13
302. STAHL, Michael. Adm. Andrew Mann 4/18/34; Mary Mann, Susannah Cyman, Anna Patterson, Esther Resler, Henry, Jacob, Abraham T$2043.33
303. STAKES, Peter. Adm. Rosanna, Andrew Kershner 4/19/30; widow, Edward G.W., Susannah S., Andrew K. T$1548.78
304. STARTZMAN, Eve and Henry. Adm. David 4/12/28; share held by George Householder for estate of Daniel Weisell; Martin, Henry, Heirs of Margaret Weisel, Juliana Householder, Susannah Firey, David, Eve Kershner T$663.00
305. STEPHEY, Andrew. Adm. John P., Andrew 9/15/30; widow, John P., Daniel, Andrew, Jacob, Samuel, Isaac T$36.42 1/3 4/5/31 T$246.92 8/30/31 T$47.00
306. STEPHEY, Catherine. Adm. John Welty 2/2/32; Christina Wentling's heirs, Catherine Dukwalk?, Jacob Bowers, George Koler, John Singer, Mary Ann, Jonas Kaler T$838.29
307. STEPHEY, David. Adm. John Hoover 10/20/29; widow, Daniel, Ann Mary T$1348.70
308. STEPHEY, Nicholas. Adm. George, John Oswalt 2/10/35; George, Catherine Hoover, Mary, Elizabeth Harbaugh, Margaret Oswalt, Susan, John D., Mary T$720.77
309. STINE, Mathias. Adm. John, Jacob J. Yeakle 6/4/29; widow, John, Valentine Wachtel and wife, Catherine, Jacob, George T$625.91
310. STOTLER, Peter. Adm. John, Henry Fessler 3/11/35; John, John in right of Christian Hoover and wife Elizabeth, Henry Burtner, Henry Fessler T$4146.06
311. STOCKSLAGER, Henry. Adm. John 3/5/30; widow, John, George H. T$1250.25
312. STOUFFER, Christian. Adm. John 7/24/30; Catherine Spessert, Elizabeth Snyder, Nancy Rowland, Sarah Emmert, John, Ann Poffenberger, Samuel, Lydia, David, Christian, Jacob T$7041.65½ 1/25/31 T$4776.45 8/2/31; Ann P. is Amelia P. T$113.78 8/23/31 T$113.78 4/17/32 T$4356.25
313. STULTZ, Henry. Adm. George Knavel 2/9/30; Peter, David, John, Susannah Knavel $2772.65; widow $1500 in hands of Executor; children only: 3/20/30 T$863.53 3/6/32 T$1133.15
314. STULTZ, Peter. Adm. George Knavel 3/27/32; widow, Samuel T$263.83
315. TOULSON, James. Adm. Daniel Malott 5/7/30; widow, Thomas, William deceased T$260.33
316. TOULSON, William. Adm. Daniel Malott 7/27/30; to mother, Thomas $31.08
317. THOMAS, Gabriel. Adm. Daniel 3/7/28; David Rohrer, Christian Rohrer, Frederick Baker, Christian Deaner, Samuel Deaner, Jacob Keedy, Abraham Snyder, Emanuel Morrison, Daniel Weaver, Daniel T$600.33

1828 - 1835

318. THOMAS, Michael. Adm. Joseph Weast 4/8/35; Sophia Nicodemus, Christian Schoenz? and wife T$303.54
319. THOMAS, Peter. Adm. John 3/26/33; Margaret the mother, David, Peter Baker and wife, Elizabeth Boyer, Margaret Wilhelm's heirs (David, Samuel, Mary, Henry, Jacob, Ambrose C.), Rozanna Pope's heirs (Mary Ann, Josiah, Rebecca), Philip Baker and wife, Daniel Warvel and wife, Christian Blessing and wife, John, Susannah, Nancy T$264.73 equally divided
320. THOMAS, Valentine. Adm. George, David Rohrer 2/12/29; widow, George, Margaret, Sarah, Elizabeth Rohrer, Sophia, Gideon, Simon, Mary, Mary Ann T$1060.40
321. TICE, Jacob Jr. Adm. Samuel Seyster 7/24/30; Otto, Upton, Sarah Ann B. T$223.71
322. TICE, John. Adm. John 3/26/35; widow, John, Andrew Wolgamot, Jacob Crook, Jacob Alter, Henry R., William M. T$1667.55
323. TROUP, Henry. Adm. Adam 8/7/29; Group A: Adam, John Brewer and wife Mary $4500.50¼ Group B: heirs of Catherine Shively (Isaac and Adam) $1291.26 1/8 Group C: heirs of David (John, Jacob, David, Christian, Elizabeth Altzbaugh, Peggy Irwin, Nancy Kakcerise) each $368.93¼ T$7671.93 10/17/29 T$2390.79 2/27/30 T$267.36
324. TROVINGER, Christopher. Adm. John, Joseph 3/15/31; Jacob's heirs, Samuel, John, William, Daniel, Joseph, Mary Keller, Rebecca, Yandis, Sarah Hatter, Catherine Smith T$898.02
325. TROVINGER, Daniel. Adm. Joseph 2/6/33; widow, Amos, David T$131.23
326. TUCKERMAN, Thomas. Adm. Thomas 4/16/35; John, Elizabeth, Mary, Sarah, Rachel, Thomas T$69.11
327. TURNER, Catherine L. Adm. Jane E. 3/3/31; same as Edmond H. below T$1389.84
328. TURNER, Edmond H. Adm. Jane E. 3/3/31; widow, Lewis, Susan M., Catherine S., Edmond H. T$6810.81
329. TUTEWILER, Jacob. Adm. Alexander Neill, Daniel Schnebly 12/29/29; half to John, David, Polly Barr; half to heirs of Ezekiel Chaney (Jacob, Maria Gill, John, Catherine Burnet, Ezekial, Joseph, Margaret) T$815.92 7/20/30 T$1150.52 1/4/31 T$1029.44 8/2/31 T$726.35 11/19/33 T$490.86
330. UPDEGRAFF, Samuel. Adm. George, Susannah 6/23/30; widow, Susannah, Samuel T$7.89
331. VAN BUSKIRK, John. Adm. Thomas C. Brent 6/25/31; George, Mary Linn, John, William received $230.25, 115.12½, 307.00, 307.00 respectively; David's heirs (Mary, Lawanee, Daniel) each $80; Samuel Blackmore alias Van Buskirk $76.75; Joseph Truax $46.05; Nancy Blackmore $19.18½ T$1285.56
332. VAN LEAR, Mathew. Adm. John Herr 12/24/33; William H., Samuel S., Otho H. Williams, Thomas F., Joseph, Mary Ann Holman T$571.35 Distribution voided
333. VAN LEAR, Thomas. Adm. O.H. Williams 1/9/35; Samuel L., Eliza Williams, Joseph, Mary Ann Hallman, William H. heirs T$1474.78 5/19/35 T$1474.78
334. VAN LEAR, William. Adm. Otho H. Williams 2/12/28; Samuel S., Eliza Williams, Joseph, Mary Ann Hollman, Thomas F., William H. heirs T$1200.19 10/23/34 T$369.20 5/19/35 (Samuel excluded) T$2004.28 5/19/35 T$637.77
335. VAN LEAR, William H. Adm. Mathew L. 4/19/33; widow, Mary L., Sarah S. T$4542.49
336. VERVIL, John. Adm. John 4/2/29; Group A: Mary, Elizabeth $40.00; Group B: John, Christian $66.67; Group C: John, Christopher, Mathias, Peter, Elizabeth Kretzer, Margaret Hovermail $1649.96 4/7/30; Group C T$713.87 4/11/31; Group C T$686.75
337. VERVIL, Peter. Adm. Joseph Mumma 4/20/29; widow, 8 children not named T$78.92 4/20/30 T$110.84 5/10/31 T$106.35
338. WADE, John. Adm. Henry, Elias 3/21/29; 5 heirs not named T$3915.00
339. WATTS, Barton. Adm. Henry 8/9/31; Henry, Barton, Elizabeth Steward, Juliana Ringer, Priscilla, Susanna Summers T$265.85
340. WATTS, Thomas. Adm. Sarah, Gera South 3/11/30; widow, Ann, Rachel, Joseph, Sarah Ann, Elizabeth, Thomas B., William, Frisby D., Abraham T$6527.52
341. WAUGH, Archibald M. Adm. Catherine 5/6/30; widow, James Zwisler and wife, Thomas M., Henrietta M.A., James A. T$614.79

DISTRIBUTION OF ESTATE ACCOUNTS

342. WEBB, Margaret. Adm. Samuel 8/19/34; same as Samuel below T$1067.00
343. WEBB, Samuel. Adm. Jacob Shank, Jacob Krouse 8/12/34; Margaret Bowers, George Foster, Samuel Foster, John Foster, Mary M. Foster T$158.82
344. WELTY, Henry. Adm. Daniel 5/29/32; widow, John, Jacob, Christian, Samuel, Ann T$56.15
345. WELTY, Jacob. Adm. John 12/22/35; John, Eve Bentmyer, Jacob, Elizabeth Hoover, Christian, Mary Turby, Nancy Augustine, Abraham, Susannah Barkdoll, David T$1261.38
346. WEST, David. Adm. George Fague 8/12/28; Benjamin, Abel, Isaac Robertson and wife Sarah, George Fague and wife Nancy T$188.39
347. WILES, John. Adm. William D. Brown 10/8/33; widow, Susannah, Hannah T$844.64
348. WILSON, Isaac. Adm. Jacob Miller n.d.; names widow, Elizabeth, Rachel, Walter, Isaac (voided)
349. WILSON, James. Adm. Lewis Fletcher 8/18/33; widow, grandchildren each $23.19½ T$46.39
350. WILSON, Rachel. Adm. Jacob Miller 2/27/28; mother, Elizabeth, Walter, Isaac (voided)
351. WINEBRENNER, Christian. Adm. Andrew Kershner 10/13/28; Philip, Christian, Catherine Snyder, Christiana Barnhiser, Sabastian, Peter, Jacob T$1063.47
352. WINEBRENNER, Jacob. Adm. Andrew Kershner 11/6/28; widow $14.88; John, Mary Barr, Sally, Peter, Joseph each $4.96; Catherine Snyder's heirs (Elizabeth, Andrew, Sally, Simon, John) each $.82½ T$44.65
353. WINGERT, Elizabeth. Adm. John 2/12/33; Ann Hoover, John, Samuel, Catherine, Martin, Jacob, Abraham, Maria Boyer T$491.08
354. WINTERS, Sarah. Adm. Jacob 9/20/31; Nancy Barr, Jacob, Daniel, John, Catherine Lee, Sarah T$584.64
355. WINTER, Susannah. Adm. John Hoover 10/20/29; John, Daniel, Andrew, Conrad Flory and wife, Elizabeth Harbaugh's heirs, Catherine Burckhart, Margaret Hoover, Mary Rideout's heirs T$2769.04 8/2/31 T$100.16
356. WISE (WEISE), John. Adm. John, George 2/5/35; widow, John, George, Daniel, Samuel, A. Humrichouse and wife, James Ressler and wife T$1810.24
357. WITTER, Jacob. Adm. Emanuel, Benjamin 3/31/35; Benjamin, Emanuel, Samuel Brown and wife, Joseph Hershey and wife T$96.04
358. WOLGAMOT, John. Adm. John, Andrew, John A. Keedy 9/26/35; widow 1/5; John, Andrew, John A. Keedy, David, Daniel, Alfred, Henry, John Teisher and wife, Elizabeth, Margaret, Nancy, Joshua T$530.00
359. WOOLF, Jacob. Adm. John 3/1/32; deduct advance to Jacob $2900; legacy to Nathaniel Rowland, John Rowland $500 each; Susannah Royer legacy $300; John, David, Catherine Rinehart, Susannah Royer, Magdalena Slifer each $2641.20 T$13106.00
360. WOLFEISBURGER, Susannah. Adm. George Keihl 3/13/33; Sarah, Barbara, Francis, George, Jonathan, Joseph T$372.29
361. YEAKLE, John. Adm. William, Samuel 8/20/29; William, Samuel, Mary Little, Elizabeth, Christina T$140.99
362. YOE, Benjamin. Adm. George Fechtig between 10/6-10/24/35; Benjamin F., George Fechtig and wife, George Post and wife T$497.69 Real estate sold to widow Downes (not entitled to distribution share)
363. ZEIGLER, David. Adm. Jacob 6/17/35; Barbara the mother, George, Jacob, Catherine, Elizabeth, Nancy, Barbara, Samuel T$681.75

INDEX

-A-
ABBONET,
 Hannah, 4
ABINETT,
 Ann, 1
ABRACHT,
 Mary, 32
ABRECHT,
 Mary, 48
ABRECT,
 Mary, 48
ACKENBARGER,
 Valentine, 7
ACLE,
 Judith, 43
ADAM,
 Adam, 6
ADAMS,
 Amos, 24
 Catherine, 39
 Christian, 11
 Helena, 24
 Henry, 11, 39
 Jacob, 11
 James, 24
 John, 11, 25
 Margaret, 24,
  36, 51
 Martha, 24
 Martin A., 24
 Mary, 11
 Mata, 24
 Otho, 26
 Peter, 11
 Rebecca, 39
 Samuel H., 39
 Sarah Ann, 39
 William, 11
 William H., 39
AKELBARGER,
 Catherine, 1
 David, 1
 Elizabeth, 1
 Enoch, 1
 Jacob, 1
 John, 1
 Michael, 1
 Rebecca, 1
ALBERT,
 Catherine, 39
 Eleanor, 39
 Elizabeth, 1
 Frederick, 1
 Jacob, 1

John, 1, 39
Mary, 39
William, 39
ALBRIGHT,
 William, 3
ALEY,
 Isaac, 10
ALIERON,
 Ann, 15
ALLAN,
 Barnet, 12
ALLEN,
 Archibald, 11
 Benjamin A. P., 11
 Eve, 31
 Henry, 11
 James, 11
 Martha K., 11
 Mary, 11
ALLENDER,
 Anna, 11
 John D., 11
 Thomas, 11
 William, 11
ALLILIA,
 Anna, 20
ALLISON,
 Amos, 28
 Mrs., 42
ALTER,
 Amelia, 39
 Catherine, 39
 David, 24, 39
 Elizabeth, 14, 43
 Frederick, 4, 15
 George, 24, 39
 Jacob, 14, 17, 39,
  43, 53
 Mary, 39
 Rebecca, 39
 Samuel, 24, 39
 Susan, 39
 Susanna, 24
ALTZBAUGH,
 Elizabeth, 53
ALUEBAUGH,
 Susanna, 1
AMAN,
 William, 50
AMEN,
 John, 39
AMOS,
 Margaret, 42

ANCHONY,
 Christian, 1
 Davalt, 1
ANDERSON,
 Amelia, 34
 Mary, 1
ANDREWS,
 Barbara, 1
 Christian, 1
 Elizabeth, 16
 John, 1
 William, 16
ANEKNEY,
 George, 11
ANGEL,
 Elizabeth, 10
 John, 10
 Margaret, 10
 Sary, 10
 Susa, 10
ANGLE,
 Catherine, 39
 Daniel, 39
 David, 39
 Elizabeth, 39
 Frederick, 39
 Henry, 11, 39
 Jacob, 11, 39, 48
 John, 11, 39
 Lovena, 39
 Margaret, 25
 Polly, 39
 Sally, 39
 Samuel, 39
 Statea, 19, 20
 Susanna, 39
 William, 39
ANKENEY,
 Andrew, 1
 Ann, 46
 Catherine, 11
 Christian, 20
 Christiana, 1
 Daniel, 11
 David, 11
 Devalt, 1
 Elizabeth, 1, 45
 George, 11
 Henry, 1, 11
 Jacob, 11
 John, 1, 11
 Magdalena, 1
 Margaret, 11
 Mary, 11

DISTRIBUTION OF ESTATE ACCOUNTS

Polly, 1
Samuel, 11
Susanna, 11
ANKENY,
  Ann, 30
  Catherine, 24
  Christian, 35
  Daniel, 24
  George, 24
  Henry, 24
  John, 24, 30
  Mary, 24
  Samuel, 24
  Susanna, 24
ANKEY,
  Henry, 20
ANKY,
  Harry, 36
ANN,
  Ann, 43
ANSBERGER,
  Christopher, 24
  Frederick, 24
  George, 24
  Henry, 24
  Jacob, 24
  John, 24
  Michael, 24
ARNOLD,
  Barbara, 18
  Catherine, 3
  Henry, 1
  Mary, 40, 1
  Rebecca, 33
  William, 40
ARNSBERGER,
  Catherine, 11
  Christopher, 11
  Elizabeth, 11
  Esther, 11
  Frederick, 11
  George, 11
  Henry, 11
  Jacob, 11
  John, 11
  Michael, 11
ARTZ,
  Abraham, 11
  Catherine, 31, 51
  Christian, 11, 24
  David, 27
  Elizabeth, 11, 24
  Henry, 11, 24
  John, 11, 24
  Joseph, 11
  Mary, 11, 24
  Nicholas P., 11
  Peter, 11, 24
  Philip, 11, 24
ASBERRY,
  John, 15
ASH,
  Abraham, 5
  Maria, 36
  Mary, 2
ASHBERRY,
  John, 24, 29
ASHERMAN,
  Eliza Ann, 48
  Elizabeth, 48
  Maria, 48
  Mary, 48
ASHITZ,
  Jacob, 22
ATKINSON,
  Margaret, 3
  Mary, 3
AUGUSTINE,
  Catherine, 8
  Elizabeth, 42
  Nancy, 54
AULT,
  Magdalena, 7
AVERY,
  Barbara, 1
  Mary Ann, 44
AVEY,
  Barbara, 39
  Catherine, 20, 39
  Elizabeth, 39
  Ezra, 39
  Frany, 15, 29
  George, 39
  Henry, 39
  Jacob, 39
  John, 39
  Joseph, 39
  Mary, 39
  Nancy, 39
  Peter, 9, 39
  Rachel, 39
  Samuel, 49
  Sophia, 49
  Susanna, 39
  Therasa, 39

-B-
BACHTEL,
  Andrew, 46
  Catherine, 30, 46
  David, 28, 43
  Henry, 46
  Isaac, 39, 46
  Jacob, 30, 39
  Martin, 24, 39, 46
  Samuel, 24, 39, 46, 47
  Susanna, 43
BACHTELL,
  Andrew, 39
  Elizabeth, 47
  Hamet, 39
  Henry, 39
  Isaac, 39
  Jacob, 39
  Joseph, 39
  Martin, 46, 39
  Samuel, 9, 39
BAER,
  Maria Rosanna, 29
BAIR,
  Christian, 47
BAIRD,
  Susanna, 2
  William, 2, 5, 13
BAKER,
  Abraham, 11, 24, 49
  Ames, 24
  Amos, 24
  Andrew, 1
  Ann, 39
  Barbara, 49
  Catherine, 26, 49
  Conrad, 1
  Daniel, 49
  David, 24, 39
  Elias, 44, 38
  Elizabeth, 13, 27, 49
  Frederick, 24, 26, 39, 52
  Fredericka, 39
  Jacob, 39, 11, 24, 39
  Jane, 1
  John, 11, 24, 39, 49
  Justiana, 49
  Lemuel, 24

INDEX

Lewis, 11
Lucas, 39
Magdalena, 36, 45
Margaret, 1, 38
Mary, 5, 21, 38
Nicholas, 11, 39
Peter, 1, 11, 24, 39, 53
Philip, 53
Polly, 26
Rebecca, 24, 39
Samuel, 7, 11, 24, 39
Sarah, 11, 24, 39
Susanna, 24, 39
Thomas, 1
William, 1
BALL,
  Leonard, 6
BARDONA,
  Mary, 3
BARE,
  Isaac, 39
  Jacob, 17
  John, 39
  Martin, 39
  Mary, 17
BARGDOLL,
  Susanna, 41
BARKDOLL,
  George, 25
  Susanna, 25
  Susannah, 54
BARKMAN,
  David, 42
  Dolly, 24
  Eve, 24, 39, 40
  Frederick, 1
  Hellery, 24
  Henry, 1
  Jacob, 1, 24, 39, 40
  Michael, 24, 40
  Peter, 7
  Susaniah, 51
  Susanna, 24, 36
BARKS,
  Jacob, 24, 29, 45
  John, 24, 40
BARKSTREFER,
  Adam, 40

BARNES,
  Robert, 5
BARNETT,
  Ann, 11, 24
  Casandra, 11, 24
  Catherine, 17
  David, 11, 24
  Henry, 11, 17, 24
  Jacob, 11, 24
  John, 11, 24
  Mary, 11, 24
BARNHART,
  Martha, 49
  Martin, 49
BARNHISER,
  Christiana, 54
BARR,
  Andrew, 1
  Barbara, 1
  Christian, 46
  Christine, 39
  David, 1
  George, 40
  Jacob, 1
  John, 1, 29
  Martin, 1, 52
  Mary, 1, 48, 54
  Mary R., 44
  Nancy, 54
  Nitericia, 40
  Susanna, 39
BARRICKMAN,
  Frederick, 24
  Henry, 24
BARTON,
  Elener, 1
  Jacob, 3
  Mary, 1
  Richard, 1
  Stephen, 26
  Susanna, 26
  Thomas, 1
BARTOON,
  Jacob, 11
  John, 11
BASORE,
  Mary, 49
BATEMAN,
  Catherine, 33
BAUGH,
  Barbara, 1
  Catherine, 1
  Elizabeth, 1
  Henry, 1

  John, 1
  Susanna, 1
BAUGHMAN,
  Easter, 29
BAUM,
  Barbara, 2
BAYER,
  Christian, 11
  Elizabeth, 12
  Jacob, 11, 31
  John, 11
  Magdolena, 11
BAYLY,
  Andrew, 26
  Ann, 14
  Arlimacy, 22
  Rebecca, 10
BAYOR,
  Eve, 16
BEALER,
  Christian, 4
BEALL,
  Andrew, 11
  Anthony, 11
  Catherine, 16
  Daniel, 16
  David, 11
  Elizabeth, 16
  Frederick, 11
  George B., 50
  George R., 44
  Jacob, 11
  John, 11, 16
  Lewis, 12
  Margaret, 16
  Rachel, 16
BEAM,
  Jacob, 21
BEAN,
  Barton, 40
  Charles, 40
  George W., 40
  William, 40
BEAR,
  Christina, 3
  Sarah, 12
BEARD,
  Adam, 47
  Catherine, 40
  George, 43
  John, 17, 26, 32, 33, 35
  Margaret, 6
  Mary, 41

DISTRIBUTION OF ESTATE ACCOUNTS

Nicholas, 11
Philip, 39, 46
Sarah, 28
Thomas, 50
William, 41
BEATTY,
  Ann E., 40
  Elie, 21
  James, 52
  James I., 52
  William, 40
BECK,
  Andrew, 48
  Richard, 13
  Susannah, 48
BECKLEY,
  Henry, 35
  Mathias, 2
BECKMAN,
  Joseph, 22
BECKNELL,
  Easau, 17
BEECHER,
  Jacob, 24
  Samuel, 24
  William W., 24
BEELER,
  Abraham, 1
  Christian, 1
  David, 1
  Elizabeth, 1
  Jacob, 1, 32
  Mary, 1
  Samuel, 1
  Sarah, 1
  Susannah, 1, 16
BEIRY,
  Catherine, 50
BELCH,
  Elizabeth, 46
  James, 11
  Susanna, 11
BELL,
  Catherine, 40
  Daniel, 1, 24, 40
  David, 40
  Elizabeth, 1
  Frederick, 1, 40
  George, 40
  George Ross, 50
  Jacob, 40
  John, 24, 40
  Julia, 31

Leonard, 24, 40
Margaret, 1
Mary, 40
Peggy, 24, 40
Peter, 1, 31, 40
Rosanna, 40
Sophia, 40
Thomas, 24
BELT,
  Thomas, 4
BELTZHOOVER,
  Catherine, 28
BENDER,
  Margaret, 24
BENNER,
  Christian, 24
  Elizabeth, 36, 51
  George, 20
  Henry, 24
  Jacob, 24, 46
  John, 24
  Susannah, 20
BENNET,
  Aquilla, 21
BENSON,
  Thomas, 1
BENTER,
  Susanna, 9
BENTMYER,
  Eve, 54
BENTZ,
  Catherine, 37
  Elizabeth, 38
  Jacob, 40
BERR,
  Susanna, 40
BESINGER,
  Elizabeth, 14
BETEBENNER,
  Rosanna, 24
BETEBRENNER,
  Rosanna, 39
BETT,
  Josiah, 24
  Levin, 24
  Lloyd, 24
  Sarah, 24
  Thomas, 24
BETTS,
  Ann, 1
  Christian, 1
  Frederick, 1
  John, 1
  Mary, 1

Willliam, 1
BETZ,
  Ann, 25
  Catherine, 11
  Christian, 25
  Elizabeth, 33
  Frederick, 11, 25
  Jacob, 11, 25
  John, 11, 25
  Mary, 25
  Mary Ann, 11
  Nancy, 11
  Sarah, 11, 25
  William, 11, 25
BETZEL,
  Mary, 28
BEUMBAUGH,
  George, 40
BEVINS,
  Basil, 25
  Leonard, 25
  Thomas, 25
BILES,
  Elizabeth, 16
BINKLEY,
  Barbara, 11
  Catherine, 11, 40
  Elizabeth, 40, 48
  Eve, 18
  Ferdinand, 48
  George, 40, 48
  Gutleib, 11
  Jacob, 40, 48
  Jonathan, 40
  Louisa, 48
  Thomas, 48
  William, 48
BINKLY,
  Fanny, 14
BISH,
  Amanda C., 40
  David, 40
  Henrietta H., 40
BISHOP,
  Catherine, 1
  David, 1
  George, 1
  Harry, 1
  Jacob, 1
  Margaret, 1
  Susanna, 1
  William, 1
BISSETT,
  Samuel, 1

INDEX

Thomas, 1
BLACKBURN,
  Elizabeth, 13
BLACKFORD,
  John, 35, 51
BLACKMORE,
  Caleb, 40
  Catherine, 40
  Kitty, 40
  Nancy, 53
  Samuel, 53
  Sarah, 14, 27
  William, 14, 27, 40
BLAIR,
  Andrew, 1, 25
  Catherine, 49
  Charity, 25
  John, 1
  Joseph, 25
  Samuel, 1, 47
  Sarah, 25
BLAKE,
  Ann, 40
  Burdine, 40, 48
  Charlotte, 40
  Jeffrey, 40
  John, 40
  Mary Jane, 40
  Sarah, 40
  Thomas, 40
  Wlizabeth, 40
BLEACHER,
  Barbara, 4
  Caty, 4
  Jacob, 4
  John, 4
  Magdalena, 4
  Mary, 4
BLECHER,
  Jacob, 40
  John, 17, 40, 43
  Samuel, 17
BLECKER,
  Barbara, 40
  Elizabeth, 40
  Jacob, 40
  John, 40
  Margaret, 40
  Maria A., 40
  Samuel, 40
  Susanna, 40
  William, 40

BLEECHER,
  Barbara, 27
BLESSING,
  Christian, 53
BLOOD,
  Elizabeth, 40
  Parker, 40
BOARD,
  Elizabeth, 9
BODMAN,
  Ferdinand, 40
  Lewis G., 40
  Philip, 40
  William, 40
BOERSTLER,
  Daniel, 22
BOETLER,
  Prudence, 41
BOND,
  Alexander, 11
  Ann, 1
  Edward, 1
  George, 1
  James, 11
  John, 1, 11
  Joseph, 1
  Lucy, 1
  Luke, 11
  Rosanna, 31
  Thomas, 11
  Walter, 1, 11
BOOK,
  Catherine, 11
  John, 11
  Joseph, 11
  Pricilla, 11
BOON,
  Mariah, 49
  Mary, 11, 24
  Sarah, 49
  Susannah, 20
BOONES,
  Sarah, 24
BOSART,
  Margaret, 16
BOSTER,
  Magdalena, 10
BOSTETER,
  Hannah, 50
BOTELAR,
  Alexander H., 25
  Edward, 25
  Elizabeth, 26
  Henry, 25

Martha, 25
BOTELER,
  Aleatha, 26, 42
  Alexander H., 11
  Bartholemew, 40
  Henry, 11
  Hezekiah, 11
  Lingan, 11
  Sarah, 26, 40, 42
  Thomas, 11, 40
  Thomas C., 40
  Washington, 40
  William, 11
BOUGHER,
  Elizabeth, 8
  Henry, 8
BOULTZ,
  Elizabeth, 44
  Joseph, 44
BOUSER,
  Frederick, 12
  Henry, 12
  John, 12
BOVA,
  Elizabeth, 11
  Jacob, 20
  Michael, 11, 24
BOVEY,
  Barbara, 12
  Catherine, 12, 25
  Christine, 25
  Daniel, 12, 25, 40
  Elizabeth, 25
  George, 25
  Henry, 25, 40
  Jacob, 25
  John, 25, 39
  Magdalena, 25
  Mary, 12, 25
  Michael, 12
  Susanna, 25
  Susannah, 39
BOWARD,
  Andrew, 40
  George, 40
  Jacob, 40
  Margaret, 40
  Michael, 40
BOWART,
  Andrew, 40
  Eve, 31
  George, 40
  Jacob, 40
  Margaret, 40

DISTRIBUTION OF ESTATE ACCOUNTS

Michael, 40
BOWER,
  Barbara, 1
  Catherine, 1
  Christian, 15
  Conrad, 1
  George, 1
  Hester, 2
  Jacob, 1, 2
  John, 1
  Magdalen, 1
  Mary, 1
  Susanna, 1
BOWERS,
  B., 40
  Barbara, 25, 40
  Elizabeth, 24,
    25, 40
  Esther, 16, 30
  George, 25, 40
  Jacob, 25, 40,
    52
  Margaret, 54
  Mary D., 25, 40
  Sarah Ann, 25,
    40
BOWIE,
  Charity, 25
  Jane, 25
  Thomas, 25
BOWLER,
  John, 4
BOWLES,
  Mary, 13
BOWLS,
  James, 50
  Robert, 50
BOWMAN,
  Catherine, 1
  Elizabeth, 25
  Ester, 46
  Esther, 39
  Frederick, 25
  Jacob, 1, 25,
    40, 51
  John, 1, 9, 25
  Peter, 25
  Sally, 40
  Simon, 1, 2
  Susanna, 40
  Susannah, 51
BOWSER,
  Margaret, 40
BOYD,

David, 30
John, 43
Samuel, 39
Walter, 31
BOYER,
  Anna, 50
  Catherine, 23, 41
  Christian, 1, 12
  Eleanor, 12
  Elenor, 12
  Elizabeth, 53
  Jacob, 1, 25, 40,
    41
  John, 1, 12, 25, 40
  Magdalena, 1
  Magdolena, 12
  Maria, 54
  Mary, 41
  Nancy, 12
  Obedia, 41
  Peter, 40
  Philip, 1
  Rachel, 41
  Sarah, 41
  Solomon, 16, 30
  Thomas, 41
  Upton, 41
BRADY,
  John, 41
  John A., 41
  Mary, 41
  Robert, 41
  Robert W., 41
  Susan, 41
BRAGONIER,
  Barbara, 20
  Daniel, 25
  David, 25
  Elizabeth, 25
  Jacob, 25
  Samuel, 25
  Susan, 42
BRAND,
  Keziah, 22
  Kipey, 10
BRANSTATER,
  Andrew, 25
  Daniel, 25, 28
  Elizabeth, 12
  John, 12, 25
  Mary, 12
  Mary Ann, 12
BRANSTETTER,
  Daniel, 41

Magdalena, 41
BRANTETER,
  Catherine, 43
  Daniel, 43
BRANTNER,
  Andrew, 25
  Ann, 41
  Catherine, 24
  Eliza, 25, 41
  Elizabeth, 25
  George, 25, 41
  Henry, 25
  Jacob, 25, 41
  John, 25, 41
  Jonas, 41
  Levi, 41
  Mary, 41
  Michael, 25, 41
  Nelly, 50
  Samuel, 25, 41
  Susan, 41
BREAD,
  Mary, 28
BREAKBELL,
  John, 25
BREISCH,
  John D., 42
BRENDLE,
  Hannah, 41
  John, 41
  Maria Antoinette,
    41
BRENT,
  George, 1
  Thomas, 1
  Thomas C., 53
BRENTLINGER,
  Charlotte, 43
  William, 43
BRETT,
  Frances, 1
  Henry, 1
  Margaret, 1
BREWER,
  Adam, 41, 45
  Anna, 29
  Catherine, 41
  Daniel, 12
  Elizabeth, 12, 30,
    41, 43
  Gustavius, 25
  Jacob, 12, 25, 39,
    41
  John, 12, 25, 27,

INDEX

41, 43, 53
Jonathan, 27
Joseph, 27, 43
Margaret, 12
Martin, 41
Mary, 12, 25, 39, 43, 45, 53
Matilda, 41
Peter, 25
BREWORS,
Mary, 9
BRIDENBAUGH,
John, 5
BRIM,
Henry, 12
BROADSTONE,
Catherine, 12
Christina, 12
Nicholas, 12
Philip, 12
Sophia, 12
BROCIUS,
John, 52
BROOKHART,
David, 42
BROTHERTON,
Elizabeth, 1
BROWN,
Abraham, 41
Anna, 41
Barbara, 25
Barton, 41
Benjamin, 25, 41
Daniel, 41
Eleanor, 41
George, 25, 41
Haddalla, 41
Hanson, 25, 41
Henry, 10
Ignatius, 25, 41
Jacob, 10
John, 10, 41, 49
Josiah, 3
Lewis, 25, 41
Margaret, 31
Maria, 41
Mary, 10
Mary A., 41
Nancy, 49
Peter, 10
Rachel, 22
Rosanna, 33
Rosannah, 18

Samuel, 41, 54
Susa, 10
Tobias, 41
William, 41, 49
William D., 54
BRROOKHART,
David, 26
BRUMBAUGH,
Caroline, 25, 41
Catherine, 25
Daniel, 25, 41
David, 25
Elizabeth, 17, 25, 39, 41
George, 23, 25, 28, 40, 41, 44, 45, 48
Isabella, 25, 41
Jacob, 25
John, 25
Joseph, 25
Joshua, 25
Louisa, 25, 41
Margaret, 25
Maria, 25, 41
Samuel, 25, 41
Susanna, 25, 41
Thomas, 41
___, 17
BRUMLEY,
Eliza, 15
John, 15
BRUNNER,
Elizabeth, 28
Jacob, 15, 28
BRYAN,
Stephen, 12
BUCHER,
Catherine, 49
BUCK,
Marice, 19
BUMGARNER,
M., 7
BURCH,
Samuel, 25, 41
BURCKHART,
Catherine, 54
BURGAN,
Sally, 40
BURKART,
Christopher, 1
Daniel, 1
Elizabeth, 1
George, 1

Samuel, 1
BURKHART,
Daniel, 1
John, 1
BURNETT,
Catherine, 53
BUROLL,
Roan, 38
BURREL,
Elizabeth, 48
BURRIE,
Elizabeth, 48
BURTNER,
Henry, 52
BUSSARD,
Catherine, 46
BUTTERBAUGH,
Henry, 33
BUTTS,
Barbara, 14, 20
BYERS,
Catherine, 37
Joseph, 40

-C-
CADDERMAN,
Mary, 29
CALE,
Barbara, 8
Jacob, 8
CALIOUR,
Charles, 12
James, 12
Johan, 12
William, 12
CAMER,
Benjamin, 41
CAMERON,
Elizabeth, 5
CAMUS,
Magdalena, 36
CAPP,
Catherine, 6
Michael, 6, 12
CAPPER,
Mary, 4
CARBAUGH,
Jacob, 44
Mary, 44
Nancy, 52
Susanna, 44
CARDLE,
David, 41
Mary, 41

DISTRIBUTION OF ESTATE ACCOUNTS

Sarah, 41
William, 41
CARL, Mary, 45
CARLES,
  Daniel, 41
  David, 41
  John, 41
  Moses, 41
CARNACUM,
  Jacob, 25
CARR, John, 38
CARTER,
  Elizabeth, 41
  Esther, 24
  J., 41
  Jane, 41
  Josiah, 41
  Rebecca, 41
CARVER,
  Amelia, 44
  Christopher, 1
  Daniel, 44
CARY,
  Cyrus, 12
  Eleanor, 12
  Eliza, 12
  George, 12
  James, 12
  John, 12
  Robert, 12
  Robert T., 12
  William, 12
CATEY, 14
CATHERINE,
  Catherine, 6
CAUFFMAN,
  Jacob, 41
  Samuel, 41
  Simon, 41
CAUSETT,
  Catherine, 20
CAVE,
  Elizabeth, 9
CELLAR,
  George, 41
CELLARS,
  John, 9
CELLER,
  John, 17
CHANEY,
  David, 12
  Drusilla, 41
  Eliza, 41
  Elizabeth, 11,
    12
  Ellen, 42
  Ezekiel, 53
  Jacob, 53
  Jealeur, 11
  Jelsy, 41
  Jeremiah, 12, 41
  Jeremiah of
    Charles, 41
  John, 12, 42, 53
  Johnson, 41
  Johnston, 41
  Joseph, 53
  Luke, 41
  Margaret, 53
  Mary, 41
  Matilda, 41
  Prudence, 41
  Rebecca, 41
  Robert, 11, 41
  Samuel, 42
  Sarah, 49
  Thomas, 41
  William B., 41, 42
  William J., 41
CHANY,
  Amanda, 41
  Ann, 41
  Elanora, 41
  Jeremiah, 41
  John B., 41
  Lucretia, 41
  Luke, 41
  Prudence, 41
  Robert, 41
  Samuel, 41
  William, 41
CHAPLINE,
  Elizabeth, 12, 26
  James, 10
  Jeremiah, 12
  Joseph, 26
CHARLES,
  Joseph, 29
CHARLTON,
  Adam, 26
  Allien, 6
  James, 26
  John, 1, 14, 26
  Jonathan, 26
  Joshua, 14
  Mary, 26
  Sarah, 11, 14, 26
  Thomas, 3, 14, 26
  William, 26
CHENEY,
  Charles, 1
  Jeremiah, 1
CHEYNEY,
  Ann, 1
  Ezekiel, 1
  Joseph, 1
CHRIST,
  Henry, 46
CHRISTIAN,
  Casandra, 11
  Christine, 24
  Daniel, 42
  Jacob, 42
CLAGETT,
  Alfred, 42
  Eliza, 42
  Horatio, 42
  Matilda, 42
  Priscilla, 11
  Rachel, 42
  Robert, 42
  Samuel, 44
  Zachariah, 42
CLAGGETT,
  Alfred, 26
  Eliza, 26
  Haratio, 26
  Martin, 26
  Robert, 26
  Zachariah, 26
CLAPPER,
  Catherine, 1
  Elizabeth, 1
  Harman, 1
  Henry, 19
  John, 1
  Mary, 1, 15
CLAPSADDLE,
  Daniel, 42
  Jacob, 42
  Mary, 34, 50
CLARK,
  Robert, 4
CLARKE,
  Isabella, 2
  James, 2
  Mathew, 2
  Robert, 43
  Sarah, 2, 43
CLAYTON,
  Daniel, 49
CLEMM, Adam, 2

INDEX

CLINE,
  Andrew, 37
  Catherine, 12, 36
  Daniel, 12
  George, 50
CLINESMITH,
  Barbara, 6
CLINGAN,
  William, 42
CLOM,
  Mary, 12
  Rebecca, 12
  Richard, 12
  Sarah, 12
CLOPPER,
  Christian, 2
  Elizabeth, 2
  Henry, 12
  John, 2, 29, 45
  Mathias, 12
  Matthias, 12
  Nancy, 47
CLYMER,
  Edward, 29
  Maria, 29
COAKLEY,
  Sarah, 51, 52
COBACK,
  Christine, 36
COCHENOUR,
  Feronica, 9
  Jacob, 9
COFFMAN,
  Anna, 33
  Barbara, 39
  Henry, 39
  John, 39
  Mary, 39
COLE,
  Ann, 4
COLEBACK,
  Catherine, 5
COLEMAN,
  Betsey, 24, 40
COLEVIN,
  John, 26
COLLEFLOWER,
  Catherine, 3
  George, 28
COLLIER,
  Elizabeth, 29
  William, 29

COLLIFLOWER,
  George, 42
  John, 42
  Peter, 42
COLLOFLOWER,
  ___, 15
COMBS,
  Colman, 12
  Eliza, 12
  John, 12, 13, 14
  Lewis, 12, 13
  Mary, 12, 13
  Nancy, 12
  Ruth, 12
  Thomas, 12, 13
COMFORT,
  Constant, 12
CONFER,
  Elizabeth, 40
  George, 40
CONN,
  Peter, 13, 26, 27
CONRAD,
  Daniel, 12
  Jacob, 12, 34
  Venter, 12
  William, 12
CONROD,
  Catherine, 2
  Daniel, 2
  Elizabeth, 2
  Jacob, 2
  John, 2
  Margaret, 2
CONTZ,
  Elizabeth, 47
COOK,
  Alexander, 42
  Charlotte, 42
  David, 42
  Elizabeth, 42
  George, 42
  Henry, 42
  John, 18, 42
  Samuel, 42
  William, 42
COOKE,
  Catherine, 24
COON,
  Catherine, 21
  John, 40, 42
  Joseph, 42
  Susan, 40

COPES,
  Esther, 18
  William, 18
CORE,
  Barbara, 15
  Christian, 4, 37
  Christine, 22, 24, 39
  Eliza, 22, 37
  Elizabeth, 4, 37
  Magdalena, 22, 37
  Rozanna, 4
COSSROTH,
  Conrod, 2
COST,
  Magdalen, 39
  Magdalena, 24
  William, 30
COWAN,
  Mary, 12
  Robert, 14
COX,
  Abraham, 2
  Ezekiel, 2
CRAIG,
  John, 26
  Sarah, 30
CRAMER,
  Daniel, 42
  David, 42
  Elizabeth, 12, 42
  Godfred, 12
  Jacob, 42
  John, 12
  Mary, 42
CRAMPTON,
  Ann Mary M., 26
  Elias, 26, 42
  Elie, 26, 30, 42, 45
  Elizabeth, 42
  Harmon, 42
  John, 26, 42
  Joshua, 42
  Josiah, 26, 42
  Oliver, 42
  Sarah E., 42
  Susanna, 42
  Thomas, 26
  Thomas H., 26, 42
  Thomas W., 42
CRAVER,
  John, 5
  Mary, 5

DISTRIBUTION OF ESTATE ACCOUNTS

CREAGER,
  Mary, 43
  Sarah, 40
  William, 43
CREEBAUM,
  Adam, 2
  Barbara, 2
  Christian, 2
  Eve Mary, 2
  Phillip, 2
CRESAP,
  Elizabeth, 2
  Jacob, 2
  Jeremiah, 2
  John, 2
  Mary, 2
  Michael, 2
  Sarah, 2
CRETZER,
  John, 11
CRISE,
  Elizabeth, 40
CRIST,
  Margaret, 5
CROMRINE,
  Ann Elizabeth, 51
CROMWELL,
  Maria Catherine, 12
  Richard, 12
  Susan, 17
  William, 12
CROOK,
  Jacob, 53
CROUSE,
  Peter, 10
  Rosanna, 22, 37
CRUMBAUGH,
  Catherine, 20
CULP,
  Catherine, 16, 30
CUNNINGHAM,
  Samuel S., 42
CUSHWA,
  Benjamin, 12, 30
  Benjamine, 12
  Betsey, 12
  Catherine, 20, 35, 36
  Christian, 12
  David, 12
  Elizabeth, 12
  Jacob, 12
  John, 4, 8, 12, 20, 36
  Jonathan, 12
  Margaret, 12
  Sarah, 12
  Sophia, 39
CUSTARD,
  Susanna, 31
CYMAN,
  Susannah, 52

-D-

DAGAN,
  Adam, 12
  Danise, 12
  Jacob, 12
DANIEL,
  Daniel, 43
DARBY,
  Henry, 42
  John, 42
  Noamia, 12
DARLING,
  John, 6, 12
DARR,
  Elizabeth, 2
  Jacob, 2
  John, 2
  Philip, 2
  Phillip, 2
DAVID,
  Eve, 43
DAVIE,
  Christine, 22
DAVIS,
  Abigail, 43
  Althea, 6
  Ann, 2
  Caley, 2
  Catherine, 2
  Charles, 12, 26
  Christian, 37
  Daniel 47
  David, 2
  Dennis, 7, 18
  Elizabeth, 26
  Eve, 14, 27
  George W., 26
  Hanson, 2
  Henry, 2
  James, 12, 26
  John, 2, 26
  Joshua, 2
  Kitty, 26
  Lodwick, 8
  Mary, 11, 12, 26
  Mrs., 31
  Nicholas, 2
  Raphel, 10
  Richard, 2
  Rith, 2
  Samuel, 26
  Sophia, 26
  Stephen, 12, 26
  Suzanna, 10
  Thomas, 10
  William, 12, 26
DAVISON,
  Robert, 1
DEAAN,
  Hezekeah, 48
  John, 48
  Rebecca, 48
DEAKIN,
  Esther, 4
  Thomas, 4
DEAN,
  Jacob, 31
  Linda, 31
DEANER,
  Christian, 43, 52
  Samuel, 52
DEEDS,
  Adam, 12
DEIHL,
  George, 51
DEITRICK,
  Barbara, 16
DELL,
  Catherine, 2
  Christian, 2
  George, 2
  Jacob, 2
  John, 2
  Polly, 2
DELLAHUNT,
  Catherine, 13
  John T., 26
  Mary, 26
  Mary Ann, 26
  Mordica, 26
  William, 13
DELMAR,
  Catherine, 10
DELTZ,
  Ann, 14

INDEX

DEMOND,
  Barnabas, 26
  John, 26
  Nancy, 26
DENOR,
  Catherine, 16
  Christian, 26
  Samuel, 26
  Yost, 26
DETWILER,
  Jacob, 43
  Samuel, 43
DICK,
  Adam, 42
  Catherine, 42
  Christian, 42
  David, 42
  Elizabeth, 2
  Eve, 18, 34, 42
  Henry, 42
  Jacob, 42
  John, 2, 42
  Mary, 2, 8, 42
  Peter, 2, 6
  Rebecca, 2
DICKEY,
  Archibald, 42
  Ezekiel, 42
  John, 42
  Matthew, 42
  Samuel, 42
  William, 42
DIEDIE,
  Henry, 26
  Solomon, 26
DIGON,
  Elizabeth, 40
DILLAHUNT,
  James, 13, 47
  John, 13
  Thomas, 13
  William, 13
DILLMAN,
  Harry, 12
DILLON,
  Elizabeth, 45
DITNZMAN,
  Mary, 21
DITTO,
  Abraham, 42
  Elizabeth, 50
  James B., 42
  Samuel, 43
  William, 3, 42, 43
DIXON,
  Elizabeth, 40
DOIL,
  Adam, 2
  Catherine, 2
  Conrad, 2
  George, 2
  Henry, 2
  Mary, 2
DONAVAN,
  James D., 42
  John, 42
  Robert, 42
  William, 42
DONER,
  Elizabeth, 24
DONNER,
  Elizabeth, 24
DORSEY,
  Benjamin, 42
  Edgar, 42
  Edward, 42
  Eliza, 42
  Elizabeth, 20
  Francis, 42
  John, 42
  Margaretta, 42
  Mary I., 42
  Philip, 42
DOUGLAS,
  Joseph, 2
  Mary, 2
  Rachel, 2
  Robert, 2
  Samuel, 2
  Sarah, 12
  William, 2
DOUGLASS,
  Rebecca, 13
DOUP,
  Catherine, 22, 37
DOVENBERGER,
  John, 36
  Mary, 42
DOWELIN,
  Peggy, 14
DOWIN,
  Susan, 45
DOWLAR,
  Richard, 6
DOWLER,
  Edward, 2
  Frances, 2
  George, 2
  Jane, 2
  John, 2
  Joseph, 2
  Richard, 2, 6
  Robert, 2
  Sally, 2
  Thomas, 2
DOWNER,
  Elizabeth, 39
DOWNES,
  Adaline, 42
  Arey, 42
  Lewis, 42
  Washington, 42
  Widow, 54
  William, 42
DOWNEY,
  Elizabeth, 2
  Henry, 12
  Isabella, 2
  Jean, 2
  Joseph, 2
  Polly, 2
  Robert, 2, 13
  Samuel, 2, 13
  William, 2, 13
DOWNY,
  William C., 25
DOYLE,
  Adam, 13
  Ann, 25
  Doren, 13
  George, 13
  Henry, 13
  John, 13
DREELING,
  John, 2
DRURY,
  William, 41
DUBLE,
  Henry, 31
DUFFY,
  John, 36
  Mary, 36
DUGAN,
  Mary, 26
DUKWALK,
  Catherine, 52
DUMWODIE,
  David, 2
DUNCAN,
  Daniel, 45
  Hamet A. L., 45

DISTRIBUTION OF ESTATE ACCOUNTS

DUNDORE,
  John, 26
DUNN,
  Eve, 14
  Jacob, 30, 33, 46
  John, 30, 46
  Susanna, 19
  Susannah, 18
DUSHWA,
  Catherine, 50
  David, 50
DUSING,
  Catherine, 42
  Elizabeth, 2, 32, 42, 48
  John, 2, 42
  Mary, 2
  Paul, 2
  Philip, 2, 42
  Susanna, 2
DUVALT,
  Elioner, 2
  Jeremiah, 2
  Richard, 2

-E-
EACLE,
  Absolem, 42
  Fanney, 42
  John D., 44
  Martin, 42
  William, 42
EAKLE,
  Absolom, 42
  Amos, 26
  Christian, 42, 26
  Harmon, 2
  Henry, 42, 18, 33
  Jacob, 42
  John, 42, 2
  Judith, 14, 27, 43
  Martin, 42
  Peter, 2
  Philip, 2
  William, 40, 47
EARHART,
  Jacob, 12
  Philip, 8
EASON,
  Elisha, 13

John, 13
Ruth, 13
William, 13
EASTER,
  Adam, 2
  Craile, 2
  Jacob, 2
  Mary, 4
  Mattelena, 2
  Painter, 2
  Peter, 2
EASTON,
  Elisha, 11, 26
  Heziakiah, 26
  John, 26
  Matilda, 11
  Sarah, 11
  William, 26
EATENIRE,
  Doratha, 8
EBY,
  Elizabeth, 15, 29
ECHART,
  Elizabeth, 8
ECHELBERGER,
  Rosena, 7
ECKELBERGER,
  Catherine, 12
  Devolt, 5
  Theobold, 35
ECKERT,
  Rebecca, 29
  William, 29
ECKHART,
  Margaret, 18
ECKLE,
  John, 26
  Linny, 26
  Peggy, 26
  Polly, 26
  Sally, 26
ECKLEBERGER,
  Jacob, 27
  John, 27
  Michael, 17
  Theobald, 20, 35
EDWARDS,
  Benjamin, 13
  Editha, 13
  Emmory, 13
  John, 13
  Maria, 21
  Mary, 12, 13
  Owen, 13

Paregrine, 13
Thomas, 13
EICHELBERGER,
  Theobald, 35
ELBZROTE,
  Catherine, 33
ELENBAUGH,
  Mary, 13
ELINBAUGH,
  Mary, 27
ELLIOTT,
  Jessee D., 45
ELLIS,
  Mary, 14, 27
EMERICK,
  Ludwick, 4
EMICK,
  Amelia, 42
  George, 42
  Jacob, 42
  John, 42
  John H., 42
  Susannah, 42, 43
  William, 42
EMIL,
  John, 11, 24
  Sarah, 24
  Susanna, 11
EMMERT,
  Benjamin, 13
  Catherine, 13
  Daniel, 13
  Elizabeth, 50
  George, 13
  John, 13
  Joseph, 13, 35, 44
  Leonard, 13
  Magdalena, 13
  Michael, 13
  Sarah, 50, 52
EMRECK,
  Susanna, 29
EMRICH,
  Dorothy, 2
  Elizabeth, 2
  Jacob, 2
  John, 2
  Jonas, 2
  Magdalena, 2
  Margaret, 2
  Roxanna, 2
ENGLISH,
  Uliana, 6

INDEX

ENSMINGER,
  Catherine, 27
  Christian, 27
  Chrsitian, 27
  David, 27
  Elizabeth, 27
  Eve, 27
  Margaret, 27
  Martin, 27
  Mary, 27
  Philip, 27
  Sodwick, 27
ERICKSON,
  Rebecca, 31
EVANS,
  Daniel, 42
  John, 42
EVERSOLE,
  Christian, 13, 27
  Emanuel, 13, 27
EVEY,
  Catherine, 36

-F-
FACHERHOF,
  Catherine, 19
FACHERHOOF,
  Catherine, 19
FACKLER,
  Martha, 6
FAGAN,
  Barbara, 2
  John, 2
FAGUE,
  George, 37, 54
  Nancy, 54
FAITH,
  Elizabeth, 45
  Jacob, 45
  Lewis, 45
  Margarth, 45
  Susannah, 45
FAUSNAUGHT,
  Abraham, 13
  Adam, 13
  Anna, 20
  Anna Maria, 13
  Barbara, 13, 20
  Barnett, 13
  Catherine, 13
  Conrad, 13
  Dorathy, 13
  Elizabeth, 13, 37
  Eve, 13
  George, 13
  Henry, 13, 14
  Jacob, 13
  John, 13, 14
  Julianna, 13, 14
  Maria, 13
  Motlena, 20
  Sarah, 13
  Susanna, 13
  Susannah, 13, 20
  Ulianna, 13
  ___, 27
FEAS,
  Nancy, 39
  Samuel, 39
FECHTIG,
  Christian, 42
  Christian C., 42
  Frederick, 42
  George, 42, 54
  Jacob, 42
  John H., 42
  Sarah, 24
FECTIG,
  George, 46
FEIRY,
  Catherine, 2, 27
  Henry, 2, 11, 50
  Jacob, 2
  John, 2, 27
  Joseph, 2, 27, 30
  Solomon, 27
FELKER,
  Abraham, 42
  Ezra, 42
  Henry, 42
  Jacob, 42
  John, 42
FELKERS,
  Abraham, 42
  Ezra, 42
  Henry, 42
  Jacob, 42
  John, 42
FELLER,
  Jacob, 7
FERROLL,
  Francis, 14
  John, 14
  Patrick, 14
FESLER,
  Catherine, 15
FESSLER,
  Barbara, 46
  Elizabeth, 27, 42
  Henry, 52
  Jacob, 42
  Mary, 27, 42
FIBLE,
  Ann, 8
  Frederick, 8
FIERY,
  Benjamin F., 43
  Daniel, 43
  Elizabeth, 43
  Henry, 43, 48
  Jacob, 43, 44
  John, 43
  Joseph, 43
  Solomon, 43
  Susanna, 37
  William H., 43
FIGALEY,
  Margaret, 40
FIGALY,
  William, 27
FILENGAME,
  Nancy, 48
FILLIGRIN,
  Ann, 32
FINECY,
  Nancy, 31
FINEFROCK,
  Daniel, 48
FINK,
  Andrew, 43
  Barbara, 43
  Christian, 43
  Daniel, 43
  George W., 43
  Jacob, 43
  John, 43
  Mary, 43
  Michael, 43
  Susannah, 43
FINLEY,
  Michael, 27
FIRESTONE,
  Susanna, 28
FIREY,
  John, 27
  Joseph, 27
  Solomon, 27
  Susannah, 52
FISHACK,
  Mary, 41

DISTRIBUTION OF ESTATE ACCOUNTS

FISHAWK,
  Frederick, 14, 27
FISHER,
  Ann, 1, 2
  Daniel, 2
  Eliza, 10
  Elizabeth, 2
  Jacob, 2, 5, 10
  John, 2, 5, 10
  Mary, 2
  Susanna, 1
FITZ,
  Catherine, 42
FITZPATRICK,
  Charity, 4
FLECK,
  Andrew, 3
  William, 3
FLEMING,
  Archibald, 52
FLEMMING,
  James, 40
  Mary, 40
FLENER,
  Catherine, 1
FLENNER,
  Susanne, 25
FLETCHER,
  Lewis, 40, 41, 54
FLICK,
  Andrew, 3
  William, 3
FLOCKER,
  Jacob, 22
FLORA,
  Adam, 27
  Christopher, 27
  Conrad, 14, 19, 23, 34
  Elizabeth, 14, 27
  John, 14, 27
  Margaret, 19, 34
  Nancy, 14, 27
FLOREY,
  Christopher, 26
FLORY,
  Christian, 49
  Christopher, 42
  Conrad, 54
  Elizabeth, 33
  Nancy, 47

FLUKE,
  Henry, 7
  John, 7
FOARD,
  E., 6
  Elinor, 6
  Esther, 3
  Hannah, 3
  Henry, 3
  Hugh, 3
  James, 3
  John, 3
  Rachel, 3
  Robert, 3
FOCKLER,
  Michael, 8
FOGLE,
  George, 14
  Jacob, 14
  John, 14, 20
FOGLER,
  Andrew, 3
FOGLESONG,
  Barbara, 3
  Catherine, 3
  Christian, 3
  David, 3
  Frederick, 3
  John, 3
FOGWELL,
  Catherine, 15
FOLTZ,
  Catherine, 43
  George, 43
  Jacob, 43
FOPLER,
  David, 14
  Mary, 14
  Sarah, 14
FORD,
  Abigail, 14, 27
  Henry, 14, 27
  Joseph, 14, 27
  Martha M., 31
  Thomas, 31
FOREMAN,
  Hannah, 50
  Joseph, 45
  Mary, 50
  Nancy, 50
FORMAN,
  Jacob I., 14
  John, 14
  Mary, 14

FORNEY,
  Elizabeth, 10
FORQUER,
  Elizabeth, 4
FOSSLER,
  Elizabeth, 27
  Mary, 27
FOSTER,
  George, 54
  John, 54
  Mary M., 54
  Samuel, 54
  Sarah, 19, 34
FOUTZ,
  Charlotte, 14
  David, 14, 43
  Frederick, 14, 43
  George, 14, 43
  Henry, 14, 43
  Jacob, 14, 22, 43
  John, 14
  Peggy, 14
  Susanna, 17, 43
  Susannah, 14
  William, 14, 43
FOX,
  Frederick, 6
FRANK, 14
FRANTZ,
  Catherine, 14
  Elizabeth, 14
  Emanuel, 14
  Eve, 14
  Frederick, 14
  George, 14
  Henry, 14
  Julian, 14
  Leddia, 14
  Mary, 14
  Nathaniel, 14
FRAZIER,
  Falder, 43
  Finley, 43
  Hale, 43
  Henry, 43
  Horatio, 43
  Jeremiah, 43
  Loyd, 43
  Otho H., 43
  Sophia, 43
FREDERICK,
  Frederick, 6
FRENCH,
  Barbara, 3

INDEX

Catherine, 3
George, 3, 16, 35
John, 3
Peter, 3
FRENER,
  John, 30
FRITZ,
  Catherine, 42
  Nicholas, 11
FRY,
  Christian, 3
  Lavinia, 37
  Rebecca, 3
  Susanna, 22, 37
FRYE,
  Abraham, 14
  Frederick, 14
  Jacob, 14
  John, 14
  Joseph, 14
  William, 14
FRYOR,
  Motlena, 10
FUAH,
  David, 31
FUGATE,
  John, 3, 14
  Mary, 14
  Peter, 3
FULTZ,
  Catherine, 27, 28
  George, 27
  Henry, 27
  Jacob, 27
  John, 27, 28
  Motelena, 27
  Susanna, 27
FUNK,
  Ann, 3, 27, 49
  Barbara, 10
  Catherine, 3
  Daniel, 3, 14, 42
  David, 3, 14, 20, 27, 42
  Elizabeth, 3, 28
  Hannah, 27
  Henry, 3, 6, 9, 10, 14, 27
  Henry (of John), 3, 14
  Jacob, 3, 27
  John, 3, 9, 14, 27, 42
  Joseph, 3
  Magdalena, 39, 46
  Margaret, 3
  Martin, 3, 14, 27, 46
  Mary, 3, 14
  Mary Ann, 3
  Michael, 26, 41
  Nancy, 27
  Neoma, 41
  Neomy, 41
  Peter, 26
  Sarah, 3
  Susan, 48
  Susanna, 3, 26
  Susannah, 27, 43
FURGASON,
  James, 43
FURRY,
  Catherine, 13, 27
  David, 27
  Elizabeth, 27
  Frederick, 43
  John, 27
  Martin, 27
FUSS,
  Elizabeth, 52

-G-

GABBY,
  Joseph, 38
  William, 35, 38
GABLE,
  Abraham, 3
  Ann, 3
  Isabella, 3
  William, 3
GABRIEL,
  Catherine, 43
  John, 43
  Josiah, 43
  William, 17
GACHARIA,
  George, 30
GAINER,
  Rosanna, 34
  Rosannah, 18
GALE,
  Baltzer, 1
  Benjamin, 14, 47
  Catherine, 14, 47
  James, 14
  Jim, 47
  Mary, 14
  William, 14
GANTZ,
  Nicholas, 27
GARBER,
  Elizabeth, 16, 22
  Jacob, 38
GARBRON,
  Rosana, 50
GARDENOUR,
  Catherine, 3
  Jacob, 3
  John, 3
GARLOCK,
  Catherine, 28
  Christian, 14
  Jacob, 14
  John, 14
GARRET,
  Hannah, 40
GARRETT,
  Mary Ann, 26, 42
GARVER,
  William, 46
GARVIN,
  Elizabeth, 50
GARY,
  Elizabeth, 43
  Eve, 14
  George, 14, 27, 43
  Judith, 14
  Mary, 14, 27, 43
  Sarah, 14
  Susanna, 14
GATES,
  Elizabeth, 43
  Joseph, 43
  Sarah, 43
  Susan, 43
  William, 43
  William B., 43
GAUSNAUGHT,
  Elizabeth, 37
GAYLORD,
  Elizabeth, 28
GEARHART,
  Catherine, 27
  Christian, 27, 28
  Daniel, 27, 28
  Elizabeth, 27
  Eve, 46
  Henry, 27, 28
  Jacob, 28

DISTRIBUTION OF ESTATE ACCOUNTS

John, 27, 28
Jonas, 27
Mary, 27
Sophia, 28
Susanna, 27
GEETING,
  George, 15
  George A., 15
  Henry, 15
  Jacob, 15
  John, 48
  Peter, 15
  Simon, 15
GEHR,
  Andrew, 28
  Anne, 29
  Catherine, 28, 43
  Daniel, 28, 43
  David, 28
  Denton, 43
  George, 28, 32, 43
  Isaac, 28, 43
  Margaret, 43, 27
  Mary, 43
  Samuel, 28, 29
  Susannah, 27
  William, 43
GEIER,
  Jacob, 48
GEIGER,
  Amelia, 15
  Eleanor, 15
  Eleanora, 15, 28
  Eliza, 15
  Elizabeth, 15, 28
  Frances, 15
  Francis, 28
  George, 15
  Henrietta, 15, 28
  Jacob, 15
  Jacob H., 15, 28
  John, 15, 28, 33
  Peter, 15
  Susannah, 15
GEISER,
  Elizabeth, 43
  Frederick, 28, 43
  John, 28, 43
  Martin, 28, 43

Michael, 28
Peter, 28, 43
GELTMAKER,
  E., 50
  Elizabeth, 50
  John, 50
  Margaret, 50
GELWICKS,
  Ann, 42
  Charles, 28
  Elizabeth, 28
  Frederick, 28
  George, 28
  George C., 28
  John, 28
GENTIACE,
  Eve, 3
GEORGE, 14
GETTING,
  Elizabeth, 43
GETZ,
  Catherine, 36
GIBBENY,
  John, 42
GILBERT,
  Jacob B., 28
  Margaret, 32
  Peter, 28
  Wendel, 28
GILL,
  Maria, 53
GILLET,
  Lettina, 4
GILLIUM,
  Elizabeth, 8
GINGLER,
  Mary, 12
  Michael, 12
GINGRICK,
  George, 39
  Mary, 39
GITMAN,
  Jacob, 41
GITTINGER,
  Jacob, 28
  John, 28
  Samuel, 28
  Sarah, 28
  Susanna, 28
GLECKNER,
  Devolt, 28
  Elizabeth, 28
  Jacob, 28
  Joseph, 28

Rosanna, 28
Susanna, 28
GLOSSBRENNER,
  Abraham, 3
  Adam, 3
  Gadfrey, 3
  Godfrey, 3
  Gutlep, 3
  Jacob, 3
  John, 3
  Lucretia, 35
  Preston, 3
  Susanna, 3
GOLDING,
  Palmer, 3
GOLE,
  Benjamin, 31
  Catherine, 31, 48
  James, 31
GOLL,
  Balzer, 19
  Maria, 21
GONCE,
  Nicholas, 28
GONTZ,
  Catherine, 5
  Mary, 29
  Sarah, 5
GOOD,
  Abraham, 28
  Christian, 21, 28
  David, 28
  Jacob, 28
  John, 15, 28
  Joseph, 28, 39
  Josiah, 15
  Peter, 28
  William, 15, 28
GOODY,
  Susannah, 42
GORDAN,
  Susannah, 13
GORDON,
  Henry, 40
  Mary, 47
  Matilda, 40
  Susannah, 13
GOSSARD,
  Barbara, 39
  John, 39
GOWER,
  Elizabeth, 45
  Margaret, 42

INDEX

GRAFF,
  Joseph, 32, 45
  Rebecca, 46
GRAFFIN,
  Christina, 6
GRAIL,
  Elizabeth, 21
GRAUFF,
  George, 12
GRAY,
  Abraham, 3
  Aleathea, 42
  Catherine, 3
  Easter, 3
  Elizabeth, 3,
    26, 42
  John, 3
  Joseph, 3
  Peggy, 3
  Peter, 3
  Samuel, 3, 4
GRAYBILL,
  Michael, 46
GRAYHAM,
  Elizabeth, 1
GREIDER,
  Martin, 5
GREY,
  Anna, 28
  Catherine, 28
  Elizabeth, 15,
    28
  George, 15, 28
  John, 15, 28
  Joseph, 15, 28
  Mary, 15
  Peter, 15, 17
  Samuel, 15, 28
  Susannah, 15
GRICE,
  Elizabeth, 48
GRIER,
  Jacob, 49
GRIFFIN,
  Christina, 6
GRIFFITH,
  Daniel, 22, 37
  Eliza, 15
  Elizabeth, 15
  Sarah, 22, 37
  Sylvanus, 15
GRIM,
  Abraham, 28, 41
  Amelia, 44

B., 28
Barbara, 28
Benjamin, 28
Cassandra, 44
Daniel, 46
David, 44
Elizabeth, 44
Mary, 16
Mary Ann, 44
Nathaniel, 44
Susanna, 50
GRIMES, James, 2
GRISE,
  John, 18
  Magdalena, 18
GROFF,
  Barbara, 27
  Joseph, 30
GROSH,
  Frederick, 17
GROUND,
  Elizabeth, 15
  George, 15, 28, 44
  John, 15, 28, 44
  Joseph, 15, 50
  Philip, 15, 28, 44
  Sarah, 15
GROVE,
  David, 26
  Francy, 10
  Henry, 28
  Jacob, 28
  Jacob H., 49
  John, 28
  Mary, 2
  Paul, 28
  Peter, 28
  Philip, 28
  Stephen, 28
GRUBB, Andrew, 2
GRUBER,
  David, 50
  Elizabeth, 50
  Isaac, 50
  Jacob, 50
  Nancy, 50
  Samuel, 50
  Sarah, 50
GRUSH,
  Catherine, 21
GUCHAREAH,
  Elizabeth, 14
GUISER,

Elizabeth, 3
Frederick, 3
Mathias, 3
GUNDERMAN,
  C. L. D., 28
GUSH,
  Catherine, 21

-H-
HAFLEBOWER,
  Sarah, 9
HAFLEY,
  Christian, 3
HAFTER,
  Sophia, 32
HAGER,
  Christian, 19, 29,
    44
  David, 41
  Elizabeth R., 44
  John, 9, 29, 41
  Jonathan, 44
  Jonathan J., 44
  Magdalena, 29, 44
  Margaret, 41
  Maria A., 41
  Mary, 6
  Matilda, 41
  Simon, 35
HAGERMAN,
  Christian, 3
  Christopher, 3
  John, 3
  Sarah, 3
HAHN,
  Christine, 28
  David, 28
  George, 28
  Henry, 28
  John, 28
  Margaret, 28, 46
  Mary, 22
HAINE, Barbara, 12
HAINES,
  Adam, 28
  David, 28
  Jacob, 28
  John, 28
  Mary, 28
HALL,
  Emily H., 48
  Hannah M., 48
  Henry, 46
  John, 32, 48

DISTRIBUTION OF ESTATE ACCOUNTS

Margaret, 36
HALLAMN,
  Mary Ann, 53
HALLER,
  Barbara, 15
  Daniel, 15
  Jacob, 15
  John, 15
  Samuel, 15
  Susannah, 15
HAM,
  P., 22
HAMER,
  Isaac, 27
  Susanna, 27
HAMILTON,
  Ann Mary, 44
  Henry, 44
  James H., 44
  Julian, 44
  William I., 44
HAMISH,
  Mrs., 43
HAMM,
  Catherine, 44
  George, 44
  Margaret, 44
  Peter, 44
  Sarah, 44
HAMMACKER,
  Adam, 28
  Daniel, 28
  Elizabeth, 28
  Mariah, 28
  Peter, 28
  Rebecca, 28
  Samuel, 28
  Susanna, 28
HAMMAKER,
  Polly, 47
  Stewart, 39
HAMMEL,
  Elizabeth, 15
  George, 15
  Isaac, 15
  John, 15
  Joseph, 15
HAMMETT,
  Catherine, 3
  James, 3
  Mary, 3
  McKelbie, 3
  Sarah, 3
  William, 3

HAMMOND,
  Ann, 49
  Catherine, 18, 33
  David, 44
  Elias, 44
  Elizabeth, 36
  Jacob, 29
  John, 12, 13, 29, 36, 51
  Joseph H., 44
  Levina, 44
  Luciann, 44
  Margaret, 33
  Michael, 29
  Paul, 29
  Peter, 29
  Philip, 29, 44
HAMPTON,
  John, 44
  Thomas, 44
  William, 44
HANER,
  Anthony, 44
  Daniel, 44
  George, 44
  Jacob, 29
  Jonathan, 44
  Martin, 44
  Rosannah, 44
HANN,
  Peter, 4
HANNAH,
  Sophia, 28
HANNER,
  Michael, 12
HARBAUGH,
  Elizabeth, 5, 52, 54
  George, 52
  John, 23
  Mary, 5
HAREY, John, 15
HARGRAVE,
  Jacob, 23
HARLAND,
  Braden, 44
  Daniel, 44
  Esther, 44
  James, 44
  John, 44
  Samuel, 44
  Solomon, 44
HARLIN,
  Esther, 27

HARLIS,
  Esther, 14
HARMAN,
  Catherine, 39
HARNISH,
  Mrs., 43
HARPER,
  Ann, 9
  Polly, 9
HARRY,
  Amelia, 46
  Andrew, 3
  Charles, 3
  Daniel, 22
  David, 2, 3, 18, 20, 30, 33
  Elizabeth, 8, 15
  Esther, 22
  George, 15
  George I., 15
  Hannah, 15
  Iona, 3
  Jacob, 3, 9, 10, 15, 46
  John, 3, 15, 24, 25, 28, 33
  Margaret, 46
  Martin, 3, 8, 10, 15
  Mary, 15
  Mary E., 15
  Samuel, 15
  Sarah, 15
  Susannah, 15
HART,
  Jacob, 37
HARTER,
  David, 29
  Elizabeth, 19
  George, 29
  Jacob, 19, 29
  John, 29
  Judith, 29
HARTLE,
  Bostian, 3
  Eave, 3
  Frederick, 3
  George, 3
  John, 47
  Martin, 3
  Michael, 3
  Peggy, 3
HARTMAN,
  B., 31

INDEX

Fudid, 31
HARWOOD,
  George, 3
  John, 3
HASLETT,
  Sophia, 48
HASSEN,
  P., 7
HATTER,
  Sarah, 37, 53
HAUER,
  Christian, 20
  Daniel, 47
HAUSER,
  Mary, 4
HAWKEN,
  Christian, 29
  George, 29, 44
  Jacob, 29, 44
  John, 29
  Juliana, 44
  Lewis, 44
  Nancy, 29, 44
  Samuel, 29, 44
  William, 29, 44
HAWLEYBOWER,
  Balsor, 4
HAWN,
  Elizabeth, 23
HAYES,
  Jeremiah, 29
  P., 29
  Simon, 20
HAYNES,
  Samuel, 41
HAYS,
  Christina M., 44
  Daniel, 44
  John, 44
HEAFER,
  Catherine, 4
  Elizabeth, 4
  Frederick, 4
  Howard, 4
  Jacob, 4
  John, 4
  Peter, 4
  Phetty, 4
  Rebecca, 4
  Susannah, 4
HEAFNER,
  Barbara, 5
HEALING,
  Sarah, 11

HEAVER,
  Peggy, 17
  Rosannah, 17
HEBB,
  William F., 51
HECK,
  Andrew, 15, 29
  Barbara, 15
  Drusilla, 41
  Henry, 15, 29, 41
  Jacob, 15
  John, 15
  Peter, 15
HECKMAN,
  Benjamin L., 44
  Mathias, 29
  Samuel P. C., 44
HECKROTE,
  Henry, 15
  John, 15
HECROTE,
  Daniel, 19
HEDDEMAN,
  Hannah, 50
HEDDRICK,
  George, 4, 22
  Jacob, 4
  John, 4
  Joseph, 4
  Warner, 4
HEDRICK,
  Christian, 11
  George, 44
HEFFLEICH,
  Amelia L., 29
  Ann Maria, 29
  Elizabeth, 29
  John, 29
  Magdalena, 29
  Matilda, 29
HEFFLEY,
  Charles, 15
  Elie, 4
  Henry, 15
  Jacob, 4
  Magdalena, 24
  Michael, 4, 15
  Peter, 18, 33
  Samuel, 4
HEFFLICH,
  Ann M., 44
  Elizabeth, 44
  John, 44
  Peter, 44

HEFLEIGH,
  Ann M., 44
  Elizabeth, 44
  John, 44
  Peter, 44
HEISTER,
  Catherine, 29
  Daniel J., 29
  Elizabeth Rosanna, 29
  Isaac, 29
  John P., 29
  Matilda, 41
  Rosanna, 29
  Rosannah, 44
  William, 29
HEITT,
  Catherine, 35
  Elizabeth, 35
HELLER,
  Daniel, 39, 40
  Elizabeth, 46
HELM,
  Joseph, 4, 15, 29
  Margaret, 15, 29
  Meredith, 15, 29
  Sarah, 15, 29
  Sophia, 29
  Sp___, 15
  Thomas, 4, 15, 29
  Thomas E., 48
HELTZER,
  Daniel, 4
  David, 4
  John, 4
  Mary, 4
HENRECTH,
  Peter, 4
HENRY,
  John, 50
  Michael, 50
HENSHAW,
  Catherine, 28
HERBERT,
  Sarah, 49
HERR,
  Henry, 29
  John, 53
  John P., 28
  Joseph, 29
  Mary, 20
  Rudolph, 29
HERSH,
  David, 15

DISTRIBUTION OF ESTATE ACCOUNTS

Elizabeth, 15, 44
Fanny, 15
Frederick, 44
George, 15
Henry, 15
Jacob, 15
HERSHEY,
  Andrew, 29, 39
  Catherine, 44
  Christian, 29, 44
  David, 29
  Elizabeth, 39
  Henry, 32
  Jacob, 23, 25, 29, 38
  John, 29, 46
  Joseph, 29, 54
  Margaret, 23, 38
  Mary, 44
  Nancy, 44
  Sophia, 46
  Susan, 44
HERSHY,
  Andrew, 15
  Barbara, 15
  Christian, 15
  David, 15
  Isaac, 15
  John, 15
  Joseph, 15
HESONG,
  Peter, 14
HESS,
  David, 16
  Elizabeth, 16
  George, 44
  Henry, 16
  John, 16
  Margaret, 6
  Samuel, 16
  Susannah, 16
HESSANG,
  Peter, 13
HESSONG,
  Barbara, 13
  Peter, 13
  Susanna, 13
HESTAND,
  Benjamin, 38
  Jacob, 38
  John, 38

HETRICK,
  Gattraat, 3
  Varner, 3
HETZER,
  Catherine, 45
  Charles, 45
  Eliza, 45
  George, 45
  Jane, 45
  John, 45
  Mary, 45
HEWETT,
  Betsey, 28
  Sodwick, 21
HEWIT,
  Daniel, 45
  Jacob, 45
  John, 45
  Ludwick, 45
HEYSER,
  William, 9
HIGGINS,
  Irmma, 45
  Jamima, 45
  Upton, 45
HIGHBARGER,
  John, 39
HILE,
  Elizabeth, 27
HILL,
  Abraham, 29
  Barbara, 29, 45
  Daniel, 29, 45
  Elizabeth, 27
  Jacob, 29, 45
  John, 29
  Jonathan, 29, 45
  Joseph, 29
  Peter, 29, 45
  Valentine, 29, 45
HILLIARD,
  Christopher, 29
  Jane, 29
HINE,
  Margaret, 50
HINES,
  Thomas, 4
HINKLE,
  Abraham, 12
  Catherine, 12
  Michael, 12
HITCHCOCK,
  Mary, 42

HITT,
  Samuel M., 44
HITTE,
  Samuel M., 44
HIVENER,
  Catherine, 45
  Jacob, 45
  Joseph, 45
HIWIT,
  Philip, 21
HOBLETZELL,
  Mary, 34
HOCKEY,
  Dorathy, 4
  Nicholas, 4
HOFFER,
  Jacob, 42
  Mary, 19
HOFFMAN,
  Barbara, 15, 16, 45
  Christine, 16
  Elizabeth, 16
  Jacob, 49
  James, 49
  John, 15, 16, 45, 49
  Mary, 49
  Mathew, 16
  Mathias, 30
  Nancy, 33, 49
  Rachel, 16
  Samuel, 49
  Sarah, 34
  Susanna, 32
  Susannah, 16
HOFMAN,
  Barbara, 15
HOGG,
  Aron, 4
  Christian, 4
  John, 4, 30, 45
  Thomas, 4
  William, 30
HOGMIRE,
  Andrew, 35
  Catherine, 35
  Daniel, 16, 29, 35
  Henry, 16, 29
  Jonas, 1, 9, 14, 27, 32, 43
  Margaret, 45
  Samuel, 21
  Sophia, 6

INDEX

HOLLIDAY,
  George S., 45
  Henry, 45
  James, 45
  Richard, 45
  Susan, 45
  William, 45
HOLLMAN,
  Mary Ann, 53
HOLMAN,
  Mary Ann, 53
HOLSINGER,
  Eliza, 19, 34
HOLTZINGER,
  Elizabeth, 19
HOLZINGER,
  Elizabeth, 19
HOMLES,
  Conrad, 16
  Jacob, 16
HOOBER,
  John, 5
HOOPER,
  John, 29
  Kellurah, 29
  Mary Ann, 29
HOOPINGARDNER,
  George, 21
HOOVER,
  Adam, 16
  Ann, 54
  Barbara, 21, 37
  Catherine, 52
  Christian, 29, 52
  Christopher, 16, 30
  Elizabeth, 10, 52, 54
  Henry, 16, 30
  Hester, 29
  Jacob, 16, 29
  John, 16, 23, 29, 30, 52, 54
  Leah, 29
  Margaret, 16, 23, 54
  Mary, 3, 29
  Peter, 16
  Rozana, 3
  Susanna, 29
HOOVERMAIL,
  Daniel, 30

  Elizabeth, 30
  John, 30
  John L., 38
  Joseph, 30
  Judith, 30
  Lodwick, 30
  Peter, 30
  Susannah, 30
HOOVERMAILE,
  Margaret, 30
HORINE,
  Adam, 16
  Catherine, 16
  Conrad, 12
  Daniel, 16
  Elizabeth, 16
  Esther, 10
  Henry, 16
  John, 16
  Nancy, 16
HORN,
  Catherine, 5
HOSE,
  George, 30
  Julianna, 48
  Peter, 45, 46
  Philip, 45
  Susanna, 32
  Susannah, 48
HOSKINS,
  Elizabeth, 32
  Frederick, 49
  George, 49
  Jacob, 49
HOSSELTON,
  Eve, 50
HOSTELTINE,
  Eve, 50
HOUCK,
  Catherine, 30
  Henry, 14, 27
  Jacob, 30
  John, 30
HOUK,
  Catherine, 30
  Elizabeth, 2
  Jacob, 30
  John, 30
HOUSEHOLDER,
  Adam, 4, 16
  Elizabeth, 16
  George, 4, 52
  Jacob, 4
  Juliana, 52

  Julianna, 37
  Mary, 16
HOUSELY,
  Levie, 31
HOUSER,
  Abraham, 16
  Anna, 1
  Catherine, 31
  Christian, 16
  Elizabeth, 49
  Fironica, 1
  Henry, 16
  Isaac, 13
  Jacob, 2, 4, 16, 31
  John, 1, 16
  Rachel, 1
  Rosanna, 15
  S., 31
  Susan, 31
  Susannah, 13
HOUSLAND,
  Jacob, 38
HOUSLY,
  Catherine, 23
HOUTZER,
  Margaret, 19, 34
HOVERMAIL,
  John L., 22
  Margaret, 53
HOWARD,
  Ann, 16
  Anthony, 16
HOWELL,
  Daniel, 21, 36
  Eliza, 48
  Elizabeth, 45
  Henry, 21
  Jacob, 16, 21, 29, 36
  James, 45
HOWER,
  Daniel, 51
  David, 30
  Elizabeth, 30, 45
  George, 30, 45
  Jacob, 30, 45
  John, 30, 45
  Maria, 30, 45
  Rosanna Henrietta, 29
  Rosannah H., 44
  Sarah, 30

DISTRIBUTION OF ESTATE ACCOUNTS

HUBER,
  Leonard, 50
HUFFER,
  E., 27
  Leah, 40
HUFFERT,
  John, 20
HUGHES,
  Ann, 45
  Anthony, 16
  James, 16
  Joseph, 45
  Samuel, 12, 16
HUGHIT,
  Eve, 5
  Mary, 5
HULL,
  Christine, 39
  John, 32
  Peter, 47
HUMPHREYVILLE,
  Susanna, 32
HUMRICHOUSE,
  A., 54
  Peter, 26
HUMRICKHOUSE,
  Frederick, 52
HUNT,
  Ann, 30
  Job, 30
HUNTSBERRY,
  Catherine, 50
HURST,
  Ann, 4
  Joseph, 4, 16
  Morgan, 4, 16
  Moses R., 16
  Ruth, 4
HUTCHESON,
  Catherine, 14, 27
HUTZELL,
  Adam, 45
  Elizabeth, 45
  Jacob, 45
  John, 45
  Jonathan, 45
  Matthias, 45
  Nancy, 45
  Samuel, 45
  Sarah, 45
  Susannah, 45
HUYETT,
  Jacob, 21

HYBARGER,
  Adam, 11
HYLAND,
  Ann, 30, 45
  Charlotte, 30, 45
  Denmar, 16
  Elisha, 16
  Hugh, 16, 30, 45
  John, 16
  John R., 16, 30, 45
  Joshua, 30
  Mary Ann, 30, 45
  Thomas, 45
HYNES,
  Hannah, 4
  William, 4

-I-

INDEY,
  Catherine, 4
  John, 4
INGRAM,
  John, 2, 33
  Joseph, 33
  Rachel, 33
IRVIN,
  John, 30
IRWIN,
  John, 45
  Peggy, 53
  Sarah, 45
  William, 45
ISAAC,
  Isaac, 43
ITNIRE,
  Catherine, 4
  Daniel, 4
  Elizabeth, 4
  George, 4
  Henry, 4
  John, 4
  Leonard, 4
  Martin, 4
  Mary, 4

-J-

JACK,
  Th---, 14
JACKSON,
  Ruth, 26
JACOB,
  Jacob, 6
  Ruth, 16

JACQUES,
  Ann, 16
  Anthony, 16
  Lancelot, 40, 42, 48
  Thomas, 16
JAFFER,
  Sarah, 1
JAMES,
  Abraham, 45
  Amos, 45
  Bennett, 45
  Hiram, 45
  Mathias, 30
  Rachel, 30
  Thomas, 50
  Walter, 30
  William, 45
JAMISON,
  Elizabeth, 4
  Priscilla, 49
JENNINGS,
  George, 41
JENY, 14
JOHN,
  Abraham, 16
  Daniel, 16
  Elizabeth, 16, 30
  Henry, 16, 30
  John, 16
  Peter, 16
JOHNS,
  Cahrlotte, 49
JOHNSON,
  Barbara, 18, 33
  Barnet, 4
  Benjamin, 1
  Daniel, 47
  Denton, 4
  Elinor, 4
  Elizabeth, 4
  John, 4, 16
  Joseph, 4
  Joshua, 4
  Mary, 4, 16
  Nancy, 4
  Noami, 12
  Peter, 4, 16
  William, 4
JOHNSTON,
  Catherine, 19
  George H., 45
  Jane, 45
  John, 45

INDEX

Margaret, 45
Mary, 49
Tobias, 49
JONES,
　Anthony, 16
　Barbara, 19, 34
　Catherine, 11, 24, 45
　David, 4
　Elizabeth, 16, 45
　Hannah, 4
　Henry, 45
　Jacob, 11, 45
　John, 4, 16, 19, 45
　Jonathan, 45
　Margaret, 45
　Mary, 4, 8, 10, 22, 45
　Melly, 22
　Milly, 10
　Peter, 4, 20
　Samuel, 6
　William, 1
JULIUS,
　Ann, 45
　Catherine, 45
　Elizabeth, 45
　George, 45
　John, 30, 45
　Samuel, 45

-K-
KAGY,
　Barbara, 4
　Fransy, 4
　Michael, 4
KAILOR,
　Catherine, 45
　Frederick, 45
　Jacob, 45
KAINAN,
　Mary, 27
KAKCERISE,
　Nancy, 53
KALER,
　Jonas, 52
KARMAN,
　Mary, 14
KARNES,
　Margaret, 13
KARSON,
　Margaret, 4

Richard, 4
KAUFFMAN,
　Susanna, 29
KEAGY,
　Henry, 49
KEALHOFFER,
　Catherine, 24
KEALHOOFER,
　Milly, 19, 34
KEBLER,
　George, 51
KEDERMAN,
　Michael, 4
KEDOMON,
　John, 4
KEEBLER,
　Jacob, 4
KEEDY,
　Catherine, 48
　Daniel, 27
　Henry, 49
　Jacob, 52
　John, 27
　John A., 54
　John J., 48
　Magdalena, 27
　Mary, 27
　Nancy, 49
KEEFAUVER,
　Barbara, 17
KEEFER,
　George, 4
KEEL,
　Joseph, 12
　Margaret, 12
KEELER,
　Mary, 37
KEESACRE,
　Jacob, 30
　Simon, 30
KEIFER,
　Elizabeth, 2
　George, 45
KEIHL,
　George, 54
KEIRNAN,
　Mary, 14
KELAHOFER,
　Catherine, 39
KELLER,
　Alford, 45
　Alfred, 30, 45
　Ann M., 30
　Ann Marie, 30, 45

Elizabeth, 26, 30, 45
George, 20, 36, 41, 51
Joseph C., 30, 45
Lewis, 47
Mary, 53
Thomas, 41
KELLY,
　Marie, 45
　Martha, 45
　Susan, 45
KEMMELL,
　Catherine, 23
KEMPFFER,
　Lydia, 49
KENDAL,
　Barbara, 21
　Elizabeth, 16
KENDLE,
　Elizabeth, 40
KENISTRICK,
　Frederick, 4
　Henry, 4
　John, 4
　Margaret, 4
KENNEDY,
　Alexander, 20
　Elenor, 35
　George, 16, 20
　John, 25, 43
KENSEY,
　Adam, 45
　Ann, 45
　James W., 45
　Samuel, 45
KENSLER,
　Betsey, 8
KEPHART,
　Elizabeth, 18, 33
KEPLER,
　Ann, 46
　Mathias, 20
KEPLINGER,
　George, 16
　Jacob, 16
　John, 36
　Joseph, 52
KERFLICK,
　Elizabeth, 39
KERSHNER,
　Andrew, 54, 30, 45, 46, 52, 54
　Ann, 25

77

DISTRIBUTION OF ESTATE ACCOUNTS

B., 21
Barbara, 30, 46
Benjamin, 4
Christiana, 46
Daniel, 46
David, 46
Elias, 16
Elizabeth, 30, 50
Eve, 37, 52
George, 4, 16, 46
Isaac, 46, 50
Jacob, 22, 38, 46, 50
John, 46
Jonathan, 30, 46
Joseph, 16
Martin, 7, 16, 30, 46
Mary, 4
Mary Ann, 21
Nancy, 38
Peter, 46
Philip, 7, 46
Polly, 46
Rosanna Hager, 29
Rosannah H., 44
Samuel, 46
Solomon, 30, 46
William, 50
KESAKER,
 Simon, 4
KESEKER,
 Simon, 4
KESSINGER,
 Joseph, 11
KESSLER, Ann, 39
KEYLER,
 Frederick, 4
KEYSERMAN,
 Catherine, 4
 Elizabeth, 4
 George, 4
 Michael, 4
 Rebecca, 4
 Simon, 4
KIFER,
 Christine, 40
KIMMERLY, John, 3
KING,
 Abraham, 46
 Christian, 2

Daniel, 46
John, 46
Levi, 46
Martin, 46
Mary, 24, 33
Otho, 46
William, 46
KINGEREY,
 Jacob, 49
 Polly, 49
 Rosanna, 49
 Samuel, 49
 Thomas, 49
KINGERY,
 Polly, 33
KINKLE,
 Adam, 30
 Elizabeth, 30
 Henry, 30
 Jacob, 30
KINSOE,
 Mary, 38
KIPER,
 George, 2
KISTER,
 Mary, 4
KLINE,
 Andrew, 30, 34
 Charles, 46
 Christian C., 46
 Daniel, 46
 George, 34, 46
 John, 46
 Peter, 10
 Samuel, 46
KLINK,
 George A., 46
 George F., 46
 Mary B., 46
KLUIR,
 George, 50
KNABLE,
 Susanna, 37
KNAVE,
 Leonard, 10
KNAVEL,
 George, 52
 Susannah, 52
KNEEDY,
 Elizabeth, 30
KNEPPER,
 Henrietta R., 44
KNESTRICK,
 Sarah, 45

KNIGHT,
 Elizabeth, 40
KNOCATEE,
 Barbara, 33
KNODE,
 Elizabeth, 16, 29
 George, 12, 16, 41
 Henry, 46
 Jacob, 16, 46
 Jacob M., 29
 John, 46
 Jonathan, 16
 Margaret, 16
 Mary, 16, 41, 45, 46
 Susannah, 16
KNODLE,
 George, 30
 Jacob, 30
 Leonard, 30
KNOKEL,
 Frederick, 4
KNOWLES,
 James, 3
 Mary, 14
KOALER,
 Catherine, 4, 5
 Christian, 5
 Daniel, 4
 Elizabeth, 4
 Esther, 5
 George, 4, 5, 16, 30
 John, 4, 5, 16, 30
 Jonathan, 5, 16, 30
 Mary, 4
KOHLER,
 George, 5
 John, 5
KOLER,
 Catherine, 3
 George, 52
KONSLER,
 Jacob, 8
KOOGLE,
 Dorothy, 7
KOONTZ,
 Catherine, 46, 49
 Elizabeth, 46
 John, 40, 46
 Susan, 40
 Thomas, 46
 William, 46

INDEX

KREAGER,
  Daniel, 46
  George, 46
  Henry, 46
  John, 46
  William, 46
KREIB,
  Philip, 34
  William, 34
KREICH,
  Nicholas, 13
  Philip, 13, 37
KREIGH,
  Andrew, 30
  Benjamin, 46
  Catherine, 46
  Daniel, 46
  Elie, 46
  Elizabeth, 46
  George, 46
  John, 46
  Mary, 46
  Nicholas, 46
  Philip, 30
  Phillip, 46
  William, 30, 46
KREPS,
  Christine, 16, 30
  Fanny, 29
  Jacob, 30
  John, 30
  Sodwick, 16
  William, 21, 38
KRETZER,
  Aaron, 46
  Adam, 30
  Catherine, 24
  Christian, 30
  David, 30
  Elizabeth, 53
  George, 35
  Henry, 30
  Jacob, 46
  John, 30, 46
  Leonard, 30
  Margaret, 46
  Noah, 46
  Sarah, 46
KRETZINGER,
  Charlotte, 30
  George, 30
  John, 30
  Lodwick, 30
  Nancy, 30
  Susanna, 30
KRITZER,
  Catherine, 40
KRITZINGER,
  George, 2
KROUSE,
  Jacob, 54
KYSER,
  Frederick, 17
  Hawn, 17
  Michael, 17
  Peter, 17

-L-
LAMBERT,
  Elizabeth, 28
  Eve, 46
  George, 31
  George H., 30, 45, 46
  George M., 46
  Jacob, 5, 14, 22, 28, 35, 46
  John, 46
  Jonas, 30, 46
  Shem, 46
LAMU,
  Elizabeth, 6
LANCE,
  Henry, 17
LANDIS,
  Abraham, 47
  Amelia, 47
  Henry, 47
  Mary, 47
  Rebecca, 37
  Salina, 47
  Susan, 47
LANE,
  Catherine, 23, 30
  Christian G., 30
  Drusilla, 12
LANGLEY,
  John, 4
LANTZ,
  Catherine, 2
  Christian, 2, 6, 17, 18, 19, 34
  Elizabeth, 17
  Farancia, 2
  Frederick, 17
  George, 17
  Henry, 17
  Jacob, 17
  Joseph, 12
  Samuel, 47
  Susannah, 12
LATSHAW,
  Elizabeth, 25
LAUDENBERGER,
  George, 5
  Mary, 5
LAUER,
  Jacob, 35
LAWRENCE,
  Catherine, 40
  George, 40
LAWSON,
  Jacob L., 21
LAWVER,
  John, 31
LEAR,
  Charles, 47
  Delila, 47
  Jacob, 47
  John, 1
  Mehala, 47
  Philip, 47
LEARY,
  Edward, 31, 41
  Elener, 31
  Joshua, 31
LEASURE,
  Christian, 31
  Elijah, 31
  Elizabeth, 31
  John, 28
  Michael, 28
  Susan, 31
LECKRON,
  Dorothy, 5
  Jacbo, 20
  Jacob, 5
  Simon, 5
LECKRONE,
  Catherine, 47
  Daniel, 47
  Elizabeth, 47
  Esther, 47
  Jacob, 47
  John, 47
  Jonas, 47
  Jonathan, 47
  Maria, 47
  Mary, 47
  Rebecca, 47
  Samuel, 47

DISTRIBUTION OF ESTATE ACCOUNTS

Susan, 47
LECKROON,
  Ann, 17, 47
  Catherine, 17,
    31, 47
  Daniel, 17, 47
  Elizabeth, 17,
    31, 47
  Isaac, 31
  Jacob, 17, 31,
    47, 51
  John, 17, 31, 47
  Lemuel, 47
  Margaret, 17,
    20, 47, 51
  Maria, 17, 31,
    47
  Mary, 17, 47
  Rebecca, 31
  Samuel, 17
  Sarah, 17, 47
  Simon, 17, 47
  Susanna, 17
  Susannah, 47
LEDDLY,
  Mary, 32
LEDY,
  Barbara, 49
LEE,
  Catherine, 54
  Colier, 31
LEFEVER,
  Christine, 31
  David, 31
  Elizabeth, 31
  George, 31
  Henry, 31
  Isaac, 31
  John, 31
  Maria, 31
  Mariah, 31
  Mary, 31
  Samuel, 31
  Sarah, 31
LEIB,
  Abraham, 35
  Gabriel, 35
  Jacob, 35
  John, 35
  Mary, 35
  Susanna, 35
  William, 35
LEIDER,
  Abraham, 31

John, 31, 34
LEIDY,
  Catherine, 31
LEIGHT,
  John, 2
LEIGHTER,
  Elizabeth, 6
  Eve, 5
  Jacob, 5, 17
  John, 5, 17
  Peter, 5, 17
  Polly, 52
LEISER,
  Jonas, 43
  Judith, 43
LEITER,
  Abraham, 31, 47
  Andrew, 31
  Ann Catherine, 47
  Ann Maria, 47
  Catherine, 31
  David, 47
  Elizabeth, 31
  Felix, 47
  George, 47
  Henry, 31, 47
  Jacob, 31, 47
  John, 31, 34, 47
  Jonas, 31
  Peter, 31
  Samuel, 31, 47
LEONARD,
  Mary, 21
LEOPARD,
  Mary, 21
LESSLEY,
  Alexander, 47
  Delila, 47
  Elizabeth, 47
  John, 47
  Joseph, 47
  Sarah, 47
LEVERNEICKT,
  Christopher, 47
LEVERNEIGHT,
  Christopher, 47
LEWIS,
  George, 32
  Nancy, 29
LEYDY,
  Barbara, 47
  David, 47
  Elizabeth, 47
  Henry, 47

John, 47
Mary, 47
LIDAY,
  George, 11, 17
LIEZER,
  Jonas, 28
LIGHT,
  Benjamin, 2
  Catherine, 2, 30
  John, 17, 51
  Mary, 25
  Peter, 22
LINCH,
  Andrew, 5
  Eliza, 11
  Elizabeth, 5
  Peter, 5
LIND,
  John, 47
LINE,
  George, 31
  Jacob, 31
  Mary, 27
LINN,
  Mary, 53
LITTLE,
  Elizabeth, 23
  Hester, 13
  Jacob, 47
  Mary, 54
  Susannah, 47
LOCHER,
  Ann B., 47
  Ann E., 47
  Ann M., 47
  Barbara, 17
  Charles H., 47
  Elizabeth, 12, 47
  Frederick, 17
  George, 47
  George H., 47
  Henry, 17, 34, 47
  Henry L., 47
  Jacob, 17
  John, 17
  Mary, 47
LOCKER,
  Barbara, 47
  Elizabeth, 47
  Henry, 47
  Isaac, 47
  John, 47
  Mary Ann, 47
  William, 47

INDEX

LOCKRIDGE,
  George, 47
  John, 47
  William, 47
LONG,
  Catherine, 19, 24, 31, 34, 49
  Daniel, 31
  David, 17, 18, 31
  Elizabeth, 5, 6, 9, 17, 24, 32, 45
  Emmanuel, 5
  Grace, 31
  Henry, 17, 36
  Isaac, 5, 19, 34, 39
  Jacob, 5, 36
  John, 5, 17, 31
  Joseph, 5
  Mary, 5, 17, 24, 28, 39
  Nancy, 50
  Peter, 17
  Samuel, 17
  Sarah, 5
LONGANACRE,
  Christian, 17
LOPAH,
  Mary, 2
LORSHBAUGH,
  Catherine, 5
  George, 5
  Harman, 5
  John, 5
  Margaret, 5
  Mary, 5
  William, 5
LOSHBAUGH,
  Catherine, 5, 17
  George, 5, 17
  Harman, 5
  Harmon, 5, 17
  John, 5, 17
  Margaret, 5, 17
  Mary, 5, 17
  William, 5, 17
LOWER,
  Elizabeth, 24
  Jacob, 20
LOWERY,
  Mary, 9

  Michel, 9
LOWMAN,
  Catherine, 31
  Daniel, 31
  David, 47
  George, 47
  Henry, 31, 47
  Jacob, 31, 47
  John, 31, 47
  Mary, 16, 47
  Nancy, 27
  Susanna, 47
LOWRA,
  Barbara, 17
  Elizabeth, 17
  George, 17
  Henry, 17
  John, 17
  Margaret, 17
  Mary, 12, 17
  Michael, 17
  Susannah, 17
LOWRY,
  Henry, 29
LUCKETT,
  Huzza, 5
  Mrs., 21
  Samuel, 5
  Thomas, 5
LUDY,
  David, 20
LUGH,
  Michael, 10
LUTZ,
  Elizabeth, 29
LYDAY,
  Adam, 17
  Catherine, 40
LYNCH,
  Blackison, 47
  John B., 47
  Samuel, 32
  Susan, 47
LYNN,
  Abigail, 5
  Clark, 5
  Edmond, 5
  Elijah, 5, 40
  Hannah, 4
  Hester, 40
  John, 5
  Mary, 5
LYSICKLER,
  Mary, 39

-M-
MCCAFFERTY,
  Dennis, 31
  Elizabeth, 31
  John, 31
  Robert, 31
MCCAMMEL,
  Alexander, 48
  Susannah, 48
MCCARDELL,
  Thomas, 32
MCCARDLE,
  William, 34
MCCAULEY,
  Henry, 47
MCCLAIN,
  Andrew, 47
  Ann C., 47
  Elie, 47
  Elizabeth, 47
  James, 31
  John, 31, 47, 51
  Josiah, 47
  Leonides, 47
  Lucretia, 47
  Margaret, 25, 31, 41
  Maria, 47
  Mary, 47, 51
  Otho, 47
  Owen, 47
MCCLANNAHAN,
  Alexander, 5
  Eliza, 41
  Jane, 5
MCCLELAN,
  William, 21
MCCLELAND,
  Alexander, 17
  James, 17
MCCLUNG,
  Elizabeth, 47
  Eve, 47
  Maria, 47
  Silas, 47
  William, 47
MCCOMAS,
  Susan, 42
  ___, 42
MCCOMKY,
  Sarah, 50
MCCORMICK,
  John, 43

DISTRIBUTION OF ESTATE ACCOUNTS

MCCOY,
  Archibald, 17
  Daniel, 6
  Edmund, 11
  Elinor, 6
  Emanuel, 47
  Jacob, 6
  James, 17
  John, 6
  Joseph, 31
  Margaret, 6
  Martha, 6
  Mary, 11, 12, 25, 47
  Perry, 6
  Vincent, 47
  William, 6
MCCREA,
  Adam, 31
  John, 31
  Martha, 31
  Mary Ann, 31
  Michael, 31
  Rebecca, 31
  Samuel, 31
MCCURDY,
  John, 43
MCDANIEL,
  Mary, 40
MCDILL,
  Catherine, 31
  John, 31
MCELHENNY,
  Jane, 25
MCELVES,
  Margaret, 52
MCFERRAN,
  Alexander, 47
  James B., 47
  Precila, 47
MCGLAUGHLIN,
  John, 3
MCGLOCKLAN,
  John, 3
MCGLOUGHLIN,
  John, 47
  William, 47
MCKAIN,
  Elizabeth, 14, 27
MCKEERNAN,
  Michael, 33
MCKEIRNAN,
  Elizabeth, 18

  Michael, 18
MCKESSIC,
  Henry, 47
  James, 47
  Jane, 47
  John, 47
  Tobert, 47
MCKIERNAN,
  John, 18
  Polly, 18
MCKOWN,
  Charles, 7
MCLAUGHLIN,
  Catherine, 11, 24
  Henry, 17
  John, 17
  Susannah, 17
MCLIN,
  Casandre, 25
MCNAME,
  Mary, 3
MCNAMEE,
  Adam, 5
  Alice, 5
  George, 5
  Gettee, 5
  Hannah, 5
  Hugh, 5
  Job, 5
  Moses, 5
  Thomas, 5
MCPHERSON,
  Brien, 36
  Jonas, 19, 34, 50
MAINER,
  Thomas, 20
MAINES,
  ___, 49
MAINS,
  Joseph, 5
  Mary, 5
  Thomas, 5, 22
MALONE,
  Amey, 48
  Benjamin, 31, 48
  Bryan, 31
  Daniel, 31
  Edward, 31
  Elias, 31, 48
  James, 31, 48
  John, 31
  Maria, 48
  Mary, 31, 48
  Mary Ann, 48

  Richard, 31
  Sallie, 48
  Thomas, 31
MALOTT,
  Benjamin, 31, 47, 48
  Catherine, 32
  Daniel, 17, 32, 47, 52
  Elias, 31, 47, 48
  Hannah, 32
  Hiram, 17, 32
  John, 17, 32, 47
  Joseph, 17, 32
  Kitty, 32
  Mary Ann, 31, 32, 47, 48
  Michael, 17, 32
  Peter, 17, 32
  Theodore, 17, 31, 32, 47, 48
  Thomas, 17, 32
  William, 17, 32
MANKAMAN,
  Catherine, 6
MANN,
  Andrew, 52
  Mary, 52
MANTESBAUGH,
  Jacob, 32
  William, 32
MAPHET,
  Elizabeth, 5
  Margaret, 5
  William, 5
MARKLE,
  Susanna, 34
  Susannah, 19
MARKLEY,
  Susanna, 34
MARSHALL,
  William M., 40
MARSTELLER,
  Ann, 17
  Benjamin, 17
  Elizabeth, 17
  George, 17
  John, 17
  Nicholas, 17
  Polly, 17
  Rebecca, 17
  Sarah, 17
MARTIN,
  Anna, 17

INDEX

Barbara, 28
Catherine, 49
Christian, 5, 17
David, 5, 17, 27, 48
Elizabeth, 5
Henry, 5, 17
Jacob, 5, 17
John, 5
Joseph, 45
Mary, 17, 50
Nicholas, 48
Rebecca, 45
Rosanna, 48
Rose, 18
Samuel, 48
Sophia, 29
Stephen, 28
Susanna, 9
Susannah, 17, 50
Thomas, 48
MARTZ,
  Peter, 35
MASON,
  Abraham B., 32
  Elizabeth, 32
  Elizabeth A. T., 32
  Jeremiah, 34
  John, 32
  John T., 32
  Mary B., 32
  Melchor B., 32
  Robert, 41
  Susanna, 10
  Thompson, 32
  Virginia, 32
MAUCHLER,
  Christian, 17
  Margaret, 17
MAULANE,
  Elizabeth, 10
MAYER,
  Felix, 5
MAYES,
  N., 22
MEAD,
  Benjamin, 32
  Jeremiah, 32
  Samuel, 32
MEAR,
  Mary, 5
MEAUCK,
  Catherine, 17

MEEK,
  Ann, 5
  Thomas, 5
MELTON,
  Ann, 32
  Philip, 32
  Thomas, 32
MENTZER,
  Catherine, 32, 40
  Conrad, 11, 40
  David, 40
  George, 16, 30
  Jacob, 40
  John, 32, 40
  Polly, 40
  Samuel, 32
MERCHAND,
  Frederick, 2
METZ,
  Magdalena, 28
MEYER,
  Lewis, 40
MEYERS,
  Lewis, 39
MICHAEL,
  Michael, 6
MIDDLECALF,
  Barbara, 17, 32
  Hannah, 13
MIDDLECAUFF,
  Christian, 33
MIDDLECOF,
  Christian, 7
MIDDLEKAUF,
  Hannah, 27
  ___, 19
MIDDLEKAUFF,
  Barbara, 6
  Christian, 48
  Daniel, 48
  Daniel M., 52
  Elizabeth, 48
  Jacob, 48
  John, 48
  Margaret, 48
  Mary Ann, 48
  Nancy, 48
  Peter, 27, 48
  Samuel, 48
  Sarah Ann, 48
  Susannah, 48
MILES,
  Benjamin, 5
  Catherine, 5

Charles, 17
Isaac, 17
James, 17
John, 5, 17, 31
Margaret, 5
Mary, 5
Morris, 5
Samuel, 5
Sarah, 17
Shaderick, 5
Susanna, 31
William, 17
MILLER,
  Abraham, 5
  Adam, 5, 16
  Alexander, 48
  Ann, 20, 48
  Barbara, 5, 15, 29, 48
  Catherine, 3, 5, 8, 17, 19, 34, 47, 50
  Christian, 5
  Christina, 5, 47
  Daniel, 5, 20, 32, 35, 47, 48
  David, 3, 5, 47
  Elias, 32
  Elizabeth, 2, 7, 17, 32, 35, 48, 50
  Ester, 5
  Eve, 15
  Frederick, 47, 48
  Fronica, 5
  George, 12, 17, 32
  Henry, 5, 47
  Jacob, 5, 12, 17, 32, 38, 47, 48, 52, 54
  Jacob F., 27, 48
  John, 3, 5, 6, 17, 31, 32, 47, 48
  John G., 49
  John T., 40
  Joseph F., 43
  Juliana, 29
  Leonard, 12
  Levin, 32
  Lodwick, 5
  Louisa, 48
  Magdalena, 17, 48
  Margaret, 29
  Maria, 17, 32

DISTRIBUTION OF ESTATE ACCOUNTS

Mary, 5, 11, 32
Mason, 32
Michael, 12, 48
Nancy, 17
Peter, 7, 32, 40
Philip, 5
Polly, 52
Rebecca, 9
Sally, 17, 32
Samuel, 5, 12,
  17, 26, 32,
  47
Sarah, 17
Tobias, 48
William, 32
William H., 32,
  48
MILLS,
  Eliza I., 48
  Elizabeth, 48
  Jacob, 48
  James, 48
  James P., 48
  Levin, 32, 35,
    48
  Michael, 48
  Samuel, 48
  Thomas, 48
  William, 48
MITCHELL,
  Alexander, 35
MITHCELL,
  Sarah, 47
MITTAG,
  Catherine, 48
  John F. G., 48
  John G., 48
  Maria, 48
  Sophia, 48
MITTER,
  Henry, 47
MOATS,
  Jacob, 43
  John, 49
MOATZ,
  Joseph, 49
  Mary C., 43
MOFFET, John, 50
MOFFETT,
  William, 36
MOLER,
  Susana, 31
MOMELTORFF,
  Barbara, 6

MONAGER,
  Mary, 40
MONG,
  Adam, 5
  Amelia, 32
  Barbara, 32
  Catherine, 5, 21
  Devalt, 5
  Elizabeth, 27, 32
  G. N., 5
  George, 5, 32
  Godfred, 5
  Henry, 5
  Jacob, 5, 32
  Jacob B., 32
  John, 5, 32
  Margaret, 32
  Mary, 32
  Peter, 5, 32
  Susanna, 27
  Susannah, 43
MONINGER,
  John, 40
MOONEY,
  Patrick, 46
MOORE,
  Elener, 2
  Eliza, 46
  Elizabeth, 25
  Martha, 25
  Mary A., 40
  Sarah, 21
MOORS,
  Thomas, 38
MOREHEAD,
  I., 6
MORELAND,
  Ann, 19, 20
  Hugh, 43
  John, 43
  William, 39, 43
MORGAN,
  Elizabeth, 50
  Euasilla, 11
  Judith, 31
MORRISON,
  Alexander, 48
  Emanuel, 52
  Jane, 48
  John, 48
  Nancy, 49
  Priscilla, 25
MOTES,
  Elie, 43

  Susannah, 43
MOTS,
  Eli, 27
  Susanna, 27
  Susannah, 14
MOTT,
  Elie, 14
  Susannah, 14
MOUDY,
  Adam, 5
  Baltzer, 5
  Casper, 5
  George, 5
  Henry, 5
  Jacob, 5
  John, 5
  Martin, 5
  Michael, 5
  Peter, 5
MOURER,
  Elizabeth, 35
MOWEN,
  Mary, 28
MOYER,
  Abraham, 6, 17, 32
  Ann, 6
  Barbara, 6, 32,
    46, 48
  Betsey, 6, 32
  Betsy, 17
  Catherine, 6, 32
  Christian, 6, 32,
    46, 48
  Christopher, 32
  Conrod, 6
  Elizabeth, 32
  Eve, 6
  Henry, 6, 32, 46,
    48
  Isaac, 32, 46, 48
  Jacob, 6, 17, 32,
    38, 46, 48
  John, 6, 17, 32,
    46, 48
  Margaret, 32
  Mary, 6
  Michael, 32
  Nancy, 17, 32, 48
  Peggy, 6, 17, 32
  Rose, 32
  Samuel, 17, 32,
    46, 48
  Simon, 6
  Susanna, 24, 39

INDEX

Susannah, 48
MUCK,
　Maria, 34
MUIR,
　James, 32
　Peggy, 32
MULENDORE,
　Catherine, 40
MULLEN,
　Elener, 1
MUMMA,
　Eliza, 28, 43
　Henry, 17
　Jacob, 17, 26
　John, 17
　Joseph, 17, 38, 53
　Margaret, 17
MURPHY,
　Susanna, 1
MURRAY,
　Susanna, 25
MURRY,
　Charles, 48
　John, 48
　Mary Ann, 43
　Thomas B., 43
MUSSELMAN,
　Esther, 9
MYERS,
　Adam, 17, 32, 35, 36, 51
　Ann, 10
　Benjamin, 49
　Catherine, 39
　Elizabeth, 6, 33, 48, 49
　Frederick, 17, 32, 49
　George, 6
　Henry, 33, 49
　Jacob, 17, 32, 33, 48, 49
　John, 32, 33, 40, 48, 49
　John (of Jacob), 48
　Jonathan, 16
　Joseph, 49
　Lud, 6
　Ludwig, 6
　Margaret, 24, 40, 48
　Martin, 36, 39

Mary, 32, 48, 49
Mary A., 49
Michael, 17, 32
Pegie, 6
Peter, 33, 49
Polly, 49
Rosanna, 33, 40, 48, 49
Sarah, 33, 49
T., 36

-N-

NANCE,
　Dianah, 5
NAVE,
　Abraham, 6
　David, 33
　George, 6
　Henry, 6
　Jacob, 6
　Leonard, 6
NEAD,
　Charlotte, 6
　Daniel, 6, 44
　David, 44
　Jacob, 6
　John, 44
　Mathias, 6
　Peter, 44
NEALE,
　Aquilla, 33
　James, 33
　Mary, 33
　Sarah, 33
　St. Leger, 33
　William, 33
NEALL,
　Aquilla, 18
　At. Leger, 18
　Curtis, 18
　Elizabeth, 18
　Esther, 18
　James, 18
　Mary, 18
　Rebecca, 18
　Sarah, 18
　St. Leger, 18
　William, 18
NEEDY,
　Elizabeth, 45
NEFF,
　Adam, 33, 49
　Catherine, 33
　Esther, 33

Francis, 49
Henry, 33, 49
Jacob, 33, 49
John, 33, 49
Margaret, 33
NEGLEY,
　Barbara, 49
NEIKIRK,
　Catherine, 40
　Nancy, 27
NEILL,
　Alexander, 29, 47, 50, 53
　Aquilla, 18
　William, 18
NEKARK,
　Margaret, 35
NESBITT,
　Jacob, 18
　John, 18
　Jonathan, 18
　Nathaniel, 18
　Peter, 18
NEWCOMER,
　Andrew, 33, 49
　Bran, 49
　Catherine, 33, 49
　Christian, 5, 33, 35, 49
　Christopher, 49
　Daniel, 49
　David, 39, 49
　David C., 51
　Elizabeth, 3, 27, 33, 49
　Emanuel, 49
　Henry, 33, 49
　Isaac, 33, 49
　Jacob, 33, 49
　Joel, 33
　John, 33, 42, 49
　Jonathan, 19, 49
　Joseph, 49
　Joshua, 33, 48, 49
　Maria, 49
　Martin, 49
　Michael, 49
　Nancy, 28, 33, 49
　Otilla, 1
　Peter, 1, 19, 33, 49
　Samuel, 21, 33, 41, 42
　Sarah, 49

DISTRIBUTION OF ESTATE ACCOUNTS

Susanna, 33, 36
Susannah, 49, 51
Thomas, 33
NEWELL,
  Elizabeth, 31
NEWSON,
  Abraham, 18, 33
  Alexander, 18, 33
  Jane, 18, 33
  John, 18, 33
  Joseph, 18, 33
  Mary, 18
  Rachel, 18, 33
  Susan, 41
NICHODEMUS,
  Magdalena, 49
  Valentine, 21
NICHOLLS,
  Jacob, 9
NICODEMUS,
  Sophia, 53
NIGH,
  Catherine, 1
  George, 10, 12, 16, 19, 21, 23
  John, 1
  Samuel, 50
NIGHSWANDER,
  Barbara, 37
NIGHWANDER,
  Abraham, 49
  Daniel, 49
  David, 49
  Elizabeth, 49
  Emmanuel, 49
  Jacob, 49
  John, 49
  Joseph, 49
  Samuel, 49
  Susannah, 49
NIKARK,
  Margaret, 35
NINENHELLER,
  Elizabeth, 44
NITZELL,
  John, 45
NOBLE, John, 31
NOLAND,
  Thomas, 46
NOONEMAKER,
  Elizabeth, 14
  Samuel, 13, 14

NOONEMOCKER,
  Elizabeth, 14
  Samuel, 14
NORRIS,
  Mary, 50
  William, 18
NOW,
  Delores, 20
NOWELL,
  Betsey, 49
  Elizabeth, 31
  Gilbert, 49
  James, 49
  John, 49
  Joseph, 49
  William, 49
NOWLAND,
  Susannah, 46
  Thomas, 46
NUNEMOCKER,
  Samuel, 13
NUSE,
  Mary, 47
NYMAN,
  Henry, 25, 41, 51
  Susanna, 25

-O-

O'BRIEN,
  Henry, 49
  James, 49
ODERFER,
  Barbara, 33
  Elizabeth, 33
  Esther, 33
  Henry, 33
  John, 33
  Margaret, 33
  Mary, 33
  Sarah, 33
OGLE,
  Catherine, 42
OHR,
  Elizabeth, 18
  Henry, 18
  Jacob, 18
  Margaret, 18
  Nicholas, 18
  Soloma, 18
OLDHAM,
  Mary, 48
  William, 48
OLDWINE,
  Charles, 5

OLINGER,
  Philip, 9
OLLAWALL,
  Elizabeth, 31
OLLIVER,
  John, 9
  Mary, 9
O'NEAL,
  Elias, 39
  Rebecca, 12
ONWILER,
  Joseph, 49
  Nicholas, 49
  William, 49
ORENDORFF,
  Christian, 4
  Mary, 20
ORMSTON,
  Andrew, 49
  Ann, 49
  John, 49
  Ralph, 49
ORNDORFF,
  Christian, 6
  Eliza, 6
OSHITZ,
  Jacob, 22
OSTER,
  Eve, 7
  Henry, 6
  Philip, 6
OSWALD,
  Adam, 6, 33
  Benjamin, 6, 28, 33, 43
  Catherine, 6
  Elizabeth, 6
  Eve, 6
  John, 6, 33
  Margaret, 33
  Peter, 6
  Philip, 6
  Sarah, 43
OSWALT,
  Adam, 49
  Benjamin, 18, 49
  Catherine, 49
  Elizabeth, 49
  Eve, 18, 49
  John, 18, 49, 52
  Jonathan, 49
  Lydia, 49
  Margaret, 52
  Peter, 49

INDEX

Phillip, 49
Samuel, 49
Solomon, 49
OTT,
  Adam, 5, 6, 12
  Elizabeth, 34
  Jacob, 6, 39
  Mary, 24
  Michael, 6
OTTO,
  Anna, 32
  David, 24
  Esabella, 27
  Esabelle, 14
  Henry, 33
  Isabella, 33
  Jack, 33
  Jeremiah, 33
  Mathias, 33
  Sarah, 32
OTTOWALL,
  Elizabeth, 31

-P-
PALMER,
  Ann, 10
  Christian, 10, 20
  David, 49
  Elizabeth, 49
  Jesse, 49
  Joseph, 49
  Peter, 11
  Samuel, 49
PALMORE,
  Catherine, 33
  Christian, 33
  David, 33
  Jacob, 33
  John, 33
  Jonathan, 33
  Joseph, 33
  Peter, 33
PARIS, 14
PARROLL,
  Deborah, 19, 20
PARROTT,
  Mary, 38
PARTHER,
  Catherine, 42
PATTERSON,
  Anna, 52
PATTON,
  Mary Ann, 43

PEAL,
  Catherine, 6
  Eve, 6
  Frederick, 6
  George, 6
  John, 6
  Nicholas, 6
PECK,
  Casper, 6
  Jacob, 6
  John, 6
PEEL,
  Catherine, 6
  Eve, 6
  George, 6
  John, 6
  Nicholas, 6
PENCE,
  Eliza, 23
  Elizabeth, 8
PENN,
  Mary, 1
PERREN,
  Catherine, 6
  Deborah, 6
  Eliner, 6
  John, 6
  Joseph, 6
  Rachel, 6
PERRIN,
  Debra, 33
PERRY,
  Ann, 6
  Catherine, 42
  Elenor, 6
  Isabella, 6
  James, 6
  John, 6
  Joseph, 6
PETER,
  Abraham, 6
  Elizabeth, 6
  Jacob, 6
  Michael, 6
PETERBRENNER,
  John, 6
  Leonard, 6
PETERS,
  Magdalena, 13
PETERY,
  Catherine, 18
  Elizabeth, 9, 18, 33
  Jacob, 18, 33

John, 18, 33
Ludwick, 9
Mary, 18
Peter, 18
Philip, 18, 33
Sodwick, 18
PETRE,
  Elizabeth, 21
PETRES,
  Magdalena, 27
PETTICOAT,
  Hannah, 6
  Laken, 6
  Nathan, 6
  Rachel, 6
  William, 6
PETTICORD,
  Alley, 18
  Hannah, 18
  Leakin, 18
  Rachel, 18
  William, 18
PETTYCORT,
  Hannah, 7
PFOUTZ,
  Eliza, 49
  Henry, 49
  Jacob, 49
  John, 49
  Joseph, 49
  Michael, 49
  Nancy, 46, 49
  Samuel, 49
PHILBE,
  William, 1
PHILLIP,
  Eve, 49
PHILPOT,
  Harriet, 49
PINDELL,
  Richard, 20
PIPER,
  Daniel, 18, 33
  Elizabeth, 3, 33
  Jacob, 3, 18, 33
  John, 18, 33
POARCH,
  Catherine, 44
  Jacob, 44
POE,
  Catherine, 38
POFFENBERGER,
  Adam, 18, 33
  Amelia, 52

DISTRIBUTION OF ESTATE ACCOUNTS

Ann, 52
Catherine, 7, 18
Christian, 7,
  18, 33
Elizabeth, 7
Henry, 7, 18,
  33, 40
Jacob, 40
John, 7, 18, 33,
  40
Mahala, 40
Margaret, 40
Mary, 17, 25
Polly, 7, 18
Samuel, 40
Simon, 18, 33
Susan, 40
Valentine, 7,
  18, 33
POFFENBURGER,
  Nancy, 50
POOL, Rebecca, 49
POOROMAN,
  Abraham, 49
  Elizabeth, 49
  Harry, 49
  Jacob, 49
  John, 49
POPE,
  Josiah, 53
  Mary Ann, 53
  Rebecca, 53
  Rozanna, 53
PORTERFIELD,
  John I., 35
POST, George, 54
POSTATER,
  Andrew, 18
  Elizabeth, 18
  Jacob, 18
  John, 18
  Maria, 18
  Susannah, 18
POSTATOR,
  Andrew, 33
  Jacob, 33
POTTER,
  Barbara, 49
  Daniel, 49
  John, 49
  Lewis, 49
  Maria, 49
POTTORF,
  Andrew, 49

George, 49
Henry, 49
Martin, 49
Mary, 15
Simon, 49
Susanna, 38, 50
POTTORFF,
  Susanna, 22
POTTS,
  Elizabeth, 36
  Jonathan, 18
POWELL,
  Ann, 51
  Benjamin, 48
  Eliza Ann, 48
  George, 48
  James, 48
  Jane, 31
  Mary Ann, 48
  Nancy, 48
  Sidney, 48
  Suzannah, 4
  Upton, 51
POWERS,
  Benjamin, 7
  Elizabeth, 7
  George, 7
  Hesley, 7
  James, 7
  Joshua, 7
  Mary, 7
  Thomas, 7
  William, 7
POWLES,
  Catherine, 18
  Christine, 23
  Daniel, 18
  Elizabeth, 33
  Henry, 18
  Jacob, 18, 33, 34
  Margaret, 18
PRATHER,
  Basil, 7
  Bazil, 18
  Benjamin, 7
  Catherine, 42
  Elizabeth, 7
  Friend, 18
  Henry, 7
  James, 7
  Jane, 7
  Jennett, 7
  Louisa, 49
  Lucy, 7

Perry, 18
Richard, 7, 18
Rush, 7
Ruth, 18
Samuel, 7, 18
Sarah, 18
Thomas, 7
PREAM,
  Elizabeth, 7
PRICE,
  Catherine, 28, 45
  Jacob, 24
  John, 43, 49
  Keziah, 49
  Mary Ann, 49
  Susanna, 24, 32
  William H., 49
PROTZMAN,
  Catherine, 18, 33
  Francis, 21
  Henry, 18, 33
  John, 1, 2, 18, 33
  Kitty, 18
  Lodwick, 50
  Ludwick, 25, 40
PRY, Philip, 17
PUTNAM,
  Andrew, 7

-Q-
QUIGLEY,
  Margaret, 25
QUINAN,
  Patrick, 14

-R-
RAGAN,
  Amelia, 33, 50
  Barbara, 6
  John, 50
  John Henry, 50
  Susannah, 50
RAIMER,
  Frederick, 20, 36
RAMER,
  Benjamin, 7
  Frederick, 51
  John, 7
RAPE,
  Elizabeth, 1
RAUHAUSER,
  Mr., 2
RAYNER,
  Benjamin, 7

INDEX

Frederick, 7
John, 7
REBB,
  Christian, 18
  John, 18
  Michael, 18
  Peter, 18
REED,
  John, 1
  Mary Ann, 51
  Peter, 1
REEDER,
  Alexander, 50
  Ann Elizabeth, 50
  Francis, 50
  Frederick, 18, 50
  Harmon, 18
  Hiram, 50
  Jesse, 50
  Jessee, 33
  John, 18
  Joseph, 50
  Kennllum, 18
  Mary, 18
  Philip, 33, 50
REEL,
  Barbara, 50
  Daniel, 50
  Henry, 50
  John, 50
  Joseph, 50
  Michael, 50
  Rezin, 50
  Samuel, 50
REESE,
  Margaret, 6
REICHARD,
  Daniel, 43
  Samuel, 39
REIGH,
  Barbara, 7
  Mathias, 7
RENCH,
  Barbara, 19
  Barnhart, 19
  Catherine, 34
  Elizabeth, 34
  Frederick, 19
  Henry, 19
  Jacob, 10, 18, 19, 23, 34
  John, 18, 19

John A., 34
Joseph, 44, 34
Margaret, 19, 23, 34
Mary, 34
Peter, 18, 19, 34
Philip, 19
Rebecca, 10
Samuel H., 34
Theresa, 34
William, 19
RENEBERGER,
  Catherine, 34
RENNER,
  Jacob, 46
  Rebecca, 32
RENOLD,
  Eve, 7
  Peter, 7
RENTCH,
  Andrew, 50
  Angelica, 50
  Ann, 50
  Catherine, 50
  Daniel, 50
  Daniel S., 50
  Ealenore, 50
  John, 50
  John A., 50
  Joseph, 50
  Lawrence, 50
  Margaret Y., 50
  Peter, 50
  Samuel H., 50
REPLEY,
  George, 50
  Henry, 50
  Jacob, 50
  John, 50
  Joseph, 50
  Lidia, 50
RESH,
  Daniel, 34
  Joseph, 34
RESLER,
  Esther, 52
RESSLER,
  James, 54
REUBEN,
  Richard, 47
REYDEY,
  Ludwick, 4
REYNOLD,
  Jacob, 19

Peter, 19
Samuel, 19
REYNOLDS,
  Daniel, 19
  Danise, 19
  George, 19
  Henry, 19
  John, 7, 19, 47
  Joseph, 7
  Mary, 19, 23
  Peggy, 19
  Peter, 19
RIBBLE,
  Rebecca, 19
RICE,
  Barbara, 50
  Henry, 50
  Jacob, 19, 50
  Mary, 46, 50
RICH,
  Samuel, 46
RICHABACK,
  Ann, 12
RICHARD,
  Daniel, 27
RICHARDSON,
  Margaret, 28
RICHART,
  Barbara, 19, 34
  Christian, 19, 34
  Daniel, 19, 34
  Eve, 19
  Holsinger, 19
  Jacob, 19, 34
  John, 19
RICKENBAUGH,
  Daniel, 7
  David, 7
  Henry, 7
  Jacob, 7
  Martin, 7
  Samuel, 7
RIDENOUR,
  Adam, 19, 34
  Amelia, 19, 34
  Ann, 50
  Anna, 34
  Anne, 19
  Archibald, 34, 50
  Barbara, 7
  Benjamin, 7
  Catherine, 7
  Charles, 19, 23, 34

DISTRIBUTION OF ESTATE ACCOUNTS

Conrad, 19, 34
Conrod, 7
D., 50
Daniel, 7, 19, 34, 50
David, 7, 19, 34
Dorothy, 50
Elizabeth, 7, 34, 50
Esther, 32, 48
Eve, 19, 34
Flora, 19
George, 19, 34
Henry, 7, 19, 34
Isaac, 50
Jacob, 7, 19, 25, 34, 46, 50
John, 7, 34, 50
John D., 50
Joseph, 22, 38, 50
Lydia, 50
Lydia A., 34, 50
Margaret, 34, 50
Martin, 3, 7, 10, 12, 23
Mary, 19, 21, 34, 37, 50
Mathias, 7
Matthias, 7
Nancy, 19, 34, 50
Nicholas, 7
Peter, 22, 50
Rebecca, 34, 50
Samuel, 19, 34
Sarah, 4, 34
Susanna, 30, 45
Susannah, 7
Upton, 34, 50
RIDEOUT, Mary, 54
RIELEY, Josiah, 23
RIGGES,
 Edmund, 20
 Elizabeth, 19, 20
 Mary, 19, 20
RILEY,
 Elizabeth, 11
 Josiah, 3
RINEHART,
 Andrew, 15
 Catherine, 54

Henry, 30
RINGER,
 Jacob, 1
 John, 22
RINGGOLD,
 Samuel, 18, 34
RIPLEY,
 Daniel, 50
RITCHIE,
 Archibald, 19, 34, 50
 Esther, 19, 34, 50
 John, 19, 34
RITTER,
 Elias, 19
 Jacob, 19
 John, 19
 Tobias, 10
RITZ,
 Daniel, 34
 Elizabeth, 34
 Sarah, 34
 Solomon, 34
 Valentine, 34
ROADS,
 Eve, 13
 George, 13, 14
ROBB,
 Christian, 34
 John, 34
 Michael, 34
 Peter, 34
ROBERTS,
 Ann, 45
ROBERTSON,
 Isaac, 54
 Sarah, 54
ROBEY,
 Deborah, 19
 Isaac, 19, 20
 Owen, 19, 20
 Statea, 19
 Susannah, 19, 20
 William, 19, 20
ROBINSON,
 Sarah, 6, 17, 32
ROCKAFIELD,
 Elizabeth, 30
ROCKERFIELD,
 Elizabeth, 46
RODERICK,
 Lodwick, 7
RODES,
 Barbara, 5

RODICK,
 Jacob, 34
 Joshua, 34
ROEBECK,
 Elizabeth, 29
ROHRBACK,
 David, 50
 Elizabeth, 29, 45
 Henry, 50
 John, 50
 Mary H., 50
ROHRER,
 Amanda, 50
 Barbara, 17
 Catherine, 6, 27
 Christian, 20, 52
 Christina, 9
 Daniel, 20
 David, 50, 52, 53
 Elias, 50
 Elizabeth, 26, 27, 42, 43, 50, 53
 Frederick, 20
 Henry, 42
 Jacob, 9, 10, 20, 50
 John, 3, 20, 50
 John of Martin, 14
 Jonathan, 34
 Joseph, 27
 Magdalena, 50
 Mahala, 50
 Marietta, 50
 Martin, 11, 42
 Mary, 42
 Rachel, 26
 Rose, 6
 Samuel, 20, 34, 50
 Silas, 50
 Sophia, 26
 Susanna, 27
ROLAND,
 Abraham, 3
 Barbara, 3
ROME,
 Catherine, 7
 David, 7
 Elizabeth, 7
 Henry, 7
 Jacob, 7
 Mary, 7
 Susanna, 7
RONEY,
 Margaret, 27

INDEX

Michael, 27
ROOF,
  Anthony, 8
ROOT,
  Barbara, 20
  Elizabeth, 20, 34
  Esther, 20
  Jacob, 13, 20, 34
  Mary, 20
ROPP,
  Christian, 22
ROSE,
  Mary, 4
ROSS,
  Catherine, 17, 50
  David, 50
  David C., 50
  Nelly, 49
  Samuel, 50
ROTENBELLER,
  Rachel, 34
ROUDEBUSH,
  Christian, 35
ROUDEROCK,
  Daniel, 3
ROUGH,
  Ann, 7
  Barbara, 34
  Barney, 34
  Barnhart, 34
  Catherine, 7
  Henry, 7, 34
  John, 7, 34
  Margaret, 34
  Philip, 34
  Polly, 7
  William, 34
ROULET,
  Thomas, 47
ROULETT,
  Daniel, 35
  John, 35
  Sarah Ann, 35
  William, 35
ROW,
  E., 7
  Rebecca, 47
ROWE,
  Jacob, 9
ROWLAND,
  Barbara, 3, 39, 50
  Benjamin, 50
  Christian, 20
  David, 50
  Elie, 50
  Elizabeth, 21, 37, 39
  Emanuel, 20
  Henry, 50
  Isaac, 50
  Jacob, 5, 20, 46, 50
  John, 50, 54
  Jonathan, 20
  Lidia, 50
  Nancy, 52
  Nathaniel, 54
  Rosannah, 20
ROYER,
  Susannah, 54
RUFF,
  Michael, 10
RUNNER,
  Isaac, 50
  Jacob, 15
  Priscilla, 50
  Rebecca, 50
  Sarah, 44
  William, 50
RUPALL,
  Elizabeth, 15
RUSELL,
  Ann, 38
  Elizabeth, 28
RUSH,
  John, 9
  Susanna, 9
RUSSELL,
  Catherine, 35
  Christian, 35
  Elizabeth, 44
  George, 7
  Henry, 7
  Jacob, 7
  John, 7, 35
  mary, 35
  Rebecca, 35
  Susanna, 35
RUTLEDGE,
  Ann, 1
RUTTER,
  Alexander, 7
  Edmund, 1, 7

-S-
SAILOR,
  Peter, 20
SALETY,
  Christina, 3
SAMUEL,
  Samuel, 43
SANDMAN,
  Jacob, 35
  William, 35
SCHENK,
  Christian, 35
  Christine, 35
  Daniel, 35
  John, 35
  Magdalena, 35
SCHLEIGH,
  Eza, 50
  Gideon, 50
  Henry, 24, 38, 40, 50
  Isaac, 50
  Jacob, 50
  John, 50
  Mary, 50
SCHLENKER,
  Henry, 20
SCHMUTZ,
  Abraham, 14, 35
  Catherine, 14
SCHNEBLEY,
  Elizabeth, 17
SCHNEBLY,
  Adam, 12
  Ann, 20
  Ann Maria, 50
  Calvin, 50
  Catherine, 7, 19, 50
  Christian, 9
  Christina, 7
  Conrad, 8
  Daniel, 34, 38, 50, 53
  David, 20
  David H., 50
  Elizabeth, 50
  Henry, 4, 7, 20
  I., 10
  Jacob, 6, 17, 32
  James, 20
  John, 18, 19, 20, 35
  Leonard, 7, 20, 35

DISTRIBUTION OF ESTATE ACCOUNTS

Margaret, 50
Margarette, 9
Polly, 45
Susanna, 7, 30, 35
Susannah, 46
SCHNELL,
  Eliza, 7
  Henry, 7
  Jacob, 7
  John, 7
  Judith, 7
  Philip, 7
  Phillip, 7
  Sarah, 7
SCHOENZ,
  Christian, 53
SCHRADER,
  Catherine, 38
SCHRIVER,
  Marian, 39
SCHRODER,
  Henry, 35
SCOITHER,
  Mary, 21
SCOTT,
  George, 35
SCOUTHER,
  Barbara, 21
SCYAFOOSE,
  Mary, 42
SEAGRIST,
  Esther, 10
SEIBERT,
  Catherine, 37, 50
  Elizabeth, 35, 49
  George, 34, 50
  George P., 50
  Henry, 35, 49, 50
  Jacob, 20, 35, 37
  John, 5, 37, 50
  Louisa, 50
  Margaret, 5, 46
  Mary, 35
  Mary Ann, 50
  Michael, 35, 50
  Michael Henry, 50
  Nicholas, 35
  Peter, 35

Susan, 50
Susannah, 8
SEYSTER,
  Andrew H., 50
  Daniel, 50
  Elizabeth K., 50
  Lewis C., 50
  Michael, 38
  Samuel, 53
  Sarah, 50
SHAFER,
  Ann M., 51
  Barbara, 8
  Caroline B., 51
  Catherine, 8, 21
  Charles W., 35
  Christian, 35
  D., 7
  David, 51
  Davolt, 7
  Elizabeth, 8, 51
  Fanny, 51
  George, 4, 8, 20, 35, 51
  Gustavus W., 51
  Harriet E., 51
  Henry, 8, 13, 16, 20, 21, 27, 30, 35, 37
  Henry I., 47
  John, 8, 13, 17, 33
  John S., 51
  Leonard, 8, 36, 51
  Lewis A., 51
  Mary, 8, 36, 51
  Peter, 20, 35
  Samuel B., 51
  Solomon, 35
  Sophia P., 51
  Thomas H., 51
  William A., 51
SHAFFER,
  Barbara, 20
SHAKETER,
  Wendle, 4
SHALL, George, 11
SHAME, Philip, 33
SHANAFELTZ,
  Abraham, 47
SHANBERGER,
  Margaret, 36
SHANE,
  Adam, 35
  Catherine, 35

Daniel, 35
Elizabeth, 35
George, 35
Henry, 35
Jone, 35
Mary, 35
Peter, 35
Susanna, 35
SHANEBERGER,
  John, 28
SHANEFELT,
  Andrew, 51
  Catherine, 8
  Daniel, 51
  David, 51
  Elizabeth, 8
  Eve, 8
  Frederick, 8
  Henry, 51
  Jacob, 51
  John, 8, 51
  Margaret, 8
  Mary, 8
  Susannah, 51
  William, 7, 8, 51
SHANK,
  Barbara, 19, 51
  Christian, 9, 44, 51
  David, 51
  Elizabeth, 9
  Frederick, 44
  George, 51
  Henrietta, 51
  Henry, 44, 51
  Jacob, 44, 51, 54
  John, 44
  Jonas, 44
  Margaret, 51
  Michael, 51
  Noah, 44
  Samuel, 51
  Sophia, 44
SHARER,
  Catherine, 51
  Henry, 35
SHARRICK,
  Sarah, 44
SHATTLEY,
  Christine, 18
SHAVER,
  George, 8, 9
  Henry, 5
  Peggy, 8

INDEX

Peter, 8
Philip, 8
SHAW,
  Eleanor, 22
  Frederick, 10, 22
SHEARER,
  Elizabeth, 35
  Henry, 20
  John, 20, 37
SHECTER,
  Andrew, 8
  Henry, 8
  Wendle, 8
SHECTOR,
  Daniel, 35
  Jacob, 35
  Lydia, 35
  Susanna, 37
SHEDLER,
  Catherine, 9
SHEELMAN,
  Susannah, 48
SHEES,
  Peter, 8
  Switzer, 8
  Weaver, 8
SHEETS,
  Elizabeth, 44
  Frederick, 8
SHEETZ,
  Daniel, 35
  Elizabeth, 35
  Mary Ann, 35
  Maryann, 35
  Peter, 35
  Rachel, 24, 40
SHEFLER,
  Nicholas, 4
SHEITZ,
  Daniel, 35
  Elizabeth, 35
  Mary Ann, 35
  Maryann, 35
  Peter, 35
SHELL,
  Catherine, 52
SHELLEBERGER,
  David, 51
SHELLER,
  Adam, 20
  Christian, 20
  Daniel, 20
  Henry, 20

William, 20
SHELLING,
  David, 51
  Elizabeth, 51
  Jacob, 51
  Jonas, 51
  Lewis, 51
  Philip, 51
  Susannah, 51
  William, 51
SHELLMAN,
  Catherine, 51
  Elizabeth, 51
  Jacob, 51
  John, 51
  Magdalena, 51
  Mary Ann, 51
  Susannah, 51
SHELLY,
  Magdalena, 15, 29
SHENK,
  Abraham, 35
  Andrew, 35
  Catherine, 31
  Christian, 35
  Daniel, 35
  George, 31
  Henry, 35
  Jacob, 35
  John, 35
  Julianna, 31
SHEPHERD,
  Alexander, 51
  Christian, 35
  David, 35, 51
  Elizabeth, 35
  George, 35
  Jacob, 35
  Jane, 51
  John, 35, 51
  Joseph, 35, 51
  Michael, 35
  Peter, 35
  Ruhemiah, 51
  Sally, 51
  Samuel, 35
  Sarah, 35
  Thomas, 35, 51
  William, 35
SHEPPERD,
  Amanda, 51
  Henry, 51
  James, 51
  Joseph, 51

Mary, 51
Sarah, 51
Thomas, 51
SHERLEY,
  Joseph, 35
SHIDELER,
  Magdalena, 49
SHIFFLER,
  John, 35
  Mary, 35
  Nicholas, 35
SHILLING,
  Catey, 4
  Philip, 4
SHINEFELT,
  John, 17
SHIVELY,
  Adam, 51, 53
  Catherine, 9, 53
  Isaac, 53
SHIVER,
  David, 46
SHIVES,
  Robert, 47
SHOCKEY,
  Abraham, 8
  Ann, 8
  Catherine, 8
  Christian, 8
SHONEFELT,
  Andrew, 20
  Elizabeth, 20
  Henry, 20
  Jacob, 20
  John, 20
  Peter, 20
  Sarah, 20
  Susannah, 20
  William, 20
SHONG,
  Elenor, 10
  Ellen, 51
  Irvem, 51
  Joseph, 51
  Mary E., 51
  Matthias, 51
  Shepherd, 51
SHOOK,
  Elizabeth, 20
  John, 20
  Susannah, 20
SHOOTZ,
  Daniel, 35
  Elizabeth, 35

DISTRIBUTION OF ESTATE ACCOUNTS

Mary Ann, 35
Maryann, 35
Peter, 35
SHORT,
  Jane, 20
  John, 24
  Mary, 24, 40
SHOTT,
  Margaret, 8
  Philip, 8
SHOWER, John, 1
SHOWERY, John, 35
SHOWMAN,
  Catherine, 8, 36, 51
  David, 36, 51
  George, 36, 51
  Jacob, 36, 51
  John, 36, 51
  Kesiah, 26
  Kessiah, 26
  Magdalena, 6, 17, 32
  Mary M., 36
  Peter, 36, 51
SHRADER,
  Frederick, 36
  Henry, 36
  John, 36
  Sarah, 36
SHULL,
  Jacob, 20
  Stephen, 20
SHULTZ,
  Eliza, 51
  Elizabeth, 8
  George, 8
  Mary, 8
  Nicholas, 51
SHUMAN,
  Christine, 36
  Samuel, 36
  Sarah E., 36
  Thomas, 1
SHUNK, George, 5
SHUP,
  Ann, 29
  Susanna, 29
SHUPE,
  Adam, 36, 51
  Andrew, 15
  Ann, 20
  Daniel, 20
  David, 20
  Elizabeth, 20, 36, 51
  Frederick, 20
  Henry, 11, 20
  Jacob, 20
  John, 20, 36, 51
  Jonathan, 20
  Polly, 36
  Samuel, 20
  Simon, 20
  Susanna, 20, 36
SHUTT,
  Christine, 37
SHYROCK,
  Catherine, 8
  Elizabeth, 8
  Henry, 5, 8
  John, 8
  Leonard, 8
  Mary, 8
  Michael, 8
  susanna, 8
SIBERT,
  Catherine, 22
  Elizabeth, 20, 36
  Henry, 20, 36
  Jacob, 20, 36
  John, 20
  Michael, 20, 36
  Peter, 20, 36
SIDERSTICK,
  Elizabeth, 27
SILER,
  Daniel, 20
  Elizabeth, 20
  George, 20
  John, 20
  Mary, 20
SILOR,
  Daniel, 20
  Elizabeth, 20
  George, 20
  John, 20
  Mary, 20
SILVER,
  Samuel, 33
SIMMONS,
  Jacob, 8
  Jonathan, 8
  Joseph, 8
  Sarah, 8
SIMPKINS,
  Derius, 51
  Derrius, 51
  Elizabeth, 51
  John W., 51
  Macey, 51
  Mary, 51
  Nancy Ann, 51
  Rebecca, 51
  Ruth Ann, 51
  Sarah, 51
  Susan, 51
  William, 11, 27, 51
SIMPSON,
  Sarah, 45
SINGER,
  John, 52
  Magdalena, 19, 34
SISLER,
  John, 35
  Mary, 35
SITES,
  Hester, 2
SLAGLE,
  Barbara, 28
  Elizabeth, 41
  Jacob, 41
  John, 28
  Magdolena, 12
SLICKLEATHER,
  Eve, 17
  Peter, 17
SLIFER,
  Catherine, 51
  Elmira, 51
  Ezra, 51
  Magdalena, 54
  Mary, 20
  Olinda, 51
  Oliver, 51
  Philip, 20
  Randolph, 51
  Rebecca, 51
  Samuel, 25
  Stephen, 20
SMALL,
  Sarah, 19, 34
SMALLENBERGER,
  Francis, 20
  Henry, 20
  Michael, 20
  Peter, 20
SMELTZER,
  Catherine, 20
  Elizabeth, 20
  George C., 20

INDEX

Leonard, 45
SMICE,
  John, 3
SMISER,
  Ann, 8
  Mathias, 8
SMITH,
  Alexander, 20, 36, 51
  Andrew, 8
  Ann, 19
  Ann Eliza, 36
  Catherine, 28, 20, 24, 36, 37, 39, 44, 51, 53
  Christian, 8, 18, 33, 36
  Christina, 51
  David, 8
  Elizabeth, 34, 36, 51
  George, 8, 14, 15, 27, 30, 36, 38, 42, 43, 45, 48, 51
  Henry, 36, 51
  Hezekiah, 36
  Jacob, 8, 36, 51
  John, 8, 22, 28, 36, 51, 52
  John A., 51, 52
  John H., 44
  Joseph, 2, 15, 20, 36, 39, 40, 51
  Magdalena, 6, 17, 36
  Margaret, 20, 36, 39
  Maria, 36
  Marian, 10
  Martin, 36
  Mary, 8, 28, 30, 45
  Mary Ann, 23
  Mathias, 36
  Matthias, 51
  Michael, 36, 51
  Michael P., 47, 51
  Nancy, 50
  Nicholas, 20, 36, 51
  Peter, 36, 51
  Polly, 8
  Rebecca, 48
  Robert, 2, 18, 33
  Sarah, 36
  Sophia, 36
  Susanna, 36
  William, 36
  William G., 51
  William S., 52
  Zebina, 31, 36, 51, 52
SMOOT,
  George, 16
SMOOTZ,
  Barbara, 14
  George, 14, 18
SMYSER,
  Matthias, 8
SNAVELY,
  Adam, 8
  Casper, 8
  Catherine, 20
  Conrad, 8
  George, 20
  Henry, 8
  Jacob, 8, 20, 23
  John, 8, 20
  Joshua, 20
SNEARY,
  James, 52
  John, 52
  Nancy, 52
SNELL,
  Margaret, 1
  Rebecca, 31, 47, 48
SNEVELY,
  Andrew, 3
  Jacob, 1, 4
  John, 1
  Susanna, 3
SNIBELY,
  Coonrod, 7
SNIVELY,
  Joseph, 46, 39
  Nancy, 39
SNYDER,
  Abraham, 8, 28, 43, 52
  Adam, 8, 21, 36
  Andrew, 54
  Barbara, 52
  Casper, 8, 21
  Catherine, 18, 21, 36, 54
  Christian, 22, 38, 52
  Daniel, 8
  David, 8, 21, 36, 37
  Elizabeth, 8, 21, 22, 52, 54
  George, 8, 21, 36, 52
  HEnry, 52
  Henry, 21, 36
  Jackson, 52
  Jacob, 21, 23, 36, 52
  John, 8, 21, 36, 37, 52, 54
  John T., 52
  Jonathan, 21
  Joseph, 52
  L., 26
  Leonard, 21, 52
  Louisa, 52
  Margaret, 2, 21, 26, 36
  Martin, 21, 36, 37, 52
  Mary, 21, 36, 43, 52
  Michael, 21, 36, 37
  Motlena, 21
  Otho, 52
  Peter, 21, 37, 51, 52
  Sally, 54
  Sarah, 21
  Sarah A., 52
  Simon, 54
  Susanna, 26
  Susannah, 21
  William B., 52
SOLLADAY,
  Christina, 3
SOUDENBERGER,
  Nancy, 50
SOUTH,
  Benjamin, 21
  Gara, 21
  Gera, 53
  Hannah, 17
SPAWN,
  John, 1

DISTRIBUTION OF ESTATE ACCOUNTS

SPEACE,
  Daniel, 37
  Margaret, 37
SPEALMAN,
  Catherine, 52
  David, 52
  Hitam W., 52
SPECK,
  Christian, 12
SPEILMAN,
  Jacob, 21
  John, 21
  Michael, 21
SPESSART,
  Elizabeth, 47
  John, 47
  Margaret, 47
  Maria, 47
  Peter, 47
  Susannah, 47
SPESSERT,
  Catherine, 52
SPICKLER,
  John, 37
  Nicholas, 37
  Samuel, 37
SPIELMAN,
  Catherine, 52
  Elizabeth, 52
  Jacob, 52
  Jeremiah, 52
  John, 52
  Margaret, 51
  Sarah, 52
SPITZNOGLE,
  Elizabeth, 22
SPONG,
  Elizabeth, 24
  Sarah, 51
SPONSLOR,
  George, 46
SPRECHER,
  Mary, 30
  Samuel, 30
SPRIGG,
  D., 24
  Daniel, 24
SPRINKLE,
  Michael, 16, 30
STAH,
  Catherine, 39
  Elizabeth, 39
  Jacob, 39
  John, 39

  Susanna, 39
STAHL,
  Abraham, 52
  Catherine, 52
  Christina, 52
  Henry, 52
  Jacob, 52
  John, 52
  Lydia, 52
  Michael, 52
  Sarah, 52
STAKE,
  Daniel, 11
  David, 11
  Susanna, 11
STAKES,
  Andrew K., 52
  Edward G. W., 52
  Peter, 52
  Rosanna, 52
  Susannah S., 52
STARTZMAN,
  David, 37, 52
  Eve, 52
  Henry, 37, 52
  Martin, 37, 52
  Rebecca, 37
STASSLER, Caty, 4
STATSMAN,
  Margaret, 9
STEAMAN,
  Mary M., 29
STEBLER,
  Mary, 43
  Sarah, 14, 27, 43
STEFFEE,
  Andrew, 8
  Elizabeth, 8
  George, 8
  Michael, 8
  Nicholas, 8
  Peter, 8
STEFFEY,
  Andrew, 21
  Catherine, 21
  Elizabeth, 21
  George, 21
  Henry, 11
  Nicholas, 21
  Peter, 21
STEFFY,
  Catherine, 17
STEINMETZ,
  Mary, 50

STEPHEN,
  Andrew, 8
  Leonard, 8
STEPHENS,
  Amanda, 37
  Andrew, 5
  Catherine, 32
  David, 37
  Elizabeth, 5
  Elmira, 37
  Harriet, 37
  James H. B., 37
  Nancy, 37
  Samuel M., 37
  Upton, 37
STEPHEY,
  Andrew, 51, 52
  Ann Mary, 52
  Catherine, 52
  Daniel, 51, 52
  David, 52
  Elizabeth, 51
  George, 52
  Isaac, 51, 52
  Jacob, 51, 52
  John D., 52
  John P., 51, 52
  Mary, 52
  Mary Ann, 52
  Nicholas, 52
  Samuel, 51, 52
  Susan, 52
STERRET,
  James, 21
  John, 46
  John W., 21
  Joseph W., 21
  Nancy, 21
  Natha, 46
  Philip, 46
  Polly, 46
STERRETT,
  Nancy, 30, 45
  Rachel, 30, 45
STEWARD,
  Elizabeth, 53
  Sarah, 32
STEWDARD,
  Elizabeth, 36
STEWETARD,
  Elizabeth, 51
STIFFLER,
  Cornelius, 38
  Sarah, 43

INDEX

STILLWELL,
  Elias, 26
  Sarah, 26
STINE,
  Catherine, 52
  E.___, 21
  Elizabeth, 21
  George, 52
  Henry, 21
  Jacob, 52
  John, 21, 52
  Julianna, 21
  Margaret, 21, 32
  Mathias, 52
  Polly, 21
  Samuel, 21
  Sophia, 51
  Susanna, 21
STITTA,
  Elizabeth, 6
STIVES,
  Sophia, 36
STOCKSLAGER,
  George H., 52
  Henry, 52
  John, 52
STOCKWELL,
  Ralph, 49
STONE,
  Elizabeth, 1, 39
  Mary, 18, 33
STONEBRAKER,
  Christian, 25
  George, 37
  Gerald, 19, 34
  Gerard, 36, 37, 39
  John, 37
  Leonard, 47
  Michael, 37
  Nancy, 47
STONEBREAKER,
  Christian, 11
  Jane, 11
STONELLING,
  Hy___, 17
STONER,
  David, 3, 37
  Fanny, 33
  John, 21
STOTLER,
  Esther, 3
  John, 3, 52
  Peter, 52

STOUFER,
  Henry, 38
STOUFFER,
  Amelia P., 52
  Ann P., 52
  Christian, 37, 52
  David, 52
  Elizabeth, 33
  Jacob, 37, 52
  John, 52
  Lydia, 52
  Samuel, 37, 52
STOUGER,
  Elizabeth, 49
STOUPS,
  Elizabeth, 48
STOVER,
  Catherine, 8
  Christian, 2, 21, 37
  David, 21, 37
  Fanny, 49
  Frederick, 8
  George, 8
  Jacob, 8, 21, 37
  John, 8, 21, 37
  Margaret, 8, 21, 37
  Mary, 10
  Michael, 8
STOWTER,
  Mary, 21
  Philip, 21
STRAUSE,
  Christina, 3
  Henry, 3
STREIGHT,
  Christian, 9
  Laurence, 9
  Leonard, 9
  Sarah, 9
  William, 9
STRITE,
  Christian, 49
  Elizabeth, 32
STROHE,
  Charlotte, 21
STROME,
  Barbara, 39
  David, 39
  George, 39
  Henry, 39
STRUMBAUGH,
  George, 9
  Magdalena, 9

  Philip, 9
STUART,
  Sarah, 17
STUCKEY,
  Abraham, 9, 20
  Daniel, 9, 20
  Eliza, 9
  Jacob, 9, 20
  Mary, 9, 20
  Samuel, 9, 20
  Simon, 9, 20
STUDANBAKER,
  Mary, 5
STUDER,
  Elizabeth, 28
  Philip, 28
STUDY,
  Margaret, 31
STULL,
  Christine, 22
  Daniel, 21
  Eliza, 21
  Emily, 21
STULTZ,
  David, 37, 52
  Henry, 37, 52
  John, 37, 52
  Peter, 37, 52
  Samuel, 52
STURR,
  Jacob, 31
STUTOR,
  Charlotte, 21
  Mary, 21
  Philip, 21
SUMMER,
  Nathaniel, 50
SUMMERS,
  Alfred, 37
  Elizabeth, 18, 33
  Henry, 6
  Jacob, 9, 18, 21, 37
  John, 9, 21
  Mary, 9, 21
  Peter, 9, 21
  Susanna, 53
  William, 37
SUNDAY,
  Elizabeth, 9
SUTER,
  Jacob, 46
SWANN,
  Alexander, 29, 44

DISTRIBUTION OF ESTATE ACCOUNTS

SWEARINGEN,
  John V., 31
SWEARINGER,
  John N., 25
SWEARINGIN,
  Charles, 37
  John V., 37
SWEIGHER,
  John, 21
  Mary, 21
SWEYER,
  John, 31
SWILER,
  Catherine, 9
SWINEHART,
  Esther, 49
SWINGLE,
  Benjamin, 51
SWINGLEY,
  Barbara, 21, 22
  Benjamin, 20, 22, 36
  Catherine E., 43
  Christine, 21
  Elizabeth, 16, 37, 45
  John, 21, 37, 45
  Mary, 33
  Nathaniel, 37, 45
  Nicholas, 37
  Philip, 21, 22
  Samuel, 22
  William, 43
SWOOPE,
  Catherine, 22, 37
  Elizabeth, 22, 37
  Jacob, 22, 50
  Jacob S. W., 37
  Magdalena, 22, 37
  Peter, 22, 37
SWOOPS,
  Peter, 23
SWOP,
  Barnett, 5
SYBERT,
  John, 4

-T-

TAILOR,
  Elizabeth, 18, 34
TANNER,
  Elizabeth, 15
TAYLOR,
  Barbara, 22
  Catherine, 22
  David, 22
  Elizabeth, 22
  John, 22
  Michael, 22
  Peter, 22
  Polly, 22
  Sophia, 28
TEACH,
  Sally, 39
TEATHERHOOF,
  Cather, 34
  Catherine, 19, 34
TECKERHOOF,
  Barbara, 10
TEISHER,
  Jacob, 37
  John, 37, 54
  Mary, 37
TENANT,
  James, 49
TETERICK,
  Barbara, 9
  Conrad, 9
  Francis, 9
  Isaiah, 9
  John, 9
  Magdalen, 9
  Peter, 9
  Philip, 9
TETRICK,
  Barbara, 16
THALLS,
  Joseph, 22
  Mary, 22
  Rebecca, 22
  Richard, 22
  Samuel, 22
  Sophia, 22
THAME,
  Philip, 18
THEDRICK,
  Robert, 48
THOMAS,
  Abraham, 22, 37
  Catherine, 22
  Christine, 37
  Daniel, 52
  David, 22, 53
  Elizabeth, 16, 22
  Gabriel, 52
  George, 22, 37, 53
  Gideon, 53
  Henry, 22, 37
  Jacob, 22, 37
  Jeremiah, 9
  John, 9, 22, 53
  Joseph, 9
  Lewis, 37
  Margaret, 22, 53
  Mary, 9, 22, 42, 53
  Mary Ann, 53
  Michael, 22, 37, 53
  Nancy, 22, 53
  Peter, 7, 22, 53
  Polly, 22
  Rosanna, 22
  Sarah, 22, 53
  Simon, 53
  Sodwick, 22, 37
  Sophia, 53
  Susanna, 22, 37
  Susannah, 53
  Thomas, 53
  Valentine, 53
  William, 9
THOME,
  Ann, 14
THOMSON,
  Daniel, 34
  Mary, 34
  Valentine, 34
THORNBURGH,
  Thomas C., 31
THRALLS,
  Casandra, 9
  Jacob, 9
  Joan, 9
  Joseph, 9
  Richard, 9
  Sigmund, 9
THUMB,
  Ann, 22
  Baltzer, 22
  David, 22
  George, 22
  Nancy, 43
  Susannah, 22
  William, 22
THUSDY,
  Ann, 9

INDEX

TICE,
  Elizabeth, 1
  Esther, 22
  Henry, 22
  Henry R., 53
  Jacob, 53
  John, 53
  Maria, 47
  Michael, 22
  Otto, 53
  Peter, 22
  Polly, 44
  Sarah Ann B., 53
  Upton, 53
  William M., 53
TINKLE,
  Daniel, 6, 17, 32
TISHER,
  John, 22
TITWILER,
  Catherine, 4
TOMS,
  Catherine, 37
  Elizabeth, 37
  Ezra, 37
  Maria, 37
TONER,
  Joseph, 6
TOOLER,
  Elizabeth, 21
  Esther, 21
TOULSON,
  James, 52
  Susannah, 44
  Thomas, 52
  William, 52
TOWER,
  Joseph, 6
TOWNSEND,
  Catherine, 49
  Delila, 49
TOWSON,
  Jacob, 35
  Jacob F., 20, 22
  Jacob T., 30, 45
  William, 36, 51, 52
TRESLER,
  Adam, 9
  Barbara, 9
  Frederick, 9
  George, 9
  Jacob, 9
  John, 9
  Mary, 9
TROUP,
  Adam, 9, 53
  Ann, 21, 37
  Christian, 53
  Christine, 37
  David, 9, 37, 53
  Henry, 9, 53
  Jacob, 37, 53
  John, 27, 37, 43, 53
  Nancy, 37
  Peggy, 37
TROVINGER,
  Amos, 53
  Christian, 37
  Christopher, 53
  Daniel, 37, 53
  David, 53
  Jacob, 53
  John, 37, 53
  Joseph, 37, 53
  Samuel, 37, 53
  William, 37, 53
TROXELL,
  Abraham, 4, 5, 9
  Anna, 9
  Catherine, 9
  Daniel, 9
  David, 9
  George, 9
  John, 24
  Magdalena, 9
  Mary, 20, 24
  Peter, 9
  Salome, 9
  Sarah, 9
  Susanna, 9
TRUAX,
  Joseph, 53
TUCKERMAN,
  Elizabeth, 53
  John, 53
  Mary, 53
  Rachel, 53
  Sarah, 53
  Thomas, 53
TUG,
  David, 9
  Frederick, 9
  Jacob, 9
  John, 9
  Mary, 9
TUPING,
  Anne Maria, 6
TURBY,
  Mary, 54
TURNER,
  Catherine L., 53
  Catherine S., 53
  Edmond H., 53
  Jane E., 53
  Lewis, 53
  Mary, 32
  Susan M., 53
TUSSING,
  Anne Maria, 6
TUTEWILER,
  David, 53
  Jacob, 53
  John, 53
TUTWILER,
  Henry, 9
  Jacob, 9
TWIGG,
  John, 9
  Rebecca, 9
TYCE,
  Catherine, 16
TYLER,
  Catherine, 21
  Daniel, 22
TYSHER,
  Dorathy, 38
  Dorotha, 22
  John, 38
  Mary, 18
  Peter, 22, 38
TYSON,
  Benjamin, 22

-U-

UMBARGER,
  Polly, 36
UMBAUGH,
  George, 51
UPDEGRAFF,
  George, 53
  Samuel, 53
  Susannah, 53
USHERMAN,
  Elizabeth, 31

-V-

VAN BUSKIRK,
  Daniel, 53
  David, 53

DISTRIBUTION OF ESTATE ACCOUNTS

George, 53
John, 53
Lawanee, 53
Mary, 53
Samuel, 53
William, 53
VAN LEAR,
  Joseph, 53
  Mary L., 53
  Mathew, 53
  Mathew L., 53
  Samuel L., 53
  Samuel S., 53
  Sarah S., 53
  Thomas, 53
  Thomas F., 53
  William, 53
  William H., 53
VANBUSKIRK,
  Daniel, 22
  Lawrence, 22
  Mary, 22
VARNER,
  Henry, 4
  Paul, 4
  Susanna, 18
VERVIL,
  Christian, 53
  Christopher, 53
  Elizabeth, 53
  John, 22, 38, 53
  Mary, 53
  Mathias, 53
  Peter, 38, 53
VOLTZ,
  Elizabeth, 22
  Maria, 22
  Ulianna, 22
VOUSSEN,
  Cosin, 22
  Henry, 22
  Nancy, 22
  Peter, 22

-W-

WACHTEL,
  Edward, 22
  Elizabeth, 22, 38
  John, 22, 38
  Valentine, 52
WADE,
  Elias, 38, 53
  Henry, 38, 42,
    53
  John, 38, 53
  Mary Ann, 26
  Priscilla, 38
  William, 38
WAGNER,
  Catherine, 50
  Joseph, 50
  Mary, 11
WAGONER,
  George, 11
  Jacob, 20, 36, 51
  John, 32
  Philip, 9
  Regana, 9
  Susanna, 11
WALLACE,
  Ruth, 13
WALLER,
  Sarah, 9
WALLS,
  Catherine, 9
  Christina, 9
  Jacob, 9
  Martin, 9
  Mary, 9
WALTER,
  Sarah, 9
WALTERS,
  Leonard, 9
WALTMIRE,
  Polly, 39
WALTZ,
  Peter, 5
WARBLE,
  Barbara, 17
  Molly, 2
WARD,
  Ellen, 48
  Isabella, 21
  Rach, 48
  Simon, 21
WARDEN,
  James, 43
WARFIELD,
  Charles A., 45
WARNER,
  George, 22
  Jacob, 22
  Margaret, 22
WARTZ,
  John, 16
WARVEL,
  Daniel, 53
WASHBAUGH,
  Ann, 9
  Catherine, 9
  Dealmer, 9
WATSON,
  Richard, 38
  Sarah, 30
WATT,
  Archibald, 38
  Eliza, 38
  John, 38
  William, 38
WATTS,
  Abraham, 53
  Ann, 53
  Barton, 53
  Elizabeth, 53
  Frisby D., 53
  Henry, 53
  Joseph, 53
  Priscilla, 53
  Rachel, 53
  Sarah, 53
  Sarah Ann, 53
  Thomas, 53
  Thomas B., 53
  William, 53
WAUGH,
  Archibald, 38
  Archibald M., 38, 53
  Catherine, 38, 53
  Henrietta M. A., 38, 53
  James, 38
  James A., 53
  Mary Ann, 38
  Thomas M., 53
WEAST,
  Joseph, 53
  Otila R., 44
WEAVER,
  Ann, 39
  Daniel, 52
  Elizabeth, 10
WEBB,
  Anna, 11
  John, 38
  Margaret, 11, 40, 54
  Mary, 11
  Peter, 38
  Pointon, 40
  Samuel, 54

INDEX

William, 1, 3, 38
WEILAND,
  Elizabeth, 37
WEIMER,
  Solime, 10
WEISE,
  Andrew, 43
  David, 43
  Henry, 43
  John, 43
WEISEL,
  Margaret, 52
WEISELL,
  Daniell, 52
WELLER,
  Adam, 38
  Jacob, 38
WELLS,
  Aaron, 10
  Ann, 22
  Aron, 22
  Elijah, 22
  Elizabeth, 22
  Isaac, 22
  Jeremiah, 22
  Jerremiah, 10
  Polly, 22
  Rachel, 22
  Rezin, 10, 22
  Susanna, 22
  Thomas, 22
WELTY,
  Abraham, 54
  Ann, 54
  Barbara, 22
  Catha, 10
  Christian, 10, 22, 54
  Christine, 22
  Christly, 10
  Daniel, 21, 38, 47, 54
  David, 54
  Elizabeth, 20, 43
  Faney, 44
  Frederick, 22, 38
  Geroge, 22
  Henry, 10, 22, 38, 54
  Jacob, 16, 22, 30, 38, 54

John, 10, 22, 27, 29, 38, 42, 48, 52, 54
Joseph, 10
Magdalena, 33
Margaret, 49
Mary, 10, 22, 28
Nancy, 20
Samuel, 22, 54
Susanna, 10, 22
Susannah, 22
WENTLING,
  Christian, 30
  Christina, 52
  Christine, 16
WERTZ,
  Harmon, 17
  John, 30
  Susanna, 17
WEST,
  Abel, 54
  Benjamin, 54
  David, 54
  John, 29
WESTENBARGER,
  Catherine, 38
  David, 38
  Elizabeth, 38
  Samuel, 38
WESTENBERGER,
  David, 21, 22
  John, 22
  Mary, 22
  Motlena, 22
  Paul, 22
  Susanna, 22
WETTLE,
  Margaret, 34
WETZEL, Peter, 46
WHEELER,
  Thomas, 8
WHETSTONE,
  Peter, 10
WHITE,
  Isaac J., 45
  Isaac S., 26, 30, 34
  James, 2
  S. S., 50
WHITEMAN,
  Andrew, 49
  Barbara, 23
  Elizabeth, 21, 23
  Jacob, 7, 21, 23

John, 21
Joseph, 7
Philip, 23
WHITMAN,
  Barbara, 21
  Philip, 21
WHITMORE,
  Christian, 10
  Mary, 10
WHITNIGHT,
  Catherine, 29
WIANY,
  Catherine, 10
  Joseph, 10
WILES,
  David, 10
  Frederick, 10
  Hannah, 54
  Henry, 10
  Jacob, 10
  John, 10, 54
  Susanna, 10
  Susannah, 54
  William, 10
WILHELM,
  Ambrose C., 53
  David, 53
  Henry, 53
  Jacob, 53
  Margaret, 53
  Mary, 53
  Samuel, 53
WILKINSON,
  Agnes, 42
  Elizabeth, 42
  Jane, 42
  Rebecca, 42
WILLBURGER,
  Margaret, 1
WILLHOUSER,
  Elizabeth, 49
  George, 49
WILLIAMS,
  Abel, 16
  Catherine, 16
  E. G., 27
  Eliza, 53
  Henry, 51
  John, 14
  O. H., 53
  Otho H., 53
  Samuel, 51
WILLIAMSON,
  Thomas, 43

101

DISTRIBUTION OF ESTATE ACCOUNTS

WILLMOUTH,
  George, 41
WILLSON,
  Edward, 10
  Philip, 19
  Rebecca, 10
  Walter, 10
WILMOUTH,
  George, 25
WILSON,
  Elias P., 38
  Elizabeth, 54
  George, 38
  Isaac, 38, 54
  James, 54
  Lidia, 38
  Martha, 42
  Mary, 38
  Phebe, 38
  Rachel, 54
  Walter, 54
WIMER,
  Hester, 3
WINDER,
  Doratha, 21
WINDERS,
  Dorathy, 21
WINEBRENNER,
  Bastian, 38
  Christian, 11, 38, 54
  Jacob, 38, 54
  John, 54
  Joseph, 54
  Peter, 38, 54
  Philip, 38, 54
  Sabastian, 54
  Sally, 54
WINGER,
  Catherine, 3
  John, 3
WINGERT,
  Abraham, 54
  Barbara, 39, 46
  Catherine, 50, 54
  Elizabeth, 39, 46, 54
  Jacob, 54
  John, 54
  Martin, 54
  Mary, 49
  Philip, 29, 44
  Samuel, 54

WINTER,
  Andrew, 23, 54
  Ann, 23
  C., 7
  Catherine, 23
  Daniel, 23, 54
  George, 10, 23
  John, 10, 23, 54
  Susanna, 23
  Susannah, 54
WINTERS,
  Catherine Lee, 54
  Daniel, 54
  George, 8
  Jacob, 54
  John, 54
  Sarah, 47, 54
WISE,
  Catherine, 1
  Daniel, 54
  George, 54
  Jacob, 34
  John, 54
  Rosanna, 34
  Samuel, 54
  Sophia, 34
  Susanna, 34
WISHORE,
  ---, 14
WISSINGER,
  Susanna, 5
WITMAN,
  John, 31
WITMANMER,
  John, 31
WITMER,
  Christian, 38
  John, 31, 33, 45
  Peter, 35
WITMYER,
  Elizabeth, 10
  George, 10
  Mary, 10
WITTEN,
  Susanna, 19
  Susannah, 20
WITTER,
  Benjamin, 54
  Emanuel, 54
  Jacob, 54
WOLF,
  Elizabeth, 28
  Joseph, 23
  Nellie, 23

WOLFELSBERGER,
  Barbara, 54
  Francis, 54
  George, 54
  Jonathan, 54
  Joseph, 54
  Sarah, 54
  Susannah, 54
WOLFELSBURGER,
  John, 47
WOLFINGER,
  Michael, 22, 38
WOLFKILL,
  Jacob, 38
  John, 38
WOLFORD,
  Catherine, 15
  Michael, 38
WOLGAMOR,
  Andrew, 53
WOLGAMOT,
  Alfred, 54
  Andrew, 54
  Daniel, 54
  David, 54
  Elizabeth, 15, 54
  Henry, 54
  John, 39, 54
  Joshua, 54
  Margaret, 54
  Mary, 39
  Nancy, 54
WOLGANST, John, 10
WOLGOMAT,
  Nancy, 39
WOLGOMOT,
  Mary Ann, 43
WOLTZ,
  Catherine, 23
  Elie, 23
  George, 23
  John, 23
  Mary, 23
  Peter, 20
  Samuel, 23
  William, 23
WOOD,
  Mary, 26
WOODALL,
  John, 23
WOODRING,
  Abraham, 35
WOOLF,
  Catherine, 9

INDEX

Daniel, 10, 23, 37, 48
David, 48, 54
Elizabeth, 10, 28, 37, 48
Frederick, 23, 36, 51
Hanna, 37
Hannah, 10, 37
Jacob, 10, 23, 28, 36, 48, 52, 54
John, 10, 37, 41, 48, 54
Jonathan, 10
Joseph, 10, 23, 25, 37
Ludwick, 23
Magdalena, 51
Maria, 46
Susanna, 10
Susannah, 48
WOOLFERSBERGER,
  John, 31
WOOLFKILL,
  Elizabeth, 38
  John, 38
WOOLFORD,
  Adam, 10
  Catherine, 10
  David, 10
  Elizabeth, 10
  Henry, 10
  Mathias, 10
  Roseena, 10
  Susannah, 10
WORLEY,
  Conrod, 42, 50
  Evan, 23
  Jacob, 23
  John, 10, 23
  Stephen, 23
WYAND,
  Christian, 23
  Elizabeth, 23
  Lena, 23
  Mary, 23
  -Y-
YAKLY,
  Barbara, 10
  Henry, 10
  Jacob, 10
YANDERS,
  Eve, 3

YANDIS,
  Rebecca, 53
YATES,
  Amos, 10
  Ignatius, 10
  John, 10
  Joseph, 10
  Joshua, 10
  Mary, 10
  Sarah, 4, 10
  Stephen, 10
  Thomas, 10
  William, 10
YEAKLE,
  Catherine, 23
  Christina, 54
  Elizabeth, 23, 54
  Henry, 18, 23
  Jacob, 23
  Jacob J., 52
  John, 54
  Samuel, 54
  William, 54
YEAKLES,
  Henry, 7
YERTY,
  Abraham, 41
YOE,
  Benjamin, 15, 29, 54
  Benjamin F., 54
  Mrs., 29
YONTZ,
  Mary, 37
  Susanna, 37
  Susannah, 22
YOST,
  George, 23
  S., 7
  Susanna, 23
YOUNG,
  Catherine, 23, 38
  George, 9, 10, 23
  Isaac, 10, 23
  Jacob, 10, 23, 38
  John, 10, 23
  Lewis, 23
  Lodwich, 7, 8
  Lodwick, 1, 10, 23, 38
  Ludwig, 3
  Magdalena, 9, 12, 23
  Margaret, 10, 23

  Martin, 23
  Mathias, 9
  Matilda, 38
  Samuel, 10, 23
  Sarah, 23, 38
YOUNTZ,
  William, 23
YOUTZ,
  Benjamin, 44

  -Z-
ZEIGLER,
  Barbara, 38, 54
  Barbara Ann, 46
  Catherine, 54
  David, 38, 54
  Elizabeth, 38, 54
  Frederick, 38
  George, 38, 54
  Jacob, 38, 54
  Lewis, 31
  Nancy, 38, 54
  Samuel, 38, 54
  William, 38
  ___, 38
ZELLAR,
  Mary Eve, 43
ZELLER,
  Jacob, 18
  Margaret, 43
ZELLERS,
  David, 50
  Elizabeth, 19
ZIMMER,
  John, 46
  Margaret, 46
ZIMMERMAN,
  Ann Mary, 2
  Daniel, 49
ZUCK,
  Jacob, 23
  Michael, 23
  ___, 15
ZUCKMAN,
  Mary, 21
ZWISLER,
  James, 53

www.ingramcontent.com/pod-product-compliance
Lightning Source LLC
Chambersburg PA
CBHW071149090426
42736CB00012B/2279